The Good Ally

The Good Ally

A guided anti-racism journey from
bystander to changemaker

Nova Reid

ONE PLACE. MANY STORIES

HQ
An imprint of HarperCollins*Publishers* Ltd
1 London Bridge Street
London SE1 9GF

www.harpercollins.co.uk

HarperCollins*Publishers*
1st Floor, Watermarque Building, Ringsend Road
Dublin 4, Ireland

1
First published in Great Britain by
HQ, an imprint of HarperCollins*Publishers* Ltd 2021

Nova Reid asserts the moral right to be
identified as the author of this work.
A catalogue record for this book is
available from the British Library.

HB ISBN: 978-0-00-843948-4
TPB ISBN: 978-0-00-843949-1

MIX
Paper from
responsible sources
FSC™ C007454

This book is produced from independently certified FSC™ paper
to ensure responsible forest management.

For more information visit: www.harpercollins.co.uk/green

This book is set in Bembo by Type-it AS, Norway

Printed and bound in the UK using 100% Renewable Electricity at
CPI Group (UK) Ltd, Croydon, CR0 4YY

This book is written as a source of information and not as a substitute for therapeutic
or medical advice. If you have been affected by any of the issues raised in the book you
should seek professional help. Neither HarperCollins Publishers ltd or Nova Reid accept
responsibility for any loss or harm that may occur from your use or misuse of this book or
your failure to seek appropriate medical advice, or for any material on third party websites.

To: my husband, I love you.
Cousin J, I found it.
Tin Tin, I did it.

In deepest gratitude to my ancestors, to all those who endured and have gone before: thank you for guiding me every step of the way throughout this process. I am changed by you.

Contents

Introduction

*'I imagine one of the reasons people cling to their
hates so stubbornly is because they sense, once hate
is gone, they will be forced to deal with pain.'*
JAMES BALDWIN[1]

So here we are: talking about racism. Again.

The fact that you have come to find this book means you probably agree that we are in the most curious of socio-political times. With social injustices rising in frequency, and an increase in far-right movements around the world, the rise in hate against 'the other' and the resistance to moving closer towards equity are palpable.

At a time when it seems like the world is imploding, it feels like I am living in an alternate universe, having an out-of-body experience that I expect to be jolted out of at any moment. But with every headline, every new 'debate' about racism, and broadcasters casually using the 'N-word' like popping bread in a toaster, the continued exposure to normalised racism, and the constant release of studies highlighting racism in healthcare, criminal justice, workplaces, media and even in primary school playgrounds, only reinforce what many have been speaking, writing, studying, protesting about and indeed, dying for, for centuries.

We are repeating cycles and patterns of behaviour. Until we take individual and, in turn, collective responsibility to address racism, nothing changes. If nothing changes, racism will continue to morph and take on new, insidious and destructive forms that strip us all of our humanity.

The good news? Well, you're here for a start and there is also a growing number of people who have been sleepwalking, who are now waking up. People like you who want to be part of change, but often feel helpless or frozen by frustration and don't fundamentally know what to do or how to help. Which often means you regularly feel frightened, angry and hopeless (or all of the above) by the state of affairs, and that generally leads to three things:

1. Inaction
2. Total disengagement
3. Ineffective allyship

All key reasons why we are still talking about race in 2021.

★

Starting to Heal

At the heart of anti-racism work, or at least my approach to anti-racism, is the process of healing – both individual and collective.

If you've ever been in therapy or perhaps broken a bone in your body, you will know it generally feels worse before it gets better. Because, for most of us, intentionally and consciously addressing anything that makes us feel any kind of discomfort, vulnerability or shame, is quite frankly, painful. So we avoid it, like the plague; we bury it.

We keep calm and carry on, we bypass human experiences with 'love and light', or 'just be kind' hashtags and put up appearances instead – because it's what many of us have come to know, what we have been taught to do and ultimately what makes us, well, *you*, feel comfortable and safe. But history has shown us change will not happen in the cosy corners of our comfort zones.

I often get asked why I do this work. I'll be honest: it was never in my career development plan to become an anti-racism activist. Growing up in Great Britain in a white-majority town meant that navigating racism was always a backdrop to my life. This only intensified as I entered the world of work, from acting and stage theatre, to working in mental wellbeing for ten years. It was during my professional training to work in mental wellbeing that I started to truly get to grips with understanding and working with human behaviour – I found and continue to find our behaviour fascinating.

It was my former wedding business, Nu Bride, birthed out of my own wedding engagement and the vast lack of representation of Black women and couples in the wedding industry, that really was the catalyst to starting this work. I eventually started being asked to consult for wedding businesses, five-star hotels and creative agencies to improve diversity and inclusion in business and I noticed the relative ease in talking about other types of inclusion, like gender, and the contrasting embarrassment, shame, awkwardness and resistance to embed change that came up every single time I spoke about race.

That was my cue to lean into anti-racism. I now have the pleasure of speaking internationally, have a TED Talk on the subject, work with courageous leaders and offer an online anti-racism course that attracts brave human beings from all around the globe who want to role-model change by courageously unlearning their racism, to reduce racial harm and change the world around them. They're a pretty awesome bunch.

I wish I didn't have to do this work. I wish that we didn't continue to live in a racist society and, as a Black woman, I wish I didn't still have to experience the dehumanising impact of racism; not even I am immune to its suffocating grip.

The truth is, I felt a strong calling that is unexplainable, the more I ignored it and pushed it away, the more it came back, a powerful call to arms, a purpose to serve something greater than me, a call that all of my life experiences, my own racial trauma and my training has led me to be in this moment, to inspire you to role-model change. I don't question it anymore, I just trust that I am acting in service for those who endured and came before me.

I do this work because I want better for us and I want better for you and I want to leave this world in a far better state than when I entered it. But, and it's a big 'but', the only way to tackle something as insidious as racism is to be honest about what we have buried; to be honest about what we have always known, what we've recently come to know, and how that makes us feel implicated. We need to be able to rip off the metaphorical plaster. To deal with the infection that has been mutating underneath the surface of us and our lineage for centuries, to see the messy and ugly reality of what lies beneath. Before we can understand the root cause of an issue, we have to look first, to really look, even if it horrifies you, even if it scares you, then seek to resolve it and finally, to heal.

★

Stages of Anti-Racism Work

In my teaching I have come to observe four key stages to anti-racism work, which you will weave in and out of in this book.

1. Listening
2. Unlearning
3. Re-learning
4. Responsive action

As you're reading this book, I suspect you're currently in the listening or unlearning phase and to be transparent, the work is never done. That's why my students (much to their dismay) will never get a certificate or cookie from me. Being a good ally isn't about achieving an academic piece of paper or impressing me or anyone else. It is about serving something greater than you. In this context it means advocating for and working alongside a group or person in a racially marginalised community, supporting them to meet a shared goal. It is about consciously addressing racism in yourself and others. Ultimately, it is about being a better human being. So it's important to remain vigilant to avoid complacency, because anti-racism is an active and intentional practice, one that should not be autonomous.

The process is not linear and you will flit between these stages of anti-racism work throughout this book, as we explore historical events and how they relate to present day experiences of racism, prompts for self-enquiry, in-depth exploration and tools to galvanise what you have learned and put it into tangible action. It is important to be consistent, but please pace yourself. You don't need to eat the pizza in one whole go. To avoid overwhelm, take it in bite-sized chunks. A huge and important component to anti-racism work is practising your own self-enquiry, being self-aware and honest with yourself. I will be sharing prompts and asking you to reflect throughout this book, so I would recommend documenting your gut responses on voice notes, journaling, and writing notes. Pay attention, not only to your thoughts, but to how this work makes you feel in your body physically. The latter is vital, because we've got very good at numbing when it comes to racism.

This is a life's work and the ultimate goal is that you don't just 'get it' and remember information – anyone with good memory recall can do that. More to the point, we Black folk can easily recognise the difference between those who are just being self-righteous parrots and those that actually embody the work. How? Because when you embody the work, you become the work and you role-model it; it becomes a part of who you are, not just something you 'do on the side'. That has a profound ripple effect in every single interaction you have and how you show up in the world. That's where exponential change happens and is exactly what this book has been created for, if you choose to move beyond the stats and data.

Before we really get cracking, I want to note that this intentionally is not a book filled with academic jargon or reams and reams of stats. Firstly, it is not my style, but more importantly, so much disproportionate weight is placed on evidence and receipt gathering in tackling anti-racism, conveniently ignoring the pre-existing data and crucial work that has already been done by academics. So whilst I will draw on them to highlight points and support your knowledge, this book intentionally centres turning anti-racism into interrogation and accessible action.

If you want a certificate for being a good human, this is not the book for you.

Whilst we will be delving into the foundation of anti-racism, this book is not for complete beginners. If you are coming to this work for the first time, this book will trigger the hell out of you – but this book is definitely for you if you are hungry for more, ready to be challenged and to roll your sleeves up.

This work is *not* comfortable. Nor should it be. Some of what I share will make you want to slam the book shut and you're probably going to hate me at times, but I urge you to keep going. Any discomfort you feel is temporary and pales in comparison to what Black people and People of Colour often have to experience on a daily basis. On the other side of some of the most difficult realisations and exchanges with yourself and others, is huge transformation – that is the work and where change happens.

If you want to be part of change, learn more about everyday and systemic racism, if you're seeking to reduce harm and the impact of racism on Black People and People of Colour including children, and you're ready to expand, experience growth, fear, messing it up, courage, vulnerability and everything in between, then you're in good company.

Welcome.

★

A Black British Lens

I intentionally approach this book with a Black British lens. As a Black woman, it's not only my experience, but is where I have chosen to focus my education and teaching and, therefore, where I can speak from integrity and my most powerful place of truth. In my experience, attempting to address multiple lenses of race and lumping anyone that isn't white into one homogenous group (something that happens all too often and ends up conflating Black experiences) dilutes the message. As a result, you miss the nuances and are less able to identify and address specific needs. I also cannot do all of these stories the justice they deserve in one book. There are some great books on racism and the impact on Indigenous communities and other Marginalised Ethnic Groups that will only add to the richness of your journey, and my recommendation is you seek those out and absolutely devour those too.

I am also intentionally choosing to centre Blackness to help you understand what the concept of race is and more importantly, where it came from.

Now, it is important for me to reinforce that race *is* a social construct. It is not real. It was born out of a race hierarchy developed primarily by Swedish botanist Carl Linnaeus in 1758[2] who felt the need to turn his passion from studying plants, to people. In doing so, Linnaeus outlined four key groups of humans that could be identified by colour. These were:

1. The Americas (Red – Indigenous Americans)
2. Europe (White – Europeans)
3. Asia (Yellow – Asians)
4. Africa (Black – Africans)

And then after that, monstrous and feral humans (yup, I'll leave you to figure that one out). This race hierarchy was then developed by several others, including a German scientist called Johann Friedrich Blumenbach who adapted this into a more rigid race hierarchy to 'classify' human races. He placed white (Europeans) at the top and Black (Africans) at the bottom with everyone else, all of these other 'colours', somewhere in between. What was ultimately an idea created by human and cultural bias and, in some cases, falsified tests, the notion of this race hierarchy became a prominent fixture from the eighteenth century. And it was this pseudoscience (aka lies) that created 'race' as we know it today and was used to justify the inhumane violence under white supremacy and the human trafficking and enslavement of millions of Black Africans.

There is absolutely no scientific evidence or biological fact that backs up the claim that white people were superior to any other human based on the colour of skin. None. But unfortunately, because we have all been fed this lie for so long, many have come to believe it, consciously and unconsciously.

> '22 per cent of UK adults still think some races
> are born less intelligent than others.'
> JUNE SARPONG[3]

What this means is that anti-Blackness has become the bedrock of racism, born out of this race hierarchy. The impact of this is so power-ful as it doesn't just feed into the subconscious of white folk, it also permeates the minds of non-Black People of Colour who can also project intercultural race hatred based on the false belief that Black people, especially those with darker skin, are least superior. And we are not unscathed either – this lie has seeped into Black people too.

This is why I choose to centre Blackness because, in order for us to truly understand the essence of what racism is, we need to understand its birthplace.

Some people think we can just end racism with statements like 'we're only one race, the human race', expecting us to just forget the race construct and merrily-we-roll-along into the sunset. Though well-intentioned, this phrase is often used as a way to shut down conversations about racism. In theory, yes, biologically this is true, however, it can be reductive. Whilst the construct of race is not real, the identities and communities we have built around this construct are real and, more importantly, the evidence of the continued impact of racism is very, very real. In fact, it's deadly.

★

Getting Uncomfortable

Racism is built on so many lies that in order for us to be anti-racist, we absolutely have to start being honest with ourselves and one another – that means choosing to take responsibility for our own complicity. For centuries, we have been taught to uphold and maintain destructive systems of oppression as the norm, without question. We've been conditioned to go along with that powerful current because it's easier than swimming in the opposite direction or, worse still, drowning.

Fear, no doubt, has also been a powerful driving force because you have learned to centre your own feelings ahead of speaking up on issues that matter, and perhaps not even noticing the injustice to begin with. You have learned to prioritise your comfort over courage. Would you say you have struggled to be a 'good ally' in the past or even now, through fear of causing offence, saying the wrong thing or not feeling like it's your place to say anything? When this happens, it subconsciously means you place your fear of causing offence as being more important than helping. No blame, no judgement.

To be truly anti-racist, to be able to withstand, and do this work without experiencing regular burnout, you will need to embed and prioritise self-care (don't worry – I've written a chapter on this which I encourage you to use as a resource whenever you need it throughout this journey). Please don't underestimate this – I would not be able to do this work without it. So before you engage with this work (or any other in-depth anti-racism work), please be self-aware and be honest with yourself about whether you currently have the emotional and psychological capacity to engage. Only you can be responsible for that.

Anti-racism work is about unlearning discrimination that has been normalised; consciously and continuously disrupting the status quo, in society, in work, in others and ultimately, in yourself.

That WILL feel uncomfortable.

It may even feel discombobulating.

You are going to feel guilt and. most probably, shame.

So when it feels tough, when you want to stop, or skip to the easy bit at the end, that is when I want you to slow it down and lean in a little closer and lean into the truth about what is making you want to disengage. To commit to doing the work properly and not undermining the process, or the labour that has gone into creating this resource for you.

We're going to go on a journey. and I will be right here with you. You'll want to laugh, curl your toes, cry, shout and scream. You'll feel joy, at times despair, but beyond that, I promise you, is hope.

The truth is, the more you do this work, the more you'll know what to do.

The more you do this work, the easier it will be to know what to say.

The more you do this work, the clearer it will be and the more glaringly obvious instances of systemic racism will become.

The more you do this work, the more clarity you will have. It will be like seeing the world with a new pair of glasses, but the difference is, instead of feeling helpless, by the end of our journey together you will know exactly how to help role-model change, because once you start, you just can't unsee it, you can't go back.

So as you go through this book, when things start to

smart a little or challenge you (because they will), I invite you to start to love the word *curious*. That is going to be your superpower in unpacking your own racism and helping others come to terms with and unlearn theirs. When something challenges you, get curious about why it feels challenging, with why your heartbeat is suddenly racing, or your jaw clenching. Just notice. And, if at times it feels overwhelming, pause if you need to, but come back to the work.

I invite you to be courageous and get comfortable with being uncomfortable, because right now, we are on the cusp of powerful and seismic change and I want you to be part of it. This is change that will go down in the history books, and we all have a chance to contribute and play a role in how this chapter will end.

Mind Your Language

One last thing before we dive into it, let me give a few notes about language. I know this is a bone of contention, and I don't want you to get too stuck on it before we've even gotten started.

In this book, I know some fellow Black and Brown people will be reading this too (I see you – please take care, as I will be sharing some racist language and experiences of racism to highlight events that can trigger racial trauma), either to unlearn their own anti-Blackness or to better understand how to navigate white supremacy in peer groups. This book, however, has been curated to talk to people who are white. When I use the term 'white' I am talking about people who are racialised as white. I understand our identities are not one-dimensional and you may also fit into a less than satisfactory 'White Other' box or be of mixed heritage, but perceived to be white – in short, if you benefit from proximity to whiteness, I am talking to you too, kiddo.

When I say 'us' or 'we', I generally mean Black people, or, if I am feeling generous, I mean all of us, perfectly imperfect humans. I hope as we get to know one another, you'll start to easily distinguish between the two.

I am not a personal fan of acronyms to describe groups of people, such as 'BIPOC' (Black, Indigenous, People of Colour) or 'POC' (People/Person of Colour). Some of my mixed-heritage and non-Black peers are fans, so I will still use these descriptions from time to time to encompass their identities, but not my own. I will generally use the terms Non-Black People of Colour or Marginalised Ethnic Groups to describe all other groups outside of the African diaspora that experience racism and, where possible, when referencing Indigenous communities, I will name them specifically.

I am definitely not a fan of 'BAME' (Black Asian, Minority Ethnic Group). None of these are racist terminologies, but they are often misused as a comfort blanket for people who are still not comfortable saying the word 'Black'. It also lumps us all in one group, which we aren't. Our ethnic groups make up thousands and as such, our experiences of the world and how racism and prejudice impacts us – though we may share common experiences – are vast. I do not speak for every Black person in the Western world. We are not a monolith.

I use 'Brown' quite fluidly to describe Black mixed-race/ mixed-heritage people from within the African diaspora, or to be literal about the actual colour of my skin. I may also use

Brown like some others, to refer to and encompass people who are of South Asian, Indian, or Pakistani heritage, for example.

Becoming anti-racist also means recognising language in this sphere changes rapidly and people will have their own individual preferences. Don't overthink it. You'll soon get used to my preferred language and others' too.

★

OK. Are you ready? Take a deep breath.

Let's get started, we have got important work to do and change to make.

★

1. The Trouble with White Privilege and its Intersection with Racism

'White supremacy is not the shark. It's the water.'
GUANTE[I]

We cannot talk about racism without talking about white privilege and we cannot talk about white privilege without talking about white supremacy. So let's start there.

In order for racism and systemic disadvantage to exist, white supremacy and systemic advantage need to co-exist. That's the core component conveniently missing from conversations about racism that gets glossed over or ignored. We have to acknowledge and name white supremacy without spiralling into shame.

Let me clarify: when other anti-racism educators and I talk about white supremacy, we are not talking about a group of 'bad' white men in pointy hoods with skinheads and swastika tattoos. We're talking about an entire system.

There are key moments in history when white supremacy and racism really started to take hold and having racist laws helped. From the early fifteenth century, the white British elite embedded slave codes in Virginia. These English common laws extended to nearly all of its American colonies, including the Caribbean, and controlled the treatment of Africans.[2] The Act prevented Black people and Indigenous Americans having protection from the law and placed them outside of civil society, with Africans given the lowest human status.[3] In 1661, another law, embedded by the British, called 'An Act for Better Ordering and Governing of Negroes' (also known as the Barbados Slave Code) was used to legalise the enslavement of Black people. The code, according to historian David Olusoga, described Africans as 'heathenish', 'brutish', and an 'uncertain and dangerous pride of people'.[4] According to Civil Rights lawyer Gloria J. Browne-Marshall, no other human community was 'designated nonhuman by law and treated as cargo'.[5] None. The seed of Black inferiority was well and truly sown and these Acts gave legal right to inflict violence as a means to control Africans.

White supremacy was galvanised in the eighteenth century when white, male European scientists started to fuse a dangerous concoction of prejudice, ignorance and science. The aforementioned Friedrich Blumenbach coined the term 'Caucasian', inspired by Mount Caucasus which straddles Europe and Asia, because he thought the most 'beautiful race of men' lived there: the Georgians. He came to the conclusion that because white people can turn from white to brown but not vice versa[6] and because their skulls were also the 'primitive colour of mankind'[7] – even though all human skulls are white – they should be referred to as Caucasian (yes, I too remain baffled).

Fellow 'scientist' Linnaeus didn't just stop at categorising humans by skin colour either. He started to assert positive or negative biases and apply them to entire groups of people. Such as Europeans (white) being 'gentle, acute and governed by laws' and Africans (Black) being 'lazy'.[8] These negative stereotypes by these scientists (that were often concocted without ever coming into any contact with Africans), still impact us today. For instance, in 2019, Research by NatCen and Runnymede Trust reported that 44 per cent of those surveyed believe some races are born harder working that others.[9]

If we look at history as far back as the Roman Empire, slavery was a common global practice, and empires would often enslave prisoners as a consequence of war, not as a consequence of the colour of one's skin.[10] Interracial relationships were commonplace. Skin colour was not a notable mark of character and you were more likely to be judged by tribe or religion.[11] Fast forward to the fifteenth century during colonial invasion, when Indigenous people were the original 'preferred choice' for white Europeans to enslave. The Taino people in Jamaica were known as a thriving community until the Spanish colonial invasion, when they started to die at alarmingly rapid rates from exposure to European diseases, such as smallpox, and from colonial enslavement, and by the mid-sixteenth century they were near extinction[12] and white elite Europeans had started to set their sights on Black Africans instead. This is where the function of slavery took on an even more sinister turn.

It was pseudoscience that created anti-Blackness, the targeted racial prejudice towards Black people – especially those with darker skin tones – and their culture and values. It was this 'science' that was used to introduce chattel slavery (where an enslaved person became the personal property of another), and it was this science that was used to legitimise kidnapping, torture, oppression and the dehumanisation of Black people. This wasn't just a blip in history. It wasn't just a social practice enforced for a couple of years. It was a social practice that was embedded in law that formed a huge part of the global economy, for centuries.

White supremacy is a system that has such a powerful and suffocating grip. It is often invisible, upheld consciously and unconsciously and continues to have a detrimental impact on society, human rights and societal disadvantage and societal advantage such as white privilege.

★

Understanding White Privilege

'A mark of maturity from white people is moving from shame and defensiveness about what we didn't know, to taking responsibility for hate we should have known.'
DAVID W SWANSON[13]

'White Privilege' is an academic term, still relatively new to the mainstream – and that is why it is so often misinterpreted and misunderstood. Understanding its origins and being able to explain examples will not only deepen your own understanding, but as an ally, will also be key to busting reductive myths.

Originally named 'White Skin Privilege' in the 1960s – it was born out of an in-depth 40-year study spearheaded by white American academic, writer and activist Theodore W. Allen, published in the height of the American civil rights movement.

Through his analysis, the data consistently revealed that there were societal privileges that benefit people identified as white *beyond* what is commonly experienced by non-white people under *the exact same* social, political, or economic circumstances. That's it. It is an inescapable consequence of the construct of white supremacy.

Of course, white (skin) privilege (and it's not clear when or why 'skin' was eventually dropped), will intersect with class, and let's face it, us Brits in particular don't have a healthy relationship with class. We often associate privilege with greed, and poverty with laziness and not working hard enough. Class disparities remain rife. However white (skin) privilege has absolutely nothing to do with wealth; it doesn't mean you haven't experienced trauma, abuse, wrongdoing or financial hardship. It just means that, as a white person, whatever challenges or circumstances you may personally face in your life, you have not received systemic racism because of the colour of your skin in addition to those challenges. Being able to acknowledge that without it taking away from your own experiences of struggle, or turning it into an 'Oppression Olympics' event, is vital.

While white (skin) privilege can't be directly compared to other 'privilege', we can better understand where we benefit from societal privilege by taking into consideration our social location. Our social location is the social position each of us holds within society, based upon social characteristics deemed to be important by any given society. Our social location can vary and be defined by many different things, from class, to skin colour, to geographical location, to gender, to body size, religion, ability and sex orientation. For example, we all have forms of societal privilege. I have societal privilege as a heterosexual woman. I can kiss my husband in public without a second thought, without fearing a homophobic attack for simply expressing a public display of affection.

A common and extreme defensive response I get (mostly from men, interestingly enough) is, 'You can't say that white homeless people are privileged, they're homeless.' Aside from displaying a strong commitment to misunderstanding the phrase 'white skin privilege', if we look through the lens of social location, unsurprisingly (given our history of social housing discrimination and private landlords who still discriminate based on race to this very day),[14] homelessness disproportionately impacts Black folk and folk in other Marginalised Ethnic Groups, with one in three homeless households being Black and other Marginalised Ethnic Groups, compared to one in seven homeless households being white[15]; Black people are three times likely to experience homelessness.[16] What statements like this also highlight is that their racial bias and perception of poverty in Britain is solely a white problem.

Whilst a white person will experience the very real systemic disadvantage of homelessness and all the dehumanisation, violence and stigma that comes with it, they will not be experiencing the abuse of racism on top. Acknowledging that doesn't take away from the real experiences of facing homelessness for anyone, nor does the suffering of white people who are homeless somehow justify the continued racial abuse of Black and Brown people who aren't.

Let's reframe privilege as advantage. Even though I experience discrimination for being a woman and racism for being

Black, in my social location, I can also recognise, as a Black able-bodied woman I still have societal advantage. As a woman and then a Black woman, whilst statistically receiving less pay than white women, nearly 40 per cent less than white men in similar roles, I will statistically receive more than my Black peers who also have a disability. Accepting and acknowledging this does not take away from my own very real and painful experiences of gender discrimination, systemic racism and anti-Blackness as a dark-skinned Black woman.

I don't feel ashamed about who I am as an individual or those 'unearned societal privileges' I have acquired for simply being born in this body, but I make sure I am continuing to be aware of the myriad of ways my disabled peers are impacted by discrimination, how I may uphold and benefit from a society that is built for able-bodied people so I can better raise awareness, advocate and support.

In the same vein, we don't want you to feel ashamed for simply being born white. That's not the work. We do, however, want you to be better aware of it, to acknowledge and interrogate how you continue to benefit, to find ways to address it, influence change and advocate for better race equity for all and to accept that white skin privilege only exists because systemic racism and anti-Blackness co-exist.

Guilt and shame are common and normal responses to people who care about tackling racism. But you staying stuck in guilt and shame is no good to any of us and certainly isn't solid grounds for allyship.

The Power of Acceptance

I will never forget Jude Kelly, CBE, founder of Women of The World Festival and someone I would describe as an ally, likening anti-racism work to the first step of the 12-step programme, an observation that deeply resonated with one of my anti-racism students who, at the time, was eight years sober. She explained to me that what was most impactful was Jude's emphasis on the power of acceptance in both addiction and anti-racism: acceptance that there is a problem and acceptance of your role as a white person or someone who benefits from white skin privilege in it, highlighting that no genuine progress in anti-racism can be made until you accept your own racism.

I witness students going through a full range of emotions before they truly get to a place of acceptance. I know it's a confronting and vulnerable place to be. This work can turn your world and self-perception upside down, and what I observe is a grieving process. From facing hard truths, to letting go of the person you thought you were and also being willing to let go of unearned societal privileges. That is a form of loss. In order to process loss, we have to go through a grieving process; we can't bypass it.

Donna Lancaster, an author, healer and therapist, explains that grief is not just about bereavement, but a natural response to any kind of loss, but there is a widespread resistance to grieve, because of a desire to avoid experiencing darker feelings, so we cut off emotions instead. Why? Because grief brings about big feelings and for some, it's simply just too painful.

The stiff upper lip and 'keep calm carry on' culture of Brits in particular, means so many get caught up in a dysfunctional relationship of dishonesty and toxic positivity in a bid to reduce emotional investment. Avoiding feelings of sadness, anger and grief in favour of 'just be kind and happy' is not realistic. Not only is this rhetoric often used as a weapon by white women to silence people who highlight racism, it is also not human to only experience one range of emotion. Sure, it might keep you comfortable and give you the illusion of being happy, but when we numb parts of our humanity in favour of 'positive vibes only', we start problematically labelling human feelings as positive or negative. We start avoiding those deemed to be 'negative' and when we don't acknowledge and process pain, we start transferring unprocessed pain onto others. And it ain't pretty.

We've all leaned into these feelings to some degree, from road rage, to trashing strangers online, to the darker side of wishing people dead, to enacting acts of mass terror. Bypassing can also look like pain avoidance, donating to charities without further anti-racist action, or as I have seen in my practice, signing up to my anti-racism course and never actually logging on to do the work.

> *'It is so important to make your peace with your own shit. If we are going to live in a higher state of consciousness, you have to do the work.'*
> DONNA LANCASTER

The truth is, we'll never be able to be anti-racist until we fully process our losses related to racism, such as loss of identity, loss of relationships, loss of so many lives, loss of who we thought we were, loss of innocence, loss of connection, loss of disproportionate power. If grief is a natural response to any kind of loss, it's no surprise you can end up going through the natural stages of grief, which can also bring up shame.

Psychiatrist Elisabeth Kübler-Ross first identified the five stages of grief in her book *Death and Dying* in 1969.[17] I have adapted these five stages to highlight common responses I witness from students in the early stages of their anti-racism journey – some that you may well experience going through this book:

Shock and denial: 'I'm so shocked!' 'How is this still happening in this day and age?' 'That wasn't racism, maybe it's just a clash of personalities or they have just misunderstood me.' 'I'm not racist, my best friend is Black.'

Anger (usually triggered by feelings of shame): shouting, screaming, resentment, blaming others, 'those disgusting racists over there' (redirected rage towards Black folk, or other friends who aren't doing the work, to avoid dealing with your own pain). 'We all have shit to deal with, there are loads of Black folk doing better than poor, working-class white folk. Why don't they just get on with it? Not everything is about race.'

Bargaining/Despair: 'Please listen to me now.' 'But I'm one of the good ones.' 'Tell me I'm one of the good ones.' 'Tell me what to do.' 'I promise from now on, I'll be the best ally I can be'. This state is generally driven by helplessness and perhaps underneath that, a realisation that you have caused harm to others, and a type of pleading that takes place.

Depression: Overwhelm – 'This is too much.' 'I'm a bad person.' Feeling heavy, sombre, leading to withdrawal from the work and potential withdrawal from self and others.

Acceptance: 'I know I have racism in me and I have unlearning to do.' Genuine acceptance of the problem, the current state of affairs, an accurate understanding of the issue and what has led us here. Acceptance of all of the losses in association with it. Acceptance of their role in it. An acceptance of their inherent racism and an acceptance that this work is necessary to reduce harm, to change systems and to live in our full humanity. It's at this point I see a real shift in how students engage in anti-racism from a place of serving something greater than them rather than managing their perception, and the real learning and allyship begins.

★

We absolutely cannot progress with any kind of effectiveness until we process grief and learn to be present with confronting feelings and get to a place of acceptance. We generally find it easier to accept the overt stuff exists and less easy to accept the coded racism that goes through your body like osmosis, harder still to own it and take responsibility for it. This is always a clear marker for me of students who are embodying this work from an honest place and those that aren't there yet. For example, a student who has come to a place of acceptance will say, without shame or flinching, 'Me and my racism.' The other will say: 'Me and my white privilege.' One is truthful, vulnerable and honest, the other is easier to say because it comes from a place of superiority and a subtle hint of 'I'm better than you' self-righteousness. It's easier to hide the parts of ourselves that make us feel shame.

Go on. Try it. How does it feel to say 'me and my racism'? What comes up for you? Then try 'me and my white privilege'. What do you notice in your body? What physical sensations do you experience?

Having white skin doesn't make you inherently superior, just like being able-bodied doesn't make me inherently superior. What I will say is this: You will not be able to be effective in your allyship and you will not be able to be truly actively anti-racist until you are honest with yourself. Because if you are honest you will recognise that inherent superiority comes with inherent inferiority. If culturally white human communities consistently chose to violently dehumanise other humans – Black Africans – in order to feel whole, better, worthy and superior, then this superiority comes from a foundation of inferiority. Being honest about racism is to accept the issue isn't just with those 'disgusting, embarrassing white people over there' but it's understanding that you have inherent racism in you too. But more to the point, it serves no purpose expending energy trying to convince Black and Brown folk and non–Black People of Colour that you're not like those racists over there. Because we have, more often than not, already experienced your racism.

If you consider yourself a feminist and can accept with relative ease that, even though you fundamentally believe in the equality of all genders, but that as a result of patriarchy, you sometimes do or say sexist things and can internalise sexism, what is the challenge to you accepting that you have consciously and unconsciously internalised white supremacy too?

As a result of white supremacy, if we – Black adults and children who fundamentally believe in racial equality and want nothing more than racism to end – can still perpetuate anti-Blackness and internalise racism, then there is no way you have come out of this unscathed.

Please note my language. I have intentionally used 'internalised white supremacy' for people racialised as white, and 'internalised racism' for Black folk and People of Colour – because they are not the same, nor do they function in the same way.

Internalised racism is succinctly described by sociologist Karen D. Pyke as the internalisation of racial oppression by the racially subordinated.[18] At its essence, internalised racism turns racist ideologies inwards, developing the same thoughts, beliefs and actions that collude with racism. It is the conscious or unconscious acceptance of the superiority of whiteness that we have swallowed, which, by default, leads to the belief in one's own inferiority and, unsurprisingly, can lead to a lot of self-hate.

I describe internalised white supremacy as something that affects people who are racialised as white, internalising the acceptance of the racial superiority of whiteness. Conscious and unconscious beliefs in negative racist stereotypes of racially marginalised groups and participation in upholding and enforcing white standards as the norm.

Until we can accept the inequality and its root cause, and start from there rather than a position of defensiveness, we will never make an in-road with this work; in another six decades, activists will be writing the same books.

No matter how many law changes there are, no matter how much shock and dismay at deaths on Black bodies, no matter how many racist governments we elect, absolutely nothing will change unless you interrogate how your racism and addiction to white racial power functions. Accepting white skin privilege means confronting the elephant in the room; addressing racism means you have to accept that your humanity is entangled and measured by the inhumanity inflicted on Black and Brown bodies. To put it simply, your disproportionate elevation in humanity is based on our genocide.

Take a breath. No blame. We are where we are.

Most don't want to accept this shared understanding because it doesn't feel great and it can be potentially exposing. You end up in defensive and child-like states because everything in your being has been taught to protect that hierarchy. Instead of addressing racism, we go round and round in defensive circles until Black folk get fatigued and stop talking about race (which, let's face it, for some, silencing us might be the end goal). The trouble is, because white people aren't used to talking about race, let alone being identified by it, it can spark huge discomfort.

Accepting that white privilege exists means acknowledging a form of complicity. It also means that you may suddenly feel like you are being compared to, or are in closer proximity than you would like, to people that society has become really good at dehumanising: 'racists'. Accepting white privilege means understanding that racism has got nothing to do with being a good or bad person. It means facing up to the fact that what we've been taught to believe about 'racists' – being exclusively abhorrent, probably unintelligent and definitely violent individuals – is false. They are also parents, academics, healthcare workers, partners, friends, neighbours, senior managers in charge of global corporations, police, politicians, the clergy and even our sweet grandparents. It also means accepting that having been raised in a society founded on white supremacy, you are going to have unconscious or conscious inherent racist programming (or internalised white supremacy) within you to some degree. It is inescapable.

Understanding this is why the subject of white privilege

elicits a huge amount of universal guilt, anger, shame, fury, embarrassment, grief, pain, frustration and an overwhelming amount of denial. Because what would it mean about you, or the people you love if it were to be true?

Breathe.

So let's look at some tangible examples of how this stuff actually manifests in society:

- White privilege means not being forty times more likely to be stopped and searched by the police.[19]
- White privilege means not having people consistently cross over the road when they see you through fear you might attack them.
- White privilege means not being four to five times more likely to die in childbirth.[20]
- White privilege means not having to worry about your child trying to lighten their skin to avoid racial bullying in the playground.
- White privilege means not having your entire race or religion stigmatised whenever there is a terrorist attack.
- White privilege means not having to Google neighbourhoods to live that aren't racist, as part of your house searching criteria.
- White privilege means not having to travel a 140-mile round trip to find a local hairdresser that is trained to work with afro-textured hair.
- White privilege means not constantly walking into your local beauty store and not being able to find one foundation that matches your skin tone. Not one.

- White privilege means it not being assumed that you are a criminal by simply wearing a tracksuit and your hoody or driving a decent car.
- White privilege means it not being assumed you don't belong in a first-class carriage.
- White privilege means not having the police called when you are waiting for a business associate in a coffee shop.
- White privilege means not being four times more likely to be detained under the Mental Health Act.[21]
- White privilege means not having to send 80–90 per cent more job applications to get a positive response from an employer because of your ethnic background.[22]
- White privilege means being able to frequently tap out of conversations about racism.

White privilege most definitely means being a British citizen, raising your family here, minding your own business and enjoying your evening tea while watching the telly and not having your home invaded by armed government officials, being told to pack up and leave, put onto a plane and physically forced to go back to a country you do not know, because you are caught up in the Windrush Scandal.

As author Reni Eddo-Lodge quite succinctly but powerfully puts it, 'White privilege is an absence of the consequences of racism.'[23]

Misunderstanding, denying or failing to engage with the concept of white skin privilege and its relationship with racism and more specifically, anti-Blackness, means we inadvertently end up sowing seeds of doubt which discredit and question the memory, validity, perception of Black people's reality, also known as gaslighting. Perhaps even more pertinent, by continuing to not be aware of the reality of the existence of systemic racism, you will remain complicit in keeping it alive.

★

Understanding Systemic Racism

Systemic racism and its powerful grip is still alive and kicking today and for many reasons is more lethal than individual overt acts of hate.* Understanding systemic racism and being able to articulate how racism exists beyond an overt act of hate will be monumental in your allyship. So let's get to it.

Systemic or institutionalised racism (also known as structural racism) is defined as 'systemic racism or racial discrimination that has become established as normal behaviour within a society or organisation.'

The term became more mainstream in 1999 after the publishing of the Macpherson Report, which played an important role in the seismic Stephen Lawrence case. The 18-year-old Black teenager Stephen was murdered in April 1993, by white youths in an unprovoked and racially-motivated attack while waiting for a bus. A credible witness account from a young Black man was deemed unreliable, and despite information being shared with the police about all of the suspects a day

---

* Systemic is not to be confused with systematic. The former is often in relation to a whole system affecting many different parts, the latter, is acting in targeted, organised cohesion to execute a plan within a system.

after the crime was committed, it took the Metropolitan Police almost nineteen years – no, that's not a typo: nineteen years – to convict just two of the previously identified suspects. An extensive two-year public inquiry led by independent High Court judge Sir William Macpherson found both conscious and unconscious racial bias and discrimination in the Police Force and determined that the Metropolitan Police was institutionally racist. This had and still has devastating consequences and has contributed to the lack of trust between the Police and the Black community in the UK.

In the report, Sir William Macpherson describes systemic racism as:

> The collective failure of an organisation to provide an appropriate and professional service to people because of their colour, culture, or ethnic origin. It can be seen or detected in processes, attitudes and behaviour which amount to discrimination through unwitting prejudice, ignorance, thoughtlessness and racist stereotyping, which disadvantage minority ethnic people.[24]

Systemic racism is a powerful force; an inevitable by-product of centuries upon centuries of white supremacy.

★

The UK's Problem with Race

> To me, this Bill is a serious thing. I feel it is directed against our people – our own people in this country. So much has been said from the Front Benches on both sides about human rights, but it always stopped short at the point of human rights and privileges and freedoms for the immigrants and did not extend to the human rights and freedoms and equality for our own people.[25]

This extract was taken from an official parliamentary transcript of Conservative MP Sir Harold Gurden, discussing concerns with a proposed Race Relations Bill to tackle racism in Britain in Parliament on 23 April 1968.

If it wasn't such corrosive persistent psychological warfare, it would be quite the spectacle watching the British Conservative government and a frightening majority of the British public continue to deny the existence of systemic racism in Britain, rather than attempt to address it.

In March 2021, the Race and Ethnic Disparities Commission (a new commission set up after Black Lives Matter protests across the country in summer 2020) published a 258-page report headed up by MPs and political advisers, some of which previously stated publicly they don't believe institutionalised racism exists.[26] [27] [28] The report concluded that the UK should be seen as model of racial equality and that the slave trade culturally transformed African people into a 're-modelled African/Britain' and concluded (after cherry-picking data to confirm their own agenda by ignoring all pre-existing data) that institutional racism no longer exists in the UK.[29]

It is evident to me this report followed a timely brief to prove, on paper, that 'Britain isn't racist'. This report was published just four months after, and in contrast to, the Black People, Racism and Human Rights report from the House of Lords and House of Commons, (which, at the time of writing, remains unaddressed) that found over 75 per cent of Black people in the UK do not believe their human rights are equally protected compared to white people's. Additionally, they found that the Equality and Human Rights Commission has persistently failed to address racial inequality and quotes:

The failings of successive governments to act in response to the successive reports and reviews shows that something is wrong with the architecture which is supposed to protect human rights and promote racial equality.'[30]

This is seismic. This is a human rights issue and a case-in-point example of what happens when you have an institution that continues to reproduce racism and buy into the racist narrative that structural inequality is merely down to individuals being 'lazy' and not working hard enough or being 'inherently flawed'. This is the devastating impact of systemic racism and this is why we all play a role in tackling it. Whether racism is unconscious or conscious, indirect or direct, intentional or unintentional, or persistent from institutions such as the government, the impact remains the same. And it is the unaddressed racism in individuals that occupies every single echelon of society that contributes to systemic racism.

Lady Doreen Lawrence, Stephen's mother – who campaigned

for justice tirelessly for two decades – stated in a meeting with British MPs in February 2019 (a couple of months shy of the twentieth anniversary of her son's murder) that institutionalised racism still very much exists in Britain and that efforts to reform institutions and racism in society remain stagnant.

One element that keeps us 'stagnant', is that when the majority of us think of racism, we *only* consider the reductive and outdated Oxford Dictionary definition: 'Prejudice, discrimination, or antagonism directed against someone of a different race based on the belief that one's own race is superior.' This limited definition that only focuses on an individual's action was first used in 1902.

We have been taught to only associate racism with a single act of overt, conscious and intentional hate, by an individual to another, based on the sole belief that their race, the colour of their skin, is superior. Most people reject the idea of overt racism. Most of us don't go around committing overt acts of violence and dehumanising other humans because of the colour of their skin. However, systemic racism turns this very definition upside down.

Systemic racism goes beyond a conscious act of overt hate, leaving most white folk completely and utterly discombobulated. Because if you have only ever positioned racism as conscious and intentional and suddenly discover it can also be unintentional, most white people either dismiss racism entirely, don't think they are contributing to it and absolve themselves from needing to address it. If you have come to understand that racism only exists in one way – committed by 'bad' and perhaps 'unintelligent' people – then if someone like me even remotely suggests that you uphold racist systems and may even have inherent racism within you, the automatic response is to vehemently reject the notion, defend your position and prove to everyone that you have been misunderstood. The idea that you could have inherent racism too is incongruent with what you have come to learn 'racists' are and therefore, nothing changes and systemic racism continues to thrive and is as toxic as hell.

This may go some way to explaining why an activist colleague recently described the corrosive nature of racism in Britain as being worse than what she experienced living and being imprisoned during apartheid South Africa.

Systemic racism is a social and political construct built on systems of oppression that directly contributed to Britain's wealth. It has enabled us to do anything but consciously and intentionally address inherent racism. It has enabled us to regularly deny and explain away 'casual racism' as a mistake, a misunderstanding, a joke, a clash of personalities, or Black people being oversensitive again.

It is a system that equates being white with automatically being right, being historically accurate and the standard of 'normal' we should all aspire to. For example, in January 2020, actor Laurence Fox drew attention to Sam Mendes' casting of a Sikh soldier in his war film, *1917*. Their very presence in a film made Fox feel agitated enough to pass comment on it. Fox stated in an article by *The Metro* that 'forcing diversity' onto the British public was 'institutionally racist'.[31]

The silent power of white supremacy and the homogenous depictions of 'our war heroes who served for Great Britain' each Remembrance Day, meant Fox believed, with conviction and self-righteousness, that only white men served as British soldiers during the First World War. This is factually incorrect. It not only ignores the incorporation of the West Indies Regiment formed by over 15,600 volunteers from British colonies, but also the 1.5 million Indian troops that fought. One in every six British soldiers were of Indian heritage, and one in five of those were Sikh. These soldiers fought alongside British-born troops (which again, might I add, were not all white) in the First World War after a plea from the British Government to help them win the war. And despite colonisation, slavery and further segregation, unequal pay and ranking within the British Army, they *still* proudly served and died for Britain and yet, their very presence in a film made Fox feel completely outraged. Aside from winding up characters like Fox, more importantly, these one-dimensional depictions of war heroes also erase and disrespect the contributions of soldiers like Arthur Roberts, a Black Scottish solider who served and survived the First World War and went onto face hostile racism in Britain. He died in a care home in 1982 in Glasgow and one of his care workers recalled he often felt forgotten on Remembrance Sundays, choosing to stay in his room rather than celebrate.[32]

*

In January 2020, (it was clearly, quite *the* month) the Duke and Duchess of Sussex, commonly known as Harry and Meghan, made an announcement that turned both the British Monarchy – an institution that by their very existence is a constant visible reminder of colonisation and oppression – and bastions of the great British public into a downward spiral.

The coded racist undercurrent from the press was bubbling

from the outset, from describing an American woman as 'exotic' and 'straight outta Compton' (aka the ghetto). These dog whistles were present even before the couple were married. In fact, Prince Harry issued an unprecedented Royal statement in 2016 calling for racism towards Meghan in the press and social media to stop.

When they got engaged, it continued, with a senior UKIP politician's girlfriend stating that Meghan's race would 'taint' the Royal family.[33] A random thought for some, but not without motivation for others. This belief is synonymous with the term 'Blue Blood', derived in the late-sixteenth century which translates from the Spanish phrase 'sangre azul', meaning to belong to aristocracy. It was a term used to determine racial superiority with the belief that the lighter and paler one's skin was and the more you could see their veins, the more 'pure' they were. It was used to identify white Christian nobility, which was seen as superior to Jewish, Muslim or West African nobility. This ideology, which some still believe today, infers that you can only be a pure Royal if your skin is white. The irony of people believing Mcghan, someone who is 'part Black', would 'taint' the Royal Family by simply being in it, is not lost on me.

But when their big day arrived, for a short while, things felt hopeful. I had the pleasure of witnessing their union and attending their wedding day at Windsor Castle in May 2018 as a media expert, and my joy at watching them fuse their cultures together in such a traditional establishment was something to behold. I am certain it was no coincidence they married on 19 May, the birthday of Queen Charlotte, descendant of a Portuguese Moor described as the first Black Queen to rule Britain and Ireland for 57 years.

The intentional touches were noticed throughout, from

an animated (and very long) sermon about love from Bishop Michael Curry to hearing the mesmerising, yet reverberating gospel tones of The Kingdom Choir. My joy was palpable and, as I'd never been a royalist, completely unexpected – so much so, when I had a moment to process what I had the privilege of being part of and the historical significance of what I just witnessed, I cried.

That joy soon dissipated when I heard mutters from a royal commentator sitting in front of me, visibly aggravated as the ceremony unfolded. She eventually moaned loudly enough for me, the only Black person in her vicinity, to hear that the wedding was 'ridiculous and too Black'. She had little self-awareness at how her agitation at their wedding-day choices was doing nothing other than exposing her own racism. Fast forward to a conversation with a viscountess who stated that Meghan would never be accepted.

It was like I was in a parallel universe. Surrounded by all of this joy and vibrant celebration of diversity on the surface, but juxtaposed against an invisible, dysfunctional and disingenuous relationship with inclusion underneath – great metaphor of what systemic racism in Britain looks like. A day that pinned so much hope on having a 'half-Black' woman openly accepted into the monarchy being an opportunity to resolve Britain's age-old problems with race relations.

The toxicity and scrutiny only gained momentum after their wedding day. A BBC journalist (at the time), compared Archie, their first born, to a chimpanzee, just days after he was born. A common racist trope synonymous with comparing Black people to animals, he claimed it was just a joke. One journalist for CNN felt the need to write an article on 'how Black the royal baby will be'.[34]

It came as no surprise to witness overt toxicity coded, consistent and disproportionate scrutiny in the way Meghan was treated in comparison to other Royals. So much so, the Sussexes decided to emancipate themselves from the Royal Family and move to the United States of America, of all places, to get away from the toxicity of racism, in Britain.[35] Not even they could escape racism from the highest ranking in society.

This announcement caused TV personalities, royal experts, historians, broadcasters and MPs to spend the next few weeks having a very public and global meltdown, similar to one a few weeks prior when grime artist Stormzy was asked in an interview for Italian newspaper *La Repubblica* if Britain was still racist to which he replied 'definitely'.[36] Blaming the couple for dividing Britain, Harry was accused of not having a mind of his own and being 'pussy-whipped' by his wife (yes, really, it got that low). This incident yielded denials and debates around racism, with pundits finding bizarre pride in comparing Britain to other countries saying 'it wasn't as racist as them'. Go figure.

★

White Supremacy and White Cultural Standards

White supremacy is a system that dictates the 'default setting'; the default rhythm we all need to dance to. It is a system that has controlled false narratives about British history. The inherent, subtle, but persistent tacit agreement that 'foreigners' should speak

English when we visit their countries, on holiday; the expectation that we adhere to Eurocentric dress codes, beauty standards and hairstyles in schools or the workplace.

For example, hair discrimination has been a longstanding issue in Black communities in Britain. In 2017, a 12-year-old schoolboy Chikayzea Flanders was given an ultimatum by his secondary school in Fulham, London: to cut off his 'unprofessional' dreadlocks or face suspension.[37] Fast forward to 2019, schoolgirl Ruby Williams was repeatedly sent home from The Urswick School for simply having an afro, aka hair as it naturally grows out of one's head.[38] They both won discrimination cases.

The policing and sense of entitlement over our hair and bodies is not new. Understanding the nuances of the system we are all pawns in, is absolutely key to resisting the power of its magnetic undercurrent. Then and only then, can we start to address white skin privilege and its messy roots in racism. We must accept it is an unavoidable and inevitable by-product of colonisation, slavery and normalising white supremacy and systems of oppression for centuries, instead of using it as a weapon to shame others who 'don't yet get it' or interpreting it as a personal attack on your identity.

Systemic racism and white supremacy have always been about power over another person. If you have been systemically advantaged for so many years, the idea of giving up that 'power', societal advantage, and all too-familiar access might feel scary. It might also feel threatening and for some, just the idea of equality, of sharing that power can even feel like oppression. Ultimately, if you have enjoyed and have gotten used to the benefits of this unearned privilege, why would you or your peers want to give it up?

As our current climate is boldly revealing to us, things will not fundamentally change unless we take intentional steps to acknowledge and disrupt racism, in all of its forms, even those you find in yourself.

So let's start today. Take a moment to reflect on and consider these two questions:

1. What does it mean to be white?
2. How has your race benefited you?

★

2. Performative Allyship: The Hero and the Ego

'An embarrassment of the past has led to an ignorance in the present.'
JOSIAH ISLES[1]

We need to talk about performative allyship and your ego, fast. If left unchecked, both can lead you into thinking you are being actively anti-racist when you aren't. This leads to further wounding.

I don't know how else to say this so I'll just say it: Black people don't need you to rescue them. We don't. Buckle up. It's going to get bumpy.

We Don't Need Another Hero

In case you missed the memo, we have been rescuing ourselves and revolting against the oppressor throughout history. For example, contrary to popular belief that only great white men rescued us from slavery, it was the Haitian Revolution that began in 1791 and went on until 1804, the only successful slave revolt in history, that instigated the global abolishment of slavery. Many

44

of the freedom fighters, such as Suzanne Sanité Bélair, were Black women.

There were many other slave rebellions in British colonies, including Jamaica, that were also often led by incredible Black warrior women who were not taking any shit. Historian Stella Dadzie recounts many in her book, *A Kick in the Belly: Women, Slavery and Resistance* such as Cubah Cornwallis. Also known as Queen of Kingston, she was a healer to enslaved people, merchants and even her own slavers, using West African healing traditions of the Ashanti people of Ghana. As a warrior, she played a key role in a slave rebellion known as Tacky's Rebellion in St Mary's, Jamaica which went on for six months and included setting sugar works and cane fields on fire in 1760.[2]

She eventually won her freedom and used her knowledge to heal others, including Black people who were denied medical treatment due to the colour of their skin, and she set up one of the first recorded nursing facilities in the Caribbean, in Port Royal Jamaica, long before Mary Seacole. Her contribution to nursing and slave rebellions remains relatively unknown.

Following the Haitian Revolution, a huge contributing factor towards the decision to abolish slavery in British colonies was fear. After a number of slave rebellions in the British West Indies (now known as the Caribbean), the powers that be started to observe that enslaved people were essentially no longer giving a damn about dying and would rather lose their lives trying to get free than continue to live a life of enslavement.[3] That observation made the British government rethink whether continuing to enslave Black Africans was going to continue to be sustainable. Why? Because there was a huge fear (which is still present to this day) that Black folk would want to seek revenge and go on a murderous killing spree of white Europeans. *That* was a significant driving force that contributed to white Europeans doing a U-turn on slavery.

So, no, despite your impulse to 'fix', Black people don't need you to rescue them. We've been revolting, rescuing ourselves and rising up, in spite of systemic oppression, for centuries. We've had no choice but to, for our own self-preservation and survival. What we really need you to do is consciously, consistently and intentionally unlearn your racism. That's the one thing we can't do for you.

It's no secret that shame and guilt go hand in hand with this work – but you can't do this work in any meaningful, or truthful way without experiencing these feelings at some point, and you will consistently feel uncomfortable. They can be quite a force that can be both debilitating and disruptive and, if left unchecked, they can also stop you from doing the work at all. Trying to do anti-racism work while remaining comfortable, to actively avoid confronting feelings is just not possible. Well, I lie, it is, but this leads to performative allyship.

What is Performative Allyship?

Performative allyship actually has very little to do with reducing harm to Black folk and ending systems of oppression and more to do with white supremacy. It happens when you are not doing the work properly; when you want to skip and get to the end bit where you can demonstrate you're one of the 'good white people'. Performative allyship happens when you have leapt from half-listening, straight into action. This action is always impulsive, often linked to avoidance of feeling shame, which ends up being reactive. This can look like feeling an urgent need to 'prove' you aren't racist. In summer 2020, with so many public declarations of allyship, I recall a number of people, oddly, tagging me in social media posts, letting their followers know they signed up to my online anti-racism course and never actually signing up. This is not allyship; this is a stage performance, to manage your perception, so your ego can feel better about all that's wrong in the world, distance yourself from those 'other' white people and soothe your own guilt or shame about not acting sooner.

This all followed the abhorrent sequence of murders on Black bodies that summer, culminating in a video of George Floyd being executed in such a nonchalant manner by a police officer's knee, being passed around the internet and TV like entertainment. This led to a rightful surge of interest in the Black Lives Matter movement, a genuine desire to drive change accompanied by new swathes, and I mean swathes (my following quadrupled in days, and my colleagues' anti-racism books sold out across the globe) of white people – perhaps even you – waking up to the fact that racism exists. Many of these white people came swooping in with freshly ironed superhero capes, it having only just occurred to them, after all these years, that they, too, could do something about racism. What then ensued in an attempt to relieve feelings of guilt and anxiety related to racism, was impulsive, often fear-based, panic-driven, knee-jerk reactions. Cue social media black-out squares, using blacklivesmatter hashtags which ended up impeding grass-roots organisers coordinating Black Lives Matter (BLM) protests and flooding their feeds with random black squares that helped no one.

That's not allyship. That's your ego wanting you to be the hero of the story and feel like you're doing something to alleviate your guilt. Performative allyship provides a very seductive vessel to trick you into thinking it's coming from a place of authenticity. It's not. Performative allyship is not allyship, it is a by-product of racism and it is being governed by your ego.

Performative allyship can look like:

- Cancelling and shaming 'those white people over there' on the internet with your finest 'shame on you' comment (and hand gesture for good measure), without addressing your own racism.
- Making a corporate statement to stand in solidarity with Black Lives Matter, without checking in on any Black staff, nor addressing any of the racism and psychological unsafety present in the workplace.
- Sharing lots of links to articles that your friends should read that you haven't read yourself, whilst proudly declaring that you were one of the few that learned about 'slavery' at school, three decades ago.
- Donating to charity without any further anti-racist action.
- Fanfaring when you, or another white person, do the bare minimum to address racism.
- Begrudgingly agreeing that Black and Brown colleagues can form a staff network in the workplace, without providing any funding for it.
- Liking your Black friends' posts about racism, but not picking up the phone to check in on them in the height of Black Lives Matter protests.

- Conversations about racism becoming 'entertainment' on mainstream breakfast television shows.
- Perfectly curating a mini-styled shoot of anti-racism books and using them as props to gloss your social media feed and never actually reading any of them.
- White partners posting about racism on social media, but letting casual racism about their Black partner pass by the dinner table by white family.
- Spending energy complaining about old Christmas song lyrics or complaining about mud-packs used in an episode of *The Golden Girls* several decades ago and likening it to blackface.

Who is this actually serving?

★

Understanding White Saviourism

Performative allyship comes from a desire to soothe the guilt, shame or discomfort you are experiencing from witnessing abhorrent racism from 'those bad white people over there' who are, essentially letting the side down, so you can separate yourself from 'those' dodgy white people as quickly as possible. This behaviour, whether conscious or unconscious, functions in the same way; it is a tool to overcompensate for past transgressions, to self-soothe, and it is not new.

Another of my students shared: 'My performative allyship and saviourism is somewhere between perfectionism, people-pleasing and wanting to make everything OK in the world, so that I don't have to feel the pain, discomfort, hurt, or anger of others. I want utopia so I don't have to deal with big emotions. I wanted the answers quickly in anti-racism work, so I could do my bit and move on. I realised I can't make a difference if I can't face the thought of not being liked, or upsetting people.'

There's an impulsive desire to fix, be the hero of the story, to swoop in and rescue and, for some, it also comes from a place of superiority and/or a desire to be forgiven. It feeds into something called the 'White Saviour Industrial Complex' – a term first coined (off the back of an exasperated Twitter rant) by Harvard professor and novelist Teju Cole in 2012. Cole explains:

> White Saviour Industrial Complex is not about justice, it's about having a big emotional experience that validates privilege… There is much more to doing good work than 'making a difference.' There is the principle of first do no harm. There is the idea that those who are being helped ought to be consulted over the matters that concern them.[4]

White saviourism serves primarily to satisfy ego, an attempt to prove and show everyone, particularly Black people, that you're one of the 'good white people'. It centres your actions and intentions over and above the cause. It centres your intentions over reducing harm.

Feeling like you are helping and rescuing 'us' serves a purpose and a need for you. It immediately moves you from feeling helpless and hopeless and it feels far more satisfying than holding up a mirror to your own behaviour. It's coming from an inherent need to centre whiteness that has been role-modelled to be the societal 'norm'. Again, this isn't new or random behaviour.

The Hays Code

Media plays a firm role in social conditioning, cultural assumptions and perpetuating racist stereotypes, so let's look at it through the simple lens of storytelling and film and connect some dots.

From the 1930s until 1966, there was a filmmaking code that impacted Hollywood films for almost three decades called the 'Hays Code'. Named after Will Hays, the Hays Code was described as a 'moral code'. The code prohibited the creation of movies that 'lowered the moral standards of those who see it.'[5] This included anything from profanity and sex, through to miscegenation, meaning the reproduction of mixed-race people through inter-racial sex and relationships, and 'white' slavery. Film directors who wanted to tell stories centring the Black experience often had great difficulty gaining access to funding, something many leading Black filmmakers still experience as a by-product today.

The Hays Code censored and controlled the narrative of filmmaking to depict 'the correct standards of life' based on what was evidentially patriarchal Christian and white-supremacist standards. Nineteen pages long, it essentially undermined and stifled filmmaking to the nth degree to only tell limited stories through limited lenses. The code also imposed the following:[6]

1. Religion could never be depicted in a mocking manner.
2. Drug use, including alcohol consumption, could not be shown unless the plot called for it.

3. Topics considered 'perverse' could not be discussed or shown, including homosexuality, interracial relationships, bestiality, and venereal diseases – imagine, homosexuality and interracial relationships were considered 'perverse'.[7]

4. The sanctity of marriage needed to be upheld at all times.

5. Crime could never be portrayed in a positive light – though slavery seemed to be a common firm fixture.

6. Blasphemy was forbidden, as was nudity and any portrayals of sex in an explicit manner.

7. Scenes of childbirth were also banned.

What I find most profound is that the Hays Code also stated that 'the audience should never be thrown to the side of crime, wrong-doing, evil or 'sin' while depictions of 'Black' slavery and 'blackface' (which also gained huge popularity in Britain) continued to be perfectly acceptable under the Hays 'moral' Code. Go figure. Beloved classics like *Gone with the Wind* (1939) have been accused of perpetuating racism whilst simultaneously romanticising slavery in the American south. Hattie McDaniel's character Mammy was depicted as loving her slaver suggesting Black characters were happy with the current state of play. Hattie McDaniel became the first African American to win an Oscar for the role she played, whilst being segregated from her fellow white cast members at the Oscars.

The Defiant Ones (1958) featuring Sidney Poitier and Tony Curtis, was a film about two escaped convicts, one Black and one white, bound together in handcuffs. One scene features a young white boy who finds the two scuffling and holds them at gunpoint. In an attempt to disarm him, the white character pushes the boy and he strikes his head on a rock and knocks himself out. Poitier's character instinctively cradles the child in his lap to attend to him to check he is OK, while the white character played by Curtis is quite happy to leave him and is heard saying 'Come on, let's go.' The child wakes to see the face of a Black man cradling him and runs from him into the arms of the white man and asks him to keep him away from the Black man. Both of these films were created during the Hays Code era.

This continued controlled racist narrative of Black people in subservient, criminal or dehumanising roles continued to feed into the negative perceptions, in the minds of many, including Black people over a thirty-year period.

The legacy of this Code cannot be underestimated, and whilst the code was by recommendation only, filmmakers who didn't abide by it had difficulty getting produced by Hollywood Studios. It also fed into the belief that we still hear batted around now by leading film producers that Black doesn't sell, and that a white audience won't be able to engage with a narrative that is centred around Blackness. Two words: *Black Panther*. It was *Black Panther* that spectacularly debunked the myth that Black doesn't sell. Premiering in February 2018, it was the first superhero film centring Black empowerment, which smashed box office records, grossing $1.3 billion worldwide, earning more in its opening weekend than *Iron Man*, *Thor* and good old *Captain America* combined.

The ingrained perception that took firm root in the Hays Code era was that white audiences would not be able to relate to stories that centre Blackness, even including those that were about Black struggle in the height of slavery or segregation, unless those stories were told through the eyes of a 'good white person': the *hero* of the story. This often led to true stories being misinterpreted, or films being 'toned down' to satisfy white mainstream audiences. To satisfy, or even to soothe egos, so the audience doesn't feel too confronted by accounts of the past, we end up diluting the message with endings in Hollywood classics like *The Help* and *Green Book* (both white directors) where we all 'Kumbaya' and 'merrily-we-roll-along happily ever after' at the end. Both films chose not to centre the Black characters and their dehumanisation at the hands of white people, but to tell the stories through the white leading characters' perspectives on racism. Both feature endings that suggest that segregation, social suffering at the hands of the white majority and the impact of continued dehumanisation and systemic racism can simply be ended with Black people just forgiving white people and swiftly moving on.

> '*The centering of whiteness and white people, white values, white norms and white feelings over everything and everyone else. The belief, whether conscious or not, that whiteness is normal and BIPOC are "other"'*.
>
> LAYLA F. SAAD[8]

A powerful example of white centring and white saviourism caught my attention in the 2016 blockbuster *Hidden Figures* based on the book by Margot Lee Shetterly. The narrative captures the untold and powerful true stories of Black women, specifically pioneering NASA mathematician Katherine Johnson, whose calculations helped launch the first American into space. I loved discovering this piece of history in this film and I had no idea about these incredible Black women who fought against racism and misogyny at the height of segregation at NASA until I first saw it. I was elated and went to read up about Katherine – it all went a bit downhill from there.

In an interview with *Vice News* in 2017, the real Katherine Johnson, played by Taraji P. Henson, discussed some scenes that featured heavily in the film – scenes that saw her character having to walk half a mile, to the 'colored people only' bathroom every time nature called.[9] This was clearly for dramatic effect because it wasn't true. The book and Katherine stated that she simply refused to entertain segregation at NASA. She refused to degrade herself. In the interview, she can be heard saying she simply just used the white woman's bathroom instead. She decided to end bathroom segregation and get on with her job. However, instead of telling the real story of Katherine's courage and resistance to segregation, we see a fictional white boss played by Kevin Costner beat the 'colored ladies room' sign hanging above door off, before heroically stating: 'Here at NASA, we all pee the same colour.'

When challenged on this depiction in the same interview, director Theodore Melfi said, 'There needs to be white people doing the right thing and Black people doing the right thing and someone does the right thing, so who cares who does the right thing, so long as the right thing is achieved?' If, using the words of Melfi, it truly doesn't matter who 'does the right thing' then why did we need this fictional white saviour scene at all? Why can't we sit in the reality of our history that many Black people courageously resisted segregation and sadly, most white people did not do the right thing?

In these instances of storytelling, it was a conscious choice to centre a white perspective. Placing a white person as the hero of a story rooted in racial injustice not only absolves accountability and glosses over the harm caused by whiteness, but invariably means that Black voices are misrepresented or completely erased – and the erasure of Black women's contributions, in particular, throughout history and to this day, is rife.

Placing you as the saviour, simultaneously places us, Black people, in the stereotypical role of the victim, being subservient and ultimately being 'less than', incapable and always needing to be rescued.

Recognising White Saviourism

White saviourism is not just rife in filmmaking, it is everywhere. It is certainly alive and kicking in church missionaries and charitable aides (which inspired Cole's original Twitter rant). British charitable organisation Comic Relief spectacularly came under fire in February 2019 when TV personality Stacey Dooley took a trip to Uganda on behalf of the charity and took a photo with a young Black toddler (who looked none too pleased), holding him in her arms cooing at how cute he looked. Labour MP David Lammy responded with a tweet[10] saying, 'The world does not need any more white saviours. As I've said before, this just perpetuates tired and unhelpful stereotypes. Let's instead promote voices from across the continent of Africa and have serious debate.' Comic Relief is regularly the target of public critique with accusations of enabling 'poverty porn', i.e. sending predominantly white celebrities out to the African continent with a camera crew, presented like nothing more than a photo opportunity with 'poor Black children', to demonstrate these 'good' deeds being done by 'good white people' on social media and beyond.

Of course, I am not challenging the need for charities and aid organisations themselves, they are important, but how aid is presented is key, and any charity that does not have a function and a core mission to empower the communities they are serving to be self-sufficient is even more problematic. Instead of this obsession with 'poverty and trauma porn', charities could intentionally choose to centre Black voices and share news about the inspiring work being done from and by people in the community and it wouldn't be remiss to share another perspective and acknowledge that more people in the African diaspora give back to Africa to aid their growth and liberation.

This is before we even start to address the irony that some of the extreme poverty that is present in parts of Africa today is a direct result of the impact of the legacy of British colonial invasion and land resource and extraction.

Don't underestimate the power of one-dimensional storytelling and representation and how they can seemingly so effortlessly inform your worldview about Black people. Journal on it, and be honest: What negative perceptions do you hold about Africa and Black people?

It's this continued misrepresentation that feeds into the narrative that Black people are all poor, destitute, and riddled with disease. A case in point: a family member and fashion designer was doing her food shop near her home in Chelsea, London in May 2020 and was told to go back to Africa and stop spreading diseases.

Even I still recall the detrimental impact of that continuous programming ringing in my ears and how that influenced my sense of self at just 7 years old. Noticing that the only people who looked like me on TV were in charity idents, with flies buzzing round their faces, with the white English man with the sombre, sad voice as a backdrop. And because of playground jibes about being brown like poo, I then naturally assumed the reason these children had flies buzzing around them was because we were 'dirty' and asking good 'white' British people to donate and save us on TV.

There is a fine line between helping and being performative, but there is a line between the two, and being an ally means being able to recognise this. To give clarity, I like to describe what allyship means to me as a Black woman. Allyship in its essence is a person who advocates and works alongside the Black community, who uplifts communities for a shared common goal, driven *solely* by the cause – to dismantle systemic racism. Meanwhile, 'a saviour', in black and white, is 'a person who saves, rescues, or delivers.' Often without consent.

To go back to Teju Cole's quote, it is important to *first do no harm*. That means acknowledging and addressing where this innate desire to rescue Black people and be one of the good white people is actually coming from. It means unlearning racism, so you don't use us as props to manage your perceptions. It means being honest about knowledge gaps and not claiming to be the fountain of all knowledge on Black people because you've read some books and watched some documentaries so don't need to do the work – perhaps maybe even thinking you are above it. It's also important, where possible, to gain consent. Be conscious of your motivations to help. This is about working alongside, not controlling and working on behalf of. It's ultimately about improving the lives of others without the need for reward and regardless of the potential impact of doing so.

If you find yourself slipping into that role of the saviour, it might be coming from your own projection of Black people, one that might not be true or positive, that comes from various narratives you've been fed in the media, one-dimensional history books, censored filmmaking and perhaps even at home. You end up with perceived knowledge based on skewed narratives and beliefs that we are weak, inferior, less-than and incapable of advancing and revolting without a white person saving us. And without a doubt, if you operate from that place, you will cause more harm. Only you can truthfully answer what your projections of us are.

Questions to consider:

- Am I acting because it's the right thing to do, to centre the needs of others, or am I doing this to centre my own needs to feel better and make myself look good?
- Am I doing this because I feel I know more, from a place of superiority, because I feel I am more capable?

★

Ego and Identity

Ego and fear are big barricades to being actively anti-racist. You may have fear around loss of identity as 'the saviour', fear of being 'found out' and exposed, fear that you're an imposter, and worse still, a real fear of being condemned, or even hated.

Your ego will hate anti-racism work with a passion and will resist doing it with mighty force – it wants to defend your position of being 'good' or 'right' at all costs, or simply turn away.

That leads to skating around the issue and going into a safe performative allyship, a 'see, I'm not racist, I'm an ally' mode. Why do you think I named this book *The Good Ally*? Because I know it speaks to that part of you that wants to be good and right; to that part of you that wants to protect that perception of yourself, that part of your identity that feels inextricably linked to being 'a decent human being'.

We all have ego. For example, my ego wants you to love this book – well, not necessarily 'love' it, but be changed by it. My ego wants everyone to read this book and unlearn racism so we can change the world. My ego wants to get it right; it wants perfection, which, during many times of this writing process left me staring at a blank screen, frozen and not writing anything at all. My wiser self, who is able to see the world beyond my own experience, knows that's not realistic and that some people will be changed by this book and some won't, and a whole lot more won't ever read it. My wiser self knows that my self-worth isn't based upon whether or not people read the book, whether you like me, or this book, or not. My ego, on the other hand, is freaking the hell out right now.

Ego, especially a healthy ego, is necessary, and can serve us well. It can also be a pain in the backside. In brief, ego forms important parts of our personality. It was most notably explored by neurologist and founder of psychoanalysis, Sigmund Freud, who is one of world's most famous psychological figures. His theories, loved and loathed, shaped our view and understanding of therapy of the mind, underpinning clinical therapy to date.

Freud believed that human personality is complex and multi-faceted. He developed a psychoanalytic theory of personality, composed of three elements. He named these three elements of personality the id, ego and superego.

The id, which I prefer to refer to as the 'Child Ego' in anti-racism because of its childlike qualities, is the only ego state that has been present since the moment we were born. It is instinctive, unconscious and it is hugely primal – this is the ego state I'll be focusing on in this chapter because this is the ego state that causes the most havoc in anti-racism work.

The others (because I know you're nosy) are:

- The ego – the component of our personality that is able to deal with reality and helps regulate those childlike impulses we get from the id. It functions in both conscious and the unconscious mind.
- The superego – this component holds all our moral stand-ards together, informing our judgements. This is our 'sense of right or wrong'.

Back to the child ego (the id). This ego state is driven by pleas-ure, with a desire to be happy, to be right, to feel good and soothed. Think of this ego state in the basic terms of a baby. A baby is hungry? The baby cries and continues to cry until their basic needs are fulfilled. This is being governed by the child ego and when basic needs are met, there is a sense of immediate gratifica-tion. However, when these needs are not met, this can result in overwhelming feelings of anxiety or some form of tension.

In anti-racism, this can show up in very-childlike ways and often intersects with racialised or white fragility – an inability to tolerate any kind of racial stress. Common behaviour includes extreme defensiveness, withdrawal, anger, belligerence, an insatiable appetite to get it right and people-please, and to have all of the information *now*. It can show up as egocentrism, self-centred expectations that people who have experienced racism should behave in the way you want, now, based on your view of the world, without any regard for them and theirs. More often than not, it also shows up as emotional immaturity, resulting in losing the ability to think critically for yourself and being unable to hold cross-racial conversations.

I recall having a meeting with a Black colleague a few years ago. She was having a board meeting with a number of white beauty practitioners. Their meeting overran, and I was invited to tag onto the end, which spilled into socialising. My colleague and I were talking about the importance of representation in beauty and, in particular, Black women and the impact of colourism – the discrimination against individuals with a darker skin tone (often within the same ethnic group) and the inherent belief that to have lighter skin and Eurocentric features is somehow better and more desirable. Colourism also impacts employment outcomes and a 2018 study[11] found Black people with darker skin tones were paid less than Black people with lighter skin within the same ethnic group. Yet another 'gift' of colonialism, slavery and white supremacy, and even though skin-bleaching products are banned in the UK, it continues to be a thriving sector in the cosmetic industry, with brands like Unilever selling skin whitening products to lots of people in the Caribbean, Africa, India, Bali and Pakistan.

One of the members from the previous board meeting over-heard our conversation and asked us to expand on what we were discussing. My colleague was happy to do so and, to give context, spoke about the root cause of colourism. When my colleague attempted to talk about racism and slavery, it was at this point, this senior member of staff – a grown adult easily in her 60s – put both fingers in her ears like a child would and said she didn't want to hear any more; her child ego state was in full swing. My colleague and I were utterly stunned, but not remotely surprised. But for me, it had an extra sting in its tail to see this type of behaviour happening at board level in the beauty industry.

As adults, we have learned to control this ego state and this part of our personality – evidently, some more than others. Otherwise, we'd be grabbing whatever we want off of shop shelves and walking out of our favourite restaurant's kitchen with food – you know when you are famished and you can see your meal on the pass just sitting there getting cold, while the waiting staff appear to be taking their sweet time? I know you know that urge, born only to serve that need for immediate gratification. However, we still flit in and out of this ego state, especially in conversations about racism.

For the most part, when you're entering into anti-racism territory, you're going to feel so uncomfortable and exposed that you'll instinctively want to seek out any opportunity to feel good again: a desire to be soothed by a Black friend or partner who can 'prove' you aren't racist; sending unsolicited messages to Black peers to let them know you're doing anti-racism work. Trust me, when you are fully immersed in anti-racism work, Black and Brown people absolutely know, and you don't need to signal it. You may attempt to relieve your feelings of anxiety related to racism by taking immediate, panic-driven, knee-jerk reactions which can cause harm or have little meaningful impact, such as going on a mission to make complaints about racist jokes in old TV shows like the British comedy *Fawlty Towers*. This is nonsensical. I'd much rather people took the time to learn about history and engage in meaningful conversations about what era those shows were born out of, what was going on in the world at the time, its impact on modern society today, and what we can learn from it, rather than spending energy complaining about old shows. Again, who is this actually serving?

Another student shared about the battle of her ego and how this showed up in her behaviour:

> I wanted to let all my white friends on social media know we are failing Black and Brown people and here's what we need to do. However, firstly, much of what I was saying was 'stealing the mic' from Black voices, and the way I did it was self-focused, with an element of 'look at me, I'm a "good" white person' virtue signal to the Black and Brown people who are following me. It was also prioritising outspoken and performative acts over actually looking after my Black friends during a very hard time, having difficult conversations with white friends and family, and also doing more inner work and research for how to teach my kids to be anti-racist. My priorities were just totally off, and the sh★t I was saying was doing more harm than good. I see now after working through your course, that my ego was on fire and I was deeply unaware of my potential for harm as a white woman.

If we have not learned how to self-regulate and self-soothe, feelings of anxiety can become overwhelming and result in these types of performative reactionary responses to alleviate your own discomfort. You end up tricking your ego into thinking the coast is clear so you can go back to playing the role of the hero, in search of a cookie and some milk from Black people for doing the bare minimum. That's not doing the work – that's you managing your perception and soothing your child ego state.

When you catch yourself in this state, remember the response you are having is instinctive and normal. Your ego is trying to protect you so don't beat yourself up about it, but notice it so you can act accordingly, or sometimes just completely surrender to it.

Notice your breathing and slow it down. Breathe in for 3 seconds, release for 5 seconds and repeat. Then let it go or respond. If you can, take breaks, move your body, go for a walk, exercise, do anything to physically change your state and energy.

Freud believed that the development of the superego and ego is what helps us control these childlike impulses. It's worth remembering that these elements of our personality don't work in isolation. They are fluid, like us, and they are always interacting with each other, influencing our personality and, of course, behaviour. Addressing any unmet needs and being self-aware in anti-racist interactions is key.

Consider these prompts if you are being activated:

1. Am I serving the cause right now or am I trying to prove I am one of the good ones?
2. Am I operating from a place of self-righteousness?
3. Am I being governed by my child ego right now?

4. Am I demanding to be heard and in turn, finding it hard to listen?
5. Am I operating from a wiser version of myself where I am able to temporarily remove my ego and remember that I am serving something bigger than me?
6. If I am feeling anxious as a result of this anti-racist interaction – what needs need to be met?

We all have basic needs that need to be met, including the need to be soothed, so learning to self-soothe (or self-parent) will help you support the child ego and its childlike urges and better sustain your anti-racism activism, and also support others in theirs. Consciously working to address your unmet needs means having to build more agility with recognising feelings.

If you're feeling anxious, try to identify your unmet needs. Ask yourself what's beneath the anxiety – is it fear? What's beneath the fear? Is it fear of rejection and not belonging? If so, who or where provides you with a sense of safety and belonging? Can you go there or reach out?

If you're feeling overwhelmed, what do you need to make you feel less so? Stability and support? Peace and quiet? Shared reality? To feel seen and heard? What can you do and who can you connect with to help you with that? If underneath the overwhelm you are ultimately feeling helpless, what can you do to feel helpful in a meaningful way? When you are resourced, what can you do to contribute?

Meet those unmet needs troops, and don't be afraid to also role model to asking for what you need.

When the child ego is running rampant, don't ruminate.

Instead, speak to a peer who is engaged in anti-racism work so you can acknowledge it with self-compassion and not a beating stick, express it and get you back to a more useful state. There, you can continue listening, learning, self-interrogating and doing important work, rather than letting your child ego go wild, steal your car keys without a licence and go out for a spin.

You're in control. Get back in the driving seat and meet those unmet needs in a more productive and useful way.

★

3. Grey Matter: Beyond Black and White

'It is not a racial problem, it's a matter of whether you're willing to look at your life and be responsible for it and then begin to change it.'
JAMES BALDWIN[1]

I witness a lot of my students feeling hugely conflicted when they begin their anti-racism journeys. Once they start peeling back the layers of themselves, a battle of identities ensues, a fight between their outer hero and their inner villain. That discovery of being someone they thought they weren't. The discovery that they, someone who previously identified as anti-racist, have perpetuated racism against people they love. I know, it doesn't feel great.

One of my anti-racism students shared with me: 'I was confronted with the fact that I wasn't the person I thought I was. I wasn't the role I had "assigned" myself. I was flooded by shame, guilt, embarrassment and disgust at myself.'

Some common responses to this battle of identities have often resulted in extremes, from complete disengagement from the work, leading to further guilt, to obsessive over-consuming and an unhealthy desire to be right and 'liked'. Sound familiar? It can also often lead to misdirected 'shame on you' anger, projecting anger and blame onto other white people who are further behind on their journeys. And then there's the other extreme: the inner conflict was so palpable for one of my clients, it induced vomiting.

The concept of 'good vs. bad' suddenly doesn't make any sense. The barrage of unwelcome contradictions leads to visible confusion – I frequently see frowning and signs of disbelief; the bewilderment at being branded 'complicit' by being silent, while also being asked not to speak up on behalf of Black and Brown folk; the internal conflict and palpable fear of saying the wrong thing, whilst having a strong desire to say and *do* something so you are no longer complicit.

Is this something you have experienced? What happened? What did you make it mean? How does this experience feel in your body? Journal on this moment.

Experiencing extreme feelings of conflict are quite common in anti-racism and that could be a sign of something called *splitting*, a common psychological process which, according to Sigmund Freud, is a defence mechanism that generally serves to protect the ego.[2]

The simplest way to describe splitting is that we start to think in simplistic black and white. We divide how we see circumstances into two parts and see things as absolutes. This is a common human response and we all do it to some degree, because our brains are used to putting things into boxes. It is an evolutionary processing tool that once helped us detect danger in prehistoric times, allowing us to determine who was part of the 'in' group and who was a threat. By grouping information this way, it also helps us to cope when we feel overwhelmed so we can process the sheer volume of information we receive.

Splitting occurs when we start to think in extremes. When we start to only associate positive or negative attributes with ourselves and others, this can create huge problems.

For example:

- Black men = criminal
- I'm right = you're wrong
- Non-racist = good person
- A racist = bad person
- Us vs them

This simplistic good vs. bad dichotomy in anti-racism fools no one (well, maybe some white people) and it does nothing other than warp reality, keep us stagnant and serve egos. Unsurprisingly, we are much more likely to personally experience splitting, or even witness others split, when an individual's anxiety increases and as we all know, just the mention of the words 'white people' or 'racism' seems to bring on the sweats. The by-product? A whole lot of splitting and cognitive dissonance (inconsistent thoughts or beliefs that are incompatible with behaviour), that are reductive and ultimately help absolutely no one.

Some common examples of splitting in anti-racism work:

- Cancel culture – the withdrawal of support, ostracising or publicly shaming someone for doing or saying something problematic, or simply making a mistake, without any opportunity to engage in conversation or atone; not to be mistaken with holding someone accountable.

- If you voted to leave the EU (or for a particular party), you're a racist.
- If you're racist, unfriend me now.

In this context, splitting also demonstrates a failure to recognise by that very definition, by the very terms that you have set, that means unfriending yourself – because, as a white person, you have inherent racism too.

Splitting means we have difficulty thinking about certain topics cohesively, or seeing things holistically. It ignores the nuance that people are not their behaviour; it bypasses the crucial fact that we all have the capacity to be good people *and* do pretty shitty things consciously. As someone racialised as white, you definitely have the capacity to do racist things that cause harm unconsciously and unintentionally. So there needs to be room for nuance, otherwise it creates a barrier to learning, empathy, growth or change – ironically four key ingredients that are necessary in becoming actively anti-racist.

★

The Trouble with Absolutes

In 2020, activist Munroe Bergdorf was challenged after she announced she would be working with L'Oréal Paris again. L'Oréal had ditched her in 2017 for writing about racism on her Facebook page following the death of activist Heather Heyer at a far-right rally in Charlottesville, USA. Bergdorf had effectively been punished for speaking up about racism and, not only did she lose her job, but received ferocious abuse online, including death threats and annihilation in British media, which had a detrimental impact on her mental health – all because L'Oréal didn't want to be associated with her comments because they felt they were at odds with company values.

Fast forward to summer 2020, after the murder of George Floyd, and L'Oréal launched a campaign 'speaking out is worth it' in support of the Black community. Bergdorf called out the racial hypocrisy following her sacking on her Instagram page. After further communication, the results were an apology from the new Vice President, a €25,000 donation to transgender and gender-variant charity Mermaids and a further €25,000 dona-tion to UK Black Pride, along with an invitation for Bergdorf to sit under the new Diversity and Inclusion Advisory board management. While we can't be a martyr to every cause and yes, some are way past redemption, many organisations and individuals often just need guidance, and that starts with letting them demonstrate atonement.

Anti-racism work is ultimately about collective healing, which cannot happen if we keep thinking in absolutes – if we keep locking people off and cancelling them when they do something shitty, how can we hold them accountable so they can learn, grow and change? We want to get to a better place of understanding and in that process accountability, boundaries and atonement are necessary; barricades do not help the cause.

★

24 June 2016. The day we were all stunned to hear Britain would be leaving the EU, even my husband – who voted for Brexit.

I remember social media timelines flooded with 'If you voted Brexit, unfriend me now' and 'If you voted Brexit, you're a disgusting human being *and* you're a racist.' None of these retorts made much sense to me because I could see the nuance; that it was perfectly possible to vote Brexit, to want better for the people, to demand better from our government, to still love the EU, to be completely loveable and not be a right-wing extremist. It was entirely possible for someone you love and respect (as I do my husband) to have a different political opinion and still love and respect them.

I remember being surprised and confused by his choice to vote Brexit, because for the most part we had voted similarly in the past, so I just asked him to tell me more about his choice and why he was voting to leave the EU to help me better understand. He simply said: 'The political system is not working, it's not designed for people like you and me and it needs a shake-up.' I'm not saying I agree with this tactic, but it was another way to look at it. Funnily enough, we didn't get divorced, and still belly-laugh together every day (I did, however, spend the next few weeks and months jibing him every time the British pound plummeted and blamed him entirely for its decline).

Splitting means being unable to acknowledge the nuance that someone like my husband, a Black man, who I love, could vote to leave the EU, care about racial justice and not be a racist.

The Trouble with Splitting in British Institutions

Increased anxiety, overwhelm and shame spirals, coupled with a new identity crisis, means you will definitely come up against splitting in yourself and others in your anti-racism journey. Splitting allows you to deflect and avoid dealing with confronting feelings. You are going to be continually seduced by absolutes and will end up filtering out important and vital pieces of information and at times, ignoring facts, in order to confirm your own bias – including bias that says the police are good and villains are bad.

If you are someone who has been raised to automatically trust and feel protected by the police, you might struggle to believe there could be power misuse and widespread institutionalised racism in the police force.

Deaths in police custody, sadly, are not isolated incidents. Between 1969 and 1999 there were over 1,000 deaths in British police custody and even though deaths in custody continue to rise at alarming rates, no officers involved have been convicted since 1969.[3] Deaths in police custody in England and Wales also disproportionately impact Black, Asian and Ethnic Minorities as a result of use of excessive force by the police.[4] For example, in 2016 Mzee Mohammed-Daley an 18-year-old student living with autism and ADHD died shortly after being forcefully detained by eighteen police officers and a further eight security guards in Liverpool ONE Shopping Centre.[5]

One of the most horrendous cases of an abuse of power was that of Christopher Alder. In 1998, the former British soldier, a Black man, choked to death while handcuffed, lying face down, motionless, with his trousers pulled down to his ankles, while officers stood around laughing and making monkey chants.

And even though the verdict from the inquest ruled unlawful killing, all police officers were acquitted.[6]

If your gut response to what I have shared above is, 'Well, what did they do to be detained and warrant that treatment?' instead of empathy, as if they somehow deserve to be treated worse than animals, that is an invitation to interrogate your racism.

In 1982, police officers were found inciting racial hatred as part of research carried out by Black sociologist John Fernandes. This research was part of a new Multicultural Unit to make a case for anti-racism training at Hendon Police College, following government recommendations as a result of growing racial tensions between the police and the Black community to tackle 'racial disadvantage'. One police officer in training stated, 'I think all Blacks are a pain and should be ejected from society.'[7]

Ken Fero, documentary filmmaker and director of *Injustice* (2001), a film showcasing true accounts of police brutality, was threatened with legal action by the Police Federation if he or any other network screened his film.[8] The police – an institution designed to protect and serve – is also an institution many families try to protect their children 'from'. Instead of believing that institutional racism remains a widespread issue in policing, some find it easier to think it's just down to a 'few bad apples' instead. However, it is entirely possible to condemn the continued abuse of power by the police, to want to hold them accountable for institutionalised racism and actually implement the recommendations made over twenty years ago in the Macpherson report *and* be proud of those in the force who protect us, uphold the law and are public servants for all of us.

It's the same with our parents. We generally get protective over them. We can put them in God–like positions. So if anyone else criticises them, we immediately get defensive and usually respond with some kind of 'Don't talk bad about my mum!' – even if their behaviour in a moment may have been questionable. We hear feedback about our parents' behaviour as a direct attack on them as individuals, and we split. For many of us this means, especially in conversations about racism, our parents' behaviour often goes unchallenged. And the same is true of our institutions.

Let's take our beloved NHS for example – an institution that we have also fetishised, that we have put on a platinum pedestal and that can't ever do anything wrong. We have framed the NHS, much like the police, to be 'heroes' and 'saviours' who rescue us, instead of looking at them as trained experts and a collective of individuals who are imperfect and doing their job – some better than others. We have romanticised the NHS and therefore struggle to hear, listen and believe stories about institutionalised racism that might tip them off that pedestal. The result? We split and fail to hold them to account, and medical racism continues to run rampant.

At the height of the COVID-19 outbreak in 2020, stories about NHS workers were the leading newspaper headlines and the British press seemed to consistently showcase predominantly white NHS workers as the heroes on front pages. This was a peculiar editorial choice in an industry that was built upon the Windrush generation and immigration where Black, Asian and Ethnic minority people make up a significant portion of staff workforce in NHS England, higher than the national average at 19.7 per cent and in London alone, representation is nearly half at 45 per cent.[9] This erasure of Black people and non–Black People of Colour irked me – there was a clear narrative being painted at the time about who was 'saving' us from this disease and who was being blamed for spreading and disproportionately dying from it.

The pandemic most certainly revealed some questionable behaviour because, when we feel like we are under attack, we go to our most primal survival state. We fend for ourselves and our ugly unaddressed prejudices come out in their most rampant forms, even at work. Some of the interviews I conducted for this book from healthcare professionals were sobering. The public were clapping for carers on a Thursday and refusing to be treated by Black, Brown, East and South-East Asian medical staff on a Friday. Because if you paid attention to the press, who were painted as the heroes of this story and who were painted as the villains?

Around this time, I was approached by a mainstream news outlet keen to explore if racism in the NHS could be contributing to disproportionate COVID deaths among Black, Asian and ethnic minority groups, and to hear some of the lived experiences of people working within it. I worked informally with the news outlet over a number of weeks to support their research by connecting them with NHS workers, speaking with them, sending articles, stats and reams of data, and even data from the British Medical Association about racial discrimination already recorded and new data being gathered from organisations like Pregnant Then Screwed, who saw an exponential increase in pregnancy discrimination in the NHS against women of colour around this time. They also sought permission to speak to some of my interviewees and hear personal accounts of workplace racism and spoke with some of them at length. They decided not to run the story in the end because there 'wasn't enough evidence'.

Even when we are presented with data, articles *and* empirical evidence, accounts of racism are still disbelieved and dismissed, as 'character' or a clash in personalities, especially when findings challenge that God-like perception of an institution or individual we love, like a parent, the NHS and even the Royal Family. It creates enormous internal conflict and goes against your bias, impacting your ability to respond or even do your job from a non-biased place. White dominance has historically been maintained by controlling the stories we read and see in the press, influencing our perception of institutions, groups of people and even individuals we have never met, such as Meghan Markle.

In an exclusive interview with Oprah Winfrey in March 2021, Meghan and Harry broke their silence about why they left the British Monarchy and, in doing so, confirmed large contributing factors were the racism in Britain and harassment from British tabloids, which had had a detrimental impact on Meghan's mental health. Meghan revealed it got to the point where she no longer wanted to live and was suicidal.[10]

This information was incompatible with many journalists' predominant view. One article in the *Daily Mail* labelled her as a 'suicidal race victim'[11] and former *Good Morning Britain* presenter and journalist Piers Morgan stated that Meghan had lied throughout her interview, including about being suicidal.[12] The idea that she was vulnerable and suicidal, and that Harry took the decision to step back and keep his family safe, goes against the character Morgan and many others had built up in their minds about Meghan being a ruthless bully who, along with Harry, should stop playing the victim because they 'brought the negative press on themselves'.[13]

Morgan was very transparent about his dislike for Meghan and had publicly assassinated her character in press articles and on TV for years. In an attempt to defend his position, bias and ego, it was easier to accuse her of lying about suicidal ideation than believe her and to perhaps even reflect on or feel remorse for his own contribution instead. Morgan's on-air comments resulted in more than 41,000 complaints to the Office of Communications (Ofcom), and mental health charity Mind issuing a statement condemning his behaviour and contacting ITV. He was also held to account by colleague Alex Beresford live on air, which resulted in Morgan storming off set and out of *Good Morning Britain*, for good.

★

Building Emotional Maturity and Healthy Relationships

Splitting can also happen in a lot in friendships. If a Black friend highlights that something you did or said was racist, that will more than likely trigger a shame spiral and an urge to defend your position and feel soothed. In the early stages of anti-racism, when you are still in a relatively fixed position of 'I'm a good white person, so I just need the tools and language and I'm good to go', you will not be used to being given feedback on your racist behaviour and will probably end up splitting. It will completely destabilise you.

As with any form of heightened anxiety or stress, our cognitive ability becomes impaired. The amygdala, the most primal part of our brain, responsible for our sense of safety and behaviour, is activated. It acts fast. It gets your body ready to do what it thinks needs to be done, including 'elimination' to make you as light as possible in case you need to run (cue upset stomach). Its role is to protect you from perceived danger. So, when your identity feels like it is under attack in anti-racist conversations or incidents, if your behaviour is impulsive and quite reactive, it's likely that this part of the brain has been activated. And sadly, for some people who have negative associations of Black people, just seeing a Black person's face can trigger this stress response.

When the amygdala is activated, it essentially takes over, preventing us from accessing the prefrontal cortex, the part we use to analyse, rationalise and make informed decisions so we can respond rather than react. The result? We end up splitting, reacting, completely shutting down, or all of the above. One thing is for sure, when we're in this state, we absolutely do not have the capacity to actively listen, make rational decisions, or engage in meaningful conversations with friends.

This means that when given feedback on racism by a Black friend you may struggle to hear and believe that you are both still loved by them, and that you've also hurt them. Instead, you might completely lock them off, deciding that they're 'attacking you', framing them – even if they're someone you love – as being 'the villain' so that you can hold onto your 'good white person' identity. You stop listening. Instead of focusing on atonement and taking responsibility for your behaviour, you do the opposite. Alternatively, you may be so consumed by shame you believe that *you* are now an inherently bad person. Either way, when you get stuck in this black-and-white thinking, that's usually the ingredients for the abrupt ending of a relationship.

Being actively anti-racist means looking for, accepting and addressing the nuances. Namely, recognising when you and others are splitting and slowing down your breathing asking yourself the following questions:

1. What is it that is causing me to split right now?
2. What information am I attempting to filter?
3. What am I struggling to hear, process and believe in this moment?

Some of the ways we can support our development are being mindful and building on our emotional and social maturity; working on our ability to be able to identify, examine, understand and regulate our emotions, whilst being open to challenging the values we have inherited from our parents or adults of influence in our lives. This doesn't mean bashing those who played a significant role in raising you – they are also imperfect and for most, did the best they could at the time with the information and resources they had available. It doesn't necessarily mean ditching those values and beliefs, but simply being open to being able to examine and question them. It means keeping what aligns with your integrity, personal growth and discovering who you are as an individual now, while soothing those identity crises that you might be confronted with.

Emotional maturity is vital for building healthy relationships. I describe it as when someone develops the ability to be present with their emotions, take responsibility for them (which can also mean asking for help) and to be able to respond to an external situation without being influenced by their own emotions, no matter their own personal circumstances. It is also very much about knowing when to act, and when to pause.

This kind of development is vital to sustain your work as an ally, hold cross-racial conversations without hearing feedback about racism as a personal attack on your identity, and help see things from perspectives that fundamentally challenge your bias and your model of the world.

We can do this by:

1. Consciously building our empathy.
2. Taking responsibility for our behaviour and when we make mistakes.
3. Meeting our unmet needs, which is absolutely vital.
4. Welcome curiosity in yourself and others.
5. Being able to first recognise and then label our emotions (and if you get stuck with emotions, notice bodily sensations) rather than bypassing them.

Many people struggle to name how they are feeling. This 'numbing' is often an avoidance response, governed by ego, to protect your identity and to keep you comfortable. For some, it may also be a survival response to past trauma. It could be a culmination of both. Check in with yourself: have you experienced this before in the past? Notice the physical sensations going on in your body and remind yourself, in this moment, you are safe. If you notice you are having a disproportionate response to anti-racist interactions in person or online when you are not in any danger, or a response that triggers past trauma, please don't be afraid to seek help from a therapist who can support you to work through this.

You cannot do this work without seeing both the light and dark. You cannot do it without acknowledging where your behaviour has negatively impacted and caused harm to others – and where it may continue to do so. You cannot do this work without accepting all parts of your personality, even the parts that aren't pretty. They are yours. Don't self-harm by beating yourself up, instead take control and own them along with your vulnerability, and take responsibility for your behaviour. If you are not happy about your behaviour, doing this work provides a beautiful opportunity to learn and grow and do better.

In case you need to hear this right now: you are not your behaviour.

You cannot do this work without accepting you don't, and won't ever, know everything. Anti-racism work will never be done and you will continue to make clumsy toe-curling mistakes along the way. Being actively anti-racist means learning to withstand and sit with this insatiable appetite to be right and immediately soothed when you slip up or feel anxious. Practise self-compassion for past and present mistakes and ask yourself: 'Now that I know this, what can I do now? Who can I continue to become?'

Until we become more honest about the parts we play and indeed, more sophisticated at having cross-racial interactions, conversations about race will continue to evoke huge anxiety and stress responses and we will end up splitting. Pausing, slowing everything down, taking some time out, reminding yourself you are safe and not in danger, can help get your prefrontal cortex back online.

Anti-racism work asks you to move beyond the black and white, to be able to sit in the discomfort of the metaphorical grey matter, to accept the contradictions, to observe the hypocrisy, to be with the uncertainty, to face the unfairness, to be present in the internal conflict and to be in the middle, as so many Black people have become masterful at.

As Black people, we have had no choice but to morph and contort ourselves to be able to exist in the grey for so long, finding ways to fit in, to observe, to read and analyse your subtle racist behaviour, to decode and read between the lines. Of course, this does not come without cost; repeatedly biting our tongues, to maintain equilibrium, continuously watching our tone and 'managing' your perception of us, existing in a continued heightened state of alert all takes its toll. But perhaps this ability has also built the most extraordinary resilience and capacity for forgiveness within us too. It has most definitely enabled us to be more sophisticated at the not knowing, to risk-assess and second-guess what happens next, without immediate gratification or resolution. By the very nature of our existence, we have had to learn to get comfortable with being uncomfortable in order to survive, live and thrive in racist systems.

Anti-racist work requires you to get comfortable with experiencing contradictions and internal conflict and to get curious about these feelings and sensations. So, question why and where they are showing up in your body. What is this information communicating to you? Instead of trying to avoid and bypass these feelings, be mindful of them, be conscious and curious about them.

I wonder what would happen if, when internal conflict and contradictions arise, instead of the endless judgements you place on yourself and others, and instead of feeling overwhelmed, you find a way to accept that both the black and white can and do co-exist and enjoy the wonder of discovering what lies within this unfamiliar grey matter instead.

★

4. Microaggressions: A Devastating Avalanche

'We are living in space-age times with stone-age minds.'

DARYL DAVIS[1]

Pay close attention to this chapter. Underline it, fold the pages. Do whatever you need to do, but pay attention because microaggressions are deeply, deeply problematic. They are the way everyday discrimination and everyday racism seep in, spread like a virus and stick to the cells of the DNA of this country.

Microaggressions contribute to what feels like an exhausting, never-ending game of ring-a-ring-a-roses, where we go round and round in exasperating circles and racism remains rife, because so many people are inactive and complicit by silent default.

So many mistakenly believe that the only people responsible for perpetuating racism are men in less-than-fetching white pointy hats, a certain breed of football fans or angry members of Britain First. They therefore think that the solution lies with organisations like the former simply disappearing off of the face of the earth, or for older generations to just die out. Capital B for Bullshit.

Generations with overtly racist views have been dying out for decades, centuries even, but lo and behold, we still have global problems with racism. It is being kept alive, evolving and morphing into new corrosive formats. The only way to address it is to first recognise it in all its forms, including racial microaggressions.

In black and white (no pun intended) the *Oxford English Dictionary* defines microaggressions as: 'A statement, action, or incident regarded as an instance of indirect, subtle, or unintentional discrimination against members of a marginalised group such as a racial or ethnic minority.'

The term was first coined by psychiatrist and Harvard academic Chester Pierce in 1970 and was further established by Dr Derald Wing Sue, psychology professor and author of *Microaggressions in Everyday Life*. Microaggressions are considered to be a form of covert everyday discrimination that happen both intentionally and unintentionally, consciously and subconsciously. Either way, the impact remains the same. They communicate that we are misplaced somehow, that we don't belong. They are the subtle ways in which people in marginalised identities are regularly not treated the same.

Microaggressions aren't often committed by overt racists. They are predominately perpetuated by well-intentioned, well-meaning liberals; people who are mostly unaware or in denial of the potential impact of their words or actions. In their original inception, microaggressions were first discovered to be discriminatory towards African Americans, but they have since been extended to include people in any ethnic minority or marginalised group (for example, based on gender, sexual orientation, disability and more) and of course, identities that intersect. For the purpose of this exploration, however, I'll be predominantly sticking with their original inception.

But first let me give you some tangible examples of both racial and other common microaggressions. These are common phrases and behaviours you may have heard, witnessed, or even unknowingly played a part in:

- 'I don't see colour.'
- 'Oh my gosh, I've just been on holiday, I'm almost as dark as you now!'
- 'Can I touch your hair?'
- 'I prefer it when your hair is straightened.'
- 'If it wasn't for your hair, you could be white.'
- 'Do you like Bob Marley?'
- 'You're pretty for a dark-skinned Black girl.'
- 'Is it true what they say about Black men in bed?'
- 'Why haven't Black people gotten over slavery yet?'
- 'You don't sound Black.'
- 'I'm shocked – how is racism still happening in this day and age?'
- 'Where are you from?'
- 'No, where are you *really* from?'

Are your toes curling yet?

Brace yourself, there's more…

- Giving a Black person a fist bump instead of a handshake.

- Actively avoiding sitting next to someone on public transport because of their race.
- Crossing the road or clutching a handbag when within close proximity to a Black man.
- Assuming a Black man with money or driving a nice car is a criminal.
- Mistaking a Person of Colour in a senior position as service staff.
- Following Black men and boys around a shop.
- Undermining and talking over Black women.

Other common microaggressions:

1. 'You don't sound gay.'
2. To someone of assumed East Asian appearance: 'I love Chinese food!'
3. 'Oh wow – your English is really good!' (when the person being racially marginalised, is in fact, English).

To a person with a visible disability:

1. To a wheelchair user: 'It must be really cool to always have your own seat!'
2. 'What happened to you?'
3. 'Can I pray for you?'

Did you wince?

I imagine feelings of guilt, shame or shock might be coming

up in the realisation that you have contributed to some of these everyday slights. Resist the urge to try to explain these away or to focus on your good intentions. The truth is, we are all capable of unknowingly committing microaggressions on a regular basis; they are a by-product of racism and a form of suppressed prejudice that we have learned as a result of participating in a society that sets white, able-bodied, heterosexual and male as the default standard.

In isolation, most of these examples seem completely harmless. An innocent statement, or a genuine attempt to connect, right? Wrong. It is the very subtlety and frequency of microaggressions that make them far from harmless or even micro in their outcomes. Consider them like snowflakes: at first fall they seem quite harmless, perhaps a nuisance, but overnight the ice starts to build up underneath that pristine surface suddenly becomes dangerous, volatile ground where we slip and fall each time we go outside. Perhaps at first spraining a wrist and then breaking a bone and, over months and years, what once were seemingly harmless snowflakes collectively cause a devastating avalanche.

*

Unpacking Racial Trauma

Research shows us that regular exposure to racial microaggressions can cause more harm to mental health than overt acts of hate. This is due to the cumulative effects of racism, resulting in increased stress hormones, which essentially cause a type of wear and tear on the body.[2] Further research from neuroscientists reveals regular exposure to this type of racial stress can have the same effects as those observed in war veterans experiencing severe post-traumatic stress disorder (PTSD).[3] In other words, racial microaggressions can show up in Black bodies as trauma.

Check in with yourself: how does this make you feel? Did you realise the link between racism and trauma before today?

Experiencing racism is trauma, so while 'post-traumatic' suggests this traumatic experience or event is in the past, you and I both know it's very much still in the present. We don't just experience it as personal trauma either. This is the direct or indirect exposure to single or multiple events that only happen to an individual. It's important to note, some can also experience personal trauma by simply witnessing or hearing about a traumatic event.

Add a layer of historical trauma on top. This is a shared collective experience by a specific cultural group related to significant traumatic experiences or events and the cumulative impact of emotional harm and social suffering to an individual or generations (not exclusive to blood relatives) that follow. In the BBC documentary, *Let's Talk About Race*, presenter Naga Munchetty interviews a Black Caribbean family. The grandmother shares her account of moving from the Caribbean to the UK as part of the Windrush generation, working as a nurse in the NHS and sick patients refusing to be treated by her because of the colour of her skin, right through to her grandson, sharing current experiences of racism and general sense of unsafety living in the UK. The grandmother concluded that when it comes to racism in Britain, nothing has really changed. I have had the same conversations with my father.

Add a layer on top of that institutional trauma. This type of

trauma breeds like wildfire in organisations that are more concerned with brand perception than taking racial microaggressions
and other types of racism seriously. Institutional trauma depends
on a failure to respond supportively, or indeed, at all, or action
that worsens the impact of trauma on individuals reliant on that
institution. And, finally, add a layer of intergenerational/transgen-
erational trauma (which we will cover more in Chapter 6). This
type of trauma is so powerful, it not only impacts psychological,
familial, social and cultural behaviour, but it can be passed down
genetically within families from generation to generation.

Because we are whole beings, it may be no surprise to learn
that trauma impacts every single system in our bodies: the nervous system, endocrine system, gastrointestinal system, muscu-
loskeletal system, respiratory system, cardiovascular system and
the reproductive system. Some common responses to trauma
include PTSD, assimilation, fawning, such as overcompliance
and befriending abusers, hypervigilance, heightened anxiety,
self-blame, avoidance, disassociation, anger, difficulty sleeping,
exhaustion, loss of or increased appetite, upset stomach, flash-
backs, nausea, pain, trembling, depression and a whole lot more.

In a journal for *Therapy Today*, psychologist and author of *Living
While Black*, Guilaine Kinouani, shares some of the consequences
of racial trauma and continuing to receive racist microaggressions
in society:

One research participant had experienced multiple instances
of racism while in hospital, but her complaints were
consistently dismissed or ignored. Over time she started
to lose confidence in her ability to trust and understand

her experience. This resulted in her minimising her own distress and ignoring her physical symptoms to the point that she did not seek treatment when she started urinating blood and lost sight in one eye.

Even Guilaine recounts a time that she was in therapy relaying a racist incident where she was spat at. The therapist said Guilaine had 'misinterpreted the situation'.[4]

Psychotherapy and psychological services that continue to fail to take the accumulative impact of racism and racial trauma into consideration in training, and in the therapy room, are not only providing inadequate services, but unethical ones too. At its furthest extreme this is malpractice.

Experiencing racism is not an isolated incidence of trauma, or just words that have no impact, but persistent, ongoing and often unaddressed trauma, for many. We have to do better than this. While I am giving you a tiny snippet into the potential impact of living with racial trauma, it is absolutely not your job to try to psychoanalyse your Black and Brown friends and colleagues.

Check in with your body. What physical sensations are you noticing? Any heat changes? Any constrictions? How is your breathing? Has your heart rate increased or decreased? Is your mouth dry? What else do you notice?

What makes microaggressions simultaneously powerfully effective and so difficult to tackle, is not only that so many people are woefully unaware of them, but that we are unsophisticated at recognising them in ourselves and in each other. For some readers, this will be the first time you are discovering the very term. It is because of these factors that microaggressions regularly go unaddressed, behaviour remains unchanged and racism continues to take on a more subtle and mutated form.

Microaggressions at work

Microaggressions run rampant in the workplace and are often ignored, denied or explained away as 'office banter', with the recipients of racism being targeted as the troublemakers or over-sensitive instead.

I was once told flat-out by a highly educated white gent and lawyer that microaggressions were not a thing, but just academic jargon used to tarnish and censor what to some is 'humorous free speech'. I was utterly flabbergasted and somewhat exasper-ated. I mean, I did also find it odd that of all the important things to advocate for in the world, given his job and the energy he'd spent maintaining he wasn't racist, he (and so many others) would want to defend his right to say racist things. Go figure.

This type of widespread denial and unwillingness to address microaggressions is one of the reasons why colleague and business psychologist Binna Kandola, OBE prefers to describe microag-gressions as 'micro-incivilities' instead. In an interview with me, he explained that you cannot dispute that civil and uncivil behaviour exist in the workplace and is directly linked to the theory of Organisational Citizenship Behaviour – a theory that observes voluntary employee behaviour outside of formal roles and the impact that this has on organisational culture. Kandola continues: 'When people engage in civil behaviour in the work-place it's supportive, it's collaborative, it's allowing people to have a voice, showing respect and value to individuals and it is directly linked to higher performance of individuals within teams and organisations.'

And yes, you guessed it, uncivil behaviour is directly linked with poor individual and organisational performance which, of course, also impacts the bottom line. Uncivil behaviour can encompass general rude behaviour and disregard for others. It can also include:

- Not making eye contact.
- Consistently mispronouncing and not bothering to learn colleagues' names.
- Completely ignoring people different to you in social environments.
- Giving poor appraisals without any specific feedback as to why.
- Constant workplace othering ('Can I touch your hair? What's it like to be Black?').
- Not allowing others to share solutions to ideas because you don't want someone in your team to get credit.
- Consistently talking over Black and Brown staff.
- Asking for feedback from everyone in the team except for the only Black person.
- Claiming others' ideas as your own, to advance your own professional development.
- Consistently undermining the authority of a Person of Colour in a senior role.
- Racist jokes in the staffroom, or staff WhatsApp groups.
- Mocking accents or mimicking cultural stereotypes.

Need some real-life examples?

I was part of a number of speakers delivering a talk to business leaders in the gig economy on inclusion. When I started to talk about racism, a director (white, male) of a well-known company sighed, leaned back in his chair, pulled out his mobile phone and started mindlessly scrolling. When I drew attention to his behaviour by directing a question at him, he said his organisation 'didn't have issues with racism'. Subtext: I don't have to nor do I want to listen to you. He carried on scrolling until I finished talking. Charmer.

Once, I was chatting with a casual member of staff in an office next door to mine about something frivolous and we engaged in conversation for a short while before I went back to my desk to get on with work. I returned to her office a few hours later and the same woman greeted me with surprising enthusiasm before proceeding to have the exact same conversation she'd had with me a couple of hours earlier. 'I was just telling your friend about this,' she said, to which I responded that the 'friend' was actually me. Cue me then having to manage her embarrassment for muddling me up with the only other Black person in our entire department, despite the fact that we looked nothing alike.

Microaggressions from those in managerial positions who have power over you can be very hard to navigate – I sadly can attest to that. There were subtle career blocks, suddenly being asked by management to be copied into all emails, having all reoccurring 1-2-1 meetings cancelled at the last minute, only communicating via email, avoiding eye contact and being moved to a smaller office. The only thing that had changed was that I raised a complaint, and I was getting more skilled in my role. I didn't know what microaggressions were back then – I didn't have the language for them – but I recognised how they made me feel, and that I was evidently being punished. I knew that I was not being treated in the same way, for example, as my white peer in the same role with less experience who was not being asked to copy our manager into emails, but had been rewarded with a bigger office.

I remember being asked to draw on my professional expertise to write about racial bias in technology, photography in particular, for a mainstream publication. They wanted their team of in-house copywriters to edit it. The article was detailed and backed up by evidence-based research on the matter. The issue was also heavily documented in the press, at the time, by filmmakers putting out a call to action for more industry training to address not only the tech limitations, but the apparent skill disparity and challenges of adequately lighting dark skin in film and TV. The first two copywriters (who also wrote for mainstream magazines at the time) flatly refused to edit it, stating my article was 'too negative'. The third copywriter edited out all of the evidence-based research and any references to racism or racial bias. All copywriters were white. I felt undermined, humiliated and silenced. When I expressed this to the PR expert who had asked me to write the article, for free, she ignored my email (yes, she was white too).

One of my interviewees for the book, who was in her 30s, has a complex relationship with her hair and her identity. She is of mixed heritage – daughter to a white mother and a Black father. She remembers her mother almost 'blocking' every opportunity to connect with her Black culture, including being left alone with Black relatives. She remembers being a little girl and her mother refusing to let her grow her hair. When she asked her mother why she had to have short hair and wasn't allowed to grow it like all her other friends, her mother told her it was because her afro hair was 'too difficult for her to comb'. Her mother made the choice to cut off her daughter's hair, rather than seek help or learn how to care for it. This resulted in her feeling like a boy, hating not only her hair, but her Black identity, and feeling like there was something wrong with her for being born with afro-textured hair. This led to self-rejection.

So for those who think racism is a thing of the past, this is just a fraction of the number of microaggressions that Black and Brown people have to deal with on a daily basis. It is exhausting. And it is traumatising.

Microaggressions and Medical Racism

In 2018, I came out in a rash all over my body. I was worried enough to go to the doctor's. The doctor, a white woman, asked me to strip so she could examine me. As I was standing in my underwear, the doctor asked me: 'Well, what exactly is it that I'm looking at then?' I was perplexed. The rash was very prevalent and *all* over my body. Humiliated, I pointed – there, there and there. The doctor then went to her computer to Google images of rashes. She started to sigh. While getting dressed, I asked her if everything was okay, and she said, 'Well, I'm trying to find pictures of rashes on, well, darker, you know, people like you.'

She printed off a document for me to read. The document featured images of white patients and descriptive text stating I needed to look out for red rashes on my skin. Never in my life has a rash shown up on my body in red. Rashes present entirely differently on darker skin tones.

It was apparent very early on in this appointment that this doctor had never seen rashes on Black skin before and was unable to provide me with proper care as a result. On top of that, when I looked at the document she printed off from the NHS website, it clearly only had an interest in catering and communicating to the white patients accessing the database. All of the images and descriptions of rashes were on white skin. I paid on my credit card to get a second opinion privately in the end, from a doctor who diagnosed straight away it was a common breakout of stress-induced eczema. I felt embarrassed, furious, dehumanised and shamed.

A similar oversight, this time with fatal consequences, revealed itself when experts for the Centers for Disease Control and Prevention[5] and the NHS warned that people should look out for signs of blue lips as a potentially life-threatening warning sign for COVID-19. Black people's and darker-skinned people's lips don't turn blue, more likely grey or whitish. But no alternative warning signs were offered to people with darker skin at the time.

In May 2020, in the middle of a global pandemic, the Great British tabloids were running with the story that Black people were 3–4 times more likely to die from contracting COVID-19.[6] The convenient spin? That this was due to the myth that is our 'genetic differences'[7] – our lack of vitamin D or carrying pre-existing 'diseases' – as well as our assumed poverty and all living in cramped houses.

While for obvious reasons societal and environmental factors make exposure risk far higher, this sole poverty narrative not only felt rooted in blame, but felt off-kilter to me. Black, Asian and Ethnic minority medical consultants, who clearly were not in poverty, were also dying disproportionately.[8] The 'genetic differences' myth clearly didn't tally up either, because Black folk living in Black-majority countries have managed the pandemic from the outset with extremely low death rates. When factors such as pre-existing conditions and environmental factors are removed from the data by the Office for National Statistics (ONS), the results were still overwhelmingly high. So, these conveniently restricted angles that we were somehow responsible for our own swansong out of life just weren't cutting it for me and I wanted to find out more.

I decided to conduct a number of interviews with NHS workers to try to understand what was happening behind the scenes at the height of a global pandemic and why so many Black and Asian doctors seemed to be so disproportionately impacted. All were keen to talk to me. Many were relieved to have their experiences heard and validated, many hadn't spoken up before through fear of being disbelieved. But all bar one wanted to remain anonymous due to the real fear of retribution.

The accounts of the impact of racial microaggressions that my interviewees shared were, at times, devastating (so much so I had to cease interviewing to preserve my own mental health), but at the height of a pandemic, not shocking. A reminder, when we feel like we are under attack, we default to our most primal survival state – we fend for ourselves and our suppressed prejudices run rampant.

I heard about white nurses having a chat in the staffroom moaning about 'BAME' staff getting special treatment. Pretty sure that's against the Nursing and Midwifery Council's code to treat all people with kindness, respect and compassion and to respect and uphold people's human rights.[9] Perhaps most sobering of all were the multiple accounts of seemingly disproportionate sanctions on common non-life-threatening mistakes made by Black staff resulting in serious disciplinary actions, in contrast to white staff being given a slap on the wrist for much more serious cases. This was all within the context of a recorded 300 per cent rise in Anti-Asian hate crime in Britain since the start of the pandemic, and the blaming of people assumed to be Chinese for spreading COVID-19.[10]

I was contacted by a Black midwife who was also pregnant at the time. Despite being on the vulnerable list, because she was pregnant and in an ethnic minority group, when she expressed her concerns for her unborn child about continuing to be exposed to the virus in hospital (heightened by the nationwide lack of PPE), she was told by her manager and head midwife that she was too junior to be able to conduct consultations and work from home and that she would have to continue working in the hospital or take unpaid leave. She recounted witnessing agency staff – who are mostly Black or non-Black People of Colour – being placed on COVID-19 wards by ward sisters who were white. They often gave agency staff five patients to look after, while non-agency staff, who were also predominately white, were given just one. At the time, it was documented that the more exposure to viral load an individual has, the higher the risk of severity of symptoms. Additionally, over her time in the NHS, my interviewee also noticed she was often last to be assigned a lunch break, if she got one at all.

Coincidentally, just a few months prior in February 2020, an investigation was carried out by the British Medical Association and the *British Medical Journal,* with a Freedom of Information request revealing that of the thirty-two medical schools that responded to the request, only half even bothered to record complaints about racism from medical students. It revealed growing fears among Black, Asian and other ethnic minority medical students in Britain that accounts of racism from co-workers and patients will be ignored or not taken seriously by white staff.[11] In an article for the *Guardian*, associate professor in medical education Katherine Woolf asked a group of eighty senior doctors in a session to raise their hands if they felt confident about handling a racism complaint from a trainee doctor. Just one person in the room put their hand up.[12]

In August 2020, CNN published an article based on a study undertaken in the United States by researchers at George Mason University analysing the data of 1.8 million births between 1992 and 2015. The article was titled 'Black newborns more likely to die when looked after by white doctors'.[13] It explained that the mortality rate of Black newborns significantly reduced, meaning they were less likely to die, when being cared for by Black physicians. On the flip side, the mortality rate for white babies was 'largely unaffected by the doctor's race'. This stopped me in my tracks, not least because a provocative headline like that will evoke a lot of fear in many. But it was also a sobering reminder of racial disparities and how systemic racism seeps into healthcare and can have devastating outcomes for Black babies.

It reminded me of regular medical experiments undertaken in the mid–nineteenth century by white American physician James

Marion Sims who, in his own autobiography, described himself as a mediocre student whose medical training only consisted of 'a year and a half of training', and yet he ended up being named the modern father of gynaecology.[14] For years, Sims would regularly, without consent, or anaesthetic, do surgical experiments on forcibly restrained Black enslaved women's genitalia[15] in his own makeshift hospital. He justified his actions by convincing himself that 'slave women were able to bear more pain because of their race.'[16] Sadly, Sims didn't stop at Black women either. He regularly experimented on Black babies who were suffering from severe malnutrition. He even went to the lengths of putting a shoe-maker's awl, a sharp pointed tool used to pierce holes in leather shoes, into Black newborn babies' heads. He justified this little 'experiment' as a means to try to solve what he believed (based on racism and pure myth), were skull malformations, caused during birth, of 'slave' babies, 'leaving the brain no space to grow and develop', which he believed were the cause of the intellectual flaws of 'slave' infants. Unsurprisingly, these inhumane experiments resulted in a 100 per cent death rate.

Some of the findings from his barbaric backyard experiments still play a firm role in racial disparities and medical racism today. From many identical accounts of Black women stating they were disbelieved when they said they were experiencing pain, including tennis star Serena Williams, to the infamous Proceedings of the National Academies of Science 2016 study, which cited that 50 per cent of white medical students still falsely believe Black people have thicker skin and can withstand more pain.[17] So, when I saw the findings of this study, while it stopped me in my tracks, it didn't surprise me, because I had just interviewed a Black British mother about her own devastating experience in the NHS.

This interviewee recalled how she wasn't feeling well following an iron infusion while she was pregnant with her second child in her final trimester. She was turned away by her GP each time, told that she was 'fine' and that there was no link to her recent iron infusion. 'I had a cold and persistent cough. I just didn't feel right and was vomiting up phlegm, nothing I would eat would stay down.'

She went into labour, still complaining of feeling unwell and was discharged after the birth of her daughter. 'I went to the doctors again two or three times after giving birth, still feeling very unwell and continued to be dismissed and was told I was fine and that the symptoms would go away.'

Her newborn daughter then started to display similar symptoms.

I raised this with my Health Visitor who also told me it would go away and to keep an eye on it if it didn't. Something didn't add up – my daughter was born on the hottest day of the year that summer and had a cold and persistent cough at just 2.5 weeks old. I knew this wasn't normal, so I went to my GP again who did some basic checks and told me the baby was fine. I told them they were not giving me any reassurance and that I would be taking her to hospital.

My interviewee explained that the GP called the hospital ahead of her arrival and shared information based on their examination and their medical opinion to the hospital. The doctor at the hospital then did a minimal assessment:

> The doctor, who was white, didn't even check her chest with a stethoscope; they did not run any blood tests or scans. I believe they based their assessment on the GP's evaluation and had already decided that my baby was "fine" and I was a "nuisance" because they did not conduct new tests, nor keep my baby in to observe her.

The doctor at the hospital advised her that the baby was too young for antibiotics and that the symptoms would go on their own and she would be fine. Three days later, the baby died.

The coroner ruled that the baby had bronchitis. Untreated, it had developed into sepsis – which led to bronchopneumonia. The judge at the inquest said the baby's death was avoidable and could have been treated with antibiotics.

Pause. Notice what's coming up for you.

- Please observe if your mind is going into victim-blaming mode – 'Why didn't she go back? Why didn't she get further opinions?'
- Interrogate why it feels easier for you to go to blame than to empathise.
- Examine where that innate response is coming from.

I asked the interviewee what she thought were contributing factors to her daughter's death and she said, unequivocally, institutionalised racism.

Multiple doctors, several white and one Asian dismissed me, ignored me, undermined me and didn't believe me time and time again. They didn't examine my baby properly because of their own assumptions and bias. One doctor even said, "It can't be bronchitis, that only happens in winter." Because it was summer, and even though both mine and my daughter's symptoms were in plain sight, it was not investigated. To this day, I have not been contacted by anyone from the hospital. I was not offered a bereavement midwife or officer. Absolutely nothing.

She then went on to say, 'You know how it is, you just have to be strong and get on with it and carry on.' After the interview she thanked me. She said it was the first time in over a year since her baby had died that she had been heard and believed. Upon sharing the CNN article on social media, I received too many comments from other Black and Brown people sharing their experiences of fear and trauma in healthcare.

We can, of course, assume with confidence that, unlike James Marion Sims, most white doctors are not out on a secret quest to intentionally kill Black people. However, since medical practices remain rooted in medical racism, it is no surprise that Black and Brown people continue to bear the brunt of disproportionately negative health outcomes. And it is these outcomes, regardless of intent, that need honesty and interrogation – and fast – to safeguard all of us.

It's far easier to condemn an overt act of hate from a 'dodgy individual' who intentionally wishes to cause us harm. It's easy to detect danger from far-right extremists whose bodies are covered in swastika tattoos – we can spot them, so in theory, we can do what we can to avoid them at all costs. But in the everyday, what about the well-meaning people we come into contact with daily on commutes, or in supermarkets, or the people we have come to love or respect? Friends, co-workers, parents, doctors, midwives, senior managers – how do we avoid you? How do we tell someone, who wouldn't for a second believe their behaviour is being triggered by unaddressed inherent racism, that they are causing us harm? Where do we even begin?

★

Surviving Covert Racism

> 'Microaggressions often appear to be small slights that in isolation cause minimal harm to the recipients. However, being exposed to a lifetime of daily insults, disregard and disrespect has been shown to be extremely harmful unless mitigated in some fashion. The effects of microaggressions may be compared to the "perennial slow death by a thousand cuts"'
>
> DERALD WING SUE[18]

The insidious nature of microaggressions is often why so many of my Black peers say if they had to choose, they would prefer to deal with an incident from an overt fascist once than have to deal with unaddressed racial microaggressions multiple times a day, every day of their lives, from people who minimise, explain away and deny their existence.

On the rare occasions when we find the courage to address microaggressions, we are often gaslighted, disbelieved and framed as troublemakers, meaning we end up facing further trauma that can lead us to question our own sanity. For example, Psychologist Monnica T. Williams PhD reports the following:

> When experiencing microaggressions, the target loses vital mental resources trying to figure out the intention of the one committing the act. These events may happen frequently, making it difficult to mentally manage the sheer volume of racial stressors. The unpredictable and anxiety-provoking nature of the events, which may be dismissed by others, can lead to victims feeling as if they are "going crazy". [19]

We end up with this constant heightened state of alert: the fear of anticipating a racial assault, even non-verbal, which can result in the body being in a constant state of hyperarousal. In a mode of fight or flight, freeze or fawn (to people-please or befriend your abuser in an attempt to avoid further harm), the body thinks it is under attack. Now imagine navigating that on a daily basis while trying to just, well, live?

I was contacted by a Black woman who shared her personal story of experiencing microaggressions with me:

> I grew up in Nigeria without any exposure to racism or microaggressions and felt like I was living my best life and

thriving. Everything changed since moving to medical school in Europe. Now working here I have become a shell of myself. Seeing my confidence dwindle, my fear has increased as a result of the poly-trauma of racism, to the point where I've started to doubt myself and see my performance suffer. I am just about managing to get by and now need to engage in therapy.

When you have been raised in a Black majority country, where your skin colour is not a defining feature or a measure of your character, that is a very different foundation from experiencing racism and the ideology of inferiority from as young as three. It's why some of my West and East African peers, especially those whose lineage was somewhat spared the trauma of enslavement, find the ideology of Black inferiority, birthed from a race hierarchy concocted by white Europeans, inconceivable and, rightly, offensive.

Microaggressions can cause both psychological and physical distress, which not only impact overall life satisfaction, but can contribute to loss of confidence, imposter syndrome, exhaustion, low self-esteem, feeling humiliated, feeling pressure to assimilate as a method of survival, causing prolonged stress and serious ill health. It may go some way to explain why the Mental Health Foundation reports that people in Black, Asian and other ethnic groups are at a higher risk of developing mental ill-health because of additional societal challenges that impact mental and physical health, like racism.[20] According to research by business psychologists and inclusion experts Pearn Kandola on the impact of racism at work in 2018, they found that those who identified as Black or Asian were least likely to report instances of racism through fear of repercussions.[21]

I appreciate this may be confronting and hard for you. Be present with any discomfort. I am not sugar-coating this chapter, because it's utterly painful for us. This is why we need more people like you who can start to understand the nuances of systemic racism and have the courage and confidence to advocate in your everyday lives and in the workplace, to stop repeating patterns of behaviour that cause harm.

The good news? In the same research by Pearn Kandola, it revealed that those who are most likely to address racism in the moment are, in fact, white people. The beautiful disaster? White people are least likely to be able to recognise subtle instances of racism, like microaggressions. You see the bind here, don't you?

Why do Microaggressions Happen?

Whether you like it or not, what is not intentionally addressed, will be expressed. And as an old drama teacher once said to me: 'Nova, you cannot not act.' The brain cannot hide prejudice.

Microaggressions are suppressed prejudice coming out and we've all been taught to suppress our prejudices. What was once normal, is now not, and unless we intentionally take steps to name and unlearn our 'isms', they still lurk beneath the surface or come out when we least expect them in the form of microaggressions in verbal and non-verbal behaviour.

The brain has naturally evolved to help us filter the enormous amounts of information we consume each day. As such, it is used to putting things and people in binary boxes; our brain and our worldview and belief systems lead us to make decisions and automatic assumptions about one another.

Assumptions about:

- Whom to trust and whom to fear
- Who is 'normal' and who isn't
- Who is guilty and who is innocent
- Who are heroes and who are villains
- Who is more likely to commit an act of terrorism and who isn't
- Who is most regularly associated with knife crime and who isn't
- Who is classically beautiful and who isn't
- Who is a better driver and who isn't

What's the first image that comes to your mind when you read the word 'pilot'? I bet it isn't a Black woman. Bias is defined as 'the inclination or prejudice for or against one person or a group especially in a way considered to be unfair'. If you're human, you have bias. You had images come to mind with just the introduction of those words and I invite you to be honest and note down the first unedited thoughts that came into your mind.

Prejudice, the preconceived opinion not based on any reason or first-hand experience, occurs when 'categories' created by your brain start being linked with positive and negative associations; 'good or bad' end up being assigned to entire groups of people.

Most of us are unaware of the preconceived thoughts and messaging that we receive from the constant stimuli around us and how this transfers through to our behaviour, thanks to a neurological process called 'mentalising'. In an interview with Professor Matthew Williams, hate expert, criminologist and author of *The Science of Hate*, he explains that mentalising and having Theory of Mind (our human capacity for empathy) is a cognitive process that starts forming during early childhood, where we develop the ability to empathise and to see the world from the perspectives of others.

This ability can vary from adult to adult and some people have low ability when it comes to engaging in mentalising and using Theory of Mind. This can be down to socialisation and genetics, but, unsurprisingly, it can also result from a lack of positive contact with people different to them: what Williams calls the 'outgroup'. A significant deficit in these cognitive processes is associated with the belief in negative stereotypes and the depersonalisation of the 'outgroup'. This, combined with a whole host of other factors that Williams calls 'accelerants' (feelings of loss or trauma, leading to frustration or anger being projected onto the outgroup), can galvanise prejudice. As a result, you may have difficulty regulating or suppressing prejudice, which can lead to committing a microaggression or outburst (as some social neuroscientists refer to them), or at the other end of the scale, an overt violent act of racism or discrimination. That difficulty in suppressing prejudice only intensifies when you add on top anonymity and the comfort of hiding behind your keypad on social media.

Microaggressions are nothing to do with being good, bad or a downright dodgy human being, but rather, deeply ingrained forms of everyday discrimination that we have learned. Some act on these impulses overtly, others suppress them and they come out in verbal and non-verbal cues. If you are not consciously and intentionally addressing your 'isms', they will keep showing up. They are an unavoidable by-product of being exposed to cultural norms that, for centuries, have normalised, and legalised structural racism.

Common Problematic Statements

At the beginning of this chapter, I mentioned a few common racial microaggressions and I want to unpack them further here:

'I'm shocked – how is racism still happening in this day and age?'

Expressing your shock and dismay to Black and Brown folk about racism is not being actively anti-racist. Get curious: when in the past has your expression of shock and dismay actually helped to actively tackle and address racism?

I can't tell you how painful it is to hear these words from white folk. Yes, acts of racism are heinous, but expressing shock and dismay is usually less about showing solidarity, and more about framing yourself as a good white person. It's also the bare minimum – a misguided attempt to show solidarity that often does the opposite. Regardless of intent, your shock at the reality of our lived experiences communicates that you have been sleepwalking – that you don't believe us, have not been listening to us and that you still don't see racism. If you can't see and you don't notice it, as discussed above, that is a fundamental barrier to ever being able to tackle racism.

Be sorry, be disappointed, commit to listening, be ready and motivated to take action, offer support; be anything but shocked.

'Can I touch your hair?'

Putting your hands on a body that is not your own is a violation no matter how 'cute', 'fluffy' or 'intriguing' our hair looks.

This common sense of entitlement or urge to want to touch afro-textured hair, isn't coming out of thin air. Fetishising Black people, and especially Black women, was common practice at the height of slavery. In fact, in the nineteenth century, human zoos were commonplace and gained popularity in Europe and the Americas, where Black and Indigenous people, including young children, were paraded around in enclosures.[22] These spectacles were visited by hundreds and thousands of white people to ogle at us like animals. The most famous case being Saartjie Baartman, a Khoikhoi woman from South Africa, whose stature and buttocks were an object of fetishisation, where fatness and Blackness were synonymous and provided cause for fear and ridicule for Europeans. She was taken from her home country and placed in what were dubbed as human 'freak shows', including being paraded around in an exhibition at London's Piccadilly Circus.

Being prodded and petted like an animal for your entertainment is utterly dehumanising and sadly, most Black people have experienced it since hair started growing out of our heads. We are not your pets.

'Where are you from? No, Where are you really from?'

This seemingly innocent question may come from curiosity, but the number of times Black folk and People of Colour are asked this question is disproportionate to being asked where you're from every now and then when you travel out of town or go on holiday. Don't conflate the two. It often communicates that we don't belong; we are perceived to be out of place. It reminds us that many have become falsely accustomed to believing that only white = British and everything else is 'other', that Black folk don't belong in the countryside and look 'out of place'.

I remember attending an art exhibition in high society in London and within ten minutes I was asked that question by three different white men. When I replied, 'England' that sparked disbelief. 'No, where are you *really* from?' A reply of 'Hertfordshire' was met with further disbelief. My very apparent English accent, accompanied by my brown skin, meant not one of them accepted my answer as fact, until they were satisfied that they had traced my ancestry.

This question can be difficult to answer for many British Black people and People of Colour, not only because it automatically 'others' us, but it also doesn't take into account that some of us don't know where we are from due to displacement and lineage lost to colonisation. It doesn't take into account having identities, language and communities torn out from under us during the height of colonisation. This line of persistent interrogation over ancestry suggests that we'll never be seen as a local and will never be accepted as British.

Consider this: Is this a complete stranger that you're asking this question of? Are there other ways to connect meaningfully without asking this question? Do you also persistently ask white people where English is their first language where they are from? Are you asking them because you are 'surprised' and don't expect to see them in a room or rural environment? What box are you trying to put them in? Are they speaking the same mother tongue as you? If so, why do you feel compelled to ask the question?

*

As demonstrated, the historical significance of our complex social, political, legal framework and collective belief system doesn't just disappear when laws change. And whilst overt acts of hate are now (arguably) condemned, years of systemic oppression and white supremacy has left us with some unaddressed and deeply ingrained racism and generational prejudice.

I was invited to attend a brilliant symposium at the launch of Zawe Ashton's play *For All The Women Who Thought They were Mad* at Hackney Showroom in 2019. It explored the impact of microaggressions on the mental health of Black women. One of the panellists was mental-health activist Dr Jayasree Kalathil, and she said something that has stayed with me ever since: 'Social injustice is at the root of all distress.' And we each have to be aware of our role in it.

I know this may be tough to read, but it is so important for collective healing and, in turn, for being able to change the discourse and stop repeating unnecessary and entirely avoidable cycles of oppression. Microaggressions turn the very definition of what we thought racism was upside down – it can lead a lot of white people to have an existential crisis, to question their morals, their identity, their values and whether they are one of the 'good' ones or not.

So I need you to hear this and understand it: This is not about you and your intentions.

Your intentions are *not* more important than the impact of your words or your behaviours. Focusing on intentions as a 'good person' is what stops us from effectively tackling microaggressions and reproduces racism. You've just read the devastating stats. This is about reducing harm.

★

What makes microaggressions so harmful is their frequency. You may have done something, only once, and felt the response was disproportionate, but as therapist and healer Donna Lancaster once said in a workshop: 'If a response is hysterical, it's historical.'

You can now start to join the dots and understand the magnitude of the bigger picture and the roles we all had and continue to have within it. It is entirely possible for good, kind people, people like you, to cause harm with your intentional and unintentional words or behaviour.

Think of it in these terms. If you're a driver – how many times have you or someone you loved had minor car bumps in supermarket car parks? It's entirely possible for good people to accidentally crash into cars and cause harm with unintentional actions. And invariably, what do we do when that happens? Apologise and take appropriate steps to repair any damage and make it right.

The same can be applied to microaggressions. Let me tell you that, as a Black woman, when you listen, acknowledge and give a genuine apology for a microaggression, it changes the outcome. It stops the shame cycle. The physiological response in my body that I have become accustomed to experiencing completely dissipates. It can also break the cycle of trauma. The resolution is so simple.

So what can you do?

Now that you understand how microaggressions exist and where they might be coming from, consider these journalling prompts:

1. How am I racist in my everyday life?
2. What racial stereotypes do I hold?
3. What common microaggressions have I committed?

Only by having the courage to name and confront your inherent 'isms' (because they are there, having a house party) can you start to address them, because we cannot fix what we do not know, or refuse to accept, is broken.

Instead of getting stuck in shame, get curious about your prejudice and biases and interrogate them. If you're truly honest with yourself, you will already know what your conscious ones are. Complete the Implicit Bias Test by Harvard or June Sarpong's Diversify ISMS test. While not an exact science, nor are these tools 'pass or fail' tests, they are starting points for anything subconscious lurking. The sooner you realise and get inquisitive about what they might be, the sooner you can bring awareness to yourself, in your social circles, in your home, in the workplace and, ultimately, the sooner you can apologise with ease when you slip up, alter your behaviour, atone and stop causing unnecessary harm.

'History, despite its wrenching pain cannot be unlived,
but if faced with courage, need not be lived again.'
MAYA ANGELOU[23]

★

5. Disrupting Racialised Fragility and Anti-Blackness

'The truth will set you free, but first it will piss you off!'
GLORIA STEINEM[1]

'I'm sick and tired of staff playing the race card.'

I will never forget those ten words uttered to me by a white male director at the start of a workshop on racism. Standing there, barely ten minutes in, among a sea of white faces (and two or three Brown ones), I was the only Black person in the room. With the combination of my training in human behaviour and hypervigilance – a trauma response that's morphed into a nifty personality trait – I can read a room like clockwork and, with the lack of eye contact from most, alongside closed body language, I knew I had no allies in the room. It was going to be a long three hours.

I thought, right, I either let that comment slide, swallow his racism and pander to white solidarity so everyone can feel comfortable for the rest of the workshop, or acknowledge that comment would have more than likely triggered the Brown staff in the room too, and use it as a learning opportunity. Since it was, after all, a workshop about racism, I assumed people were there to learn, so I chose the latter. That was a mistake, and I spent the rest of the workshop in a boxing ring with this director's ego.

I explained that 'playing the race card' was a trope used in far-right politics in the height of the 60s to gain votes by inciting fear of Black people coming over to the UK, taking jobs from white people and potentially being your neighbour. That tactic seemed to work when Conservative MP Peter Griffiths used the slogan 'If you want a nigger for a neighbour vote Labour' in his campaign – and won a seat at a general election. Fear of Black and Brown folk was rampant, even in left-wing politicians. Labour MP Patrick Gordon-Walker led Labour's opposition to the 1962 Commonwealth Immigrants Act and supported the legal restriction for right of entry to Britain of 600 million citizens of the Commonwealth.[2]

I also highlighted to the white male director that by using this phrase he was communicating an automatic lack of trust should any staff have the courage to bring accounts of racism to management and that mistrust doesn't provide the groundwork for fair and due process.

As a personal aside, I would genuinely love to know what this race card is (also referred to by some as 'brownie points') because, in reality, if this special card trick was so effective, we wouldn't still be dealing with this level of systemic racism globally and there would be a lot fewer racist senior managers in employment. Instead it seems this disingenuous statement is quite good at derailing, gaslighting and silencing people who experience racism in the workplace, which may go some way to explain why so few Black, Asian and Ethnic Minority staff bring forward formal race grievances.

This senior manager made it obvious that he didn't like me bringing this to his attention and then went into defensive mode, telling me that his daughter was mixed race (white British and white Irish). A far reach to attempt to demonstrate how he couldn't be racist. At one point he even pulled me aside to have a quiet word and told me to 'lighten up the mood'.

Later in the workshop I shared an image of a campaign called '56 Black Men' founded by Cephas Williams, a businessman with a degree in architecture, often racially profiled, who set out on a mission to change the narrative and negative stereotypes of Black men being criminals. He created a powerful visual campaign in association with advertising giants Clear Channel, featuring Black men across the UK, from politicians such as David Lammy to barristers, all wearing black hoodies encouraging people to see beyond the stereotype. It was striking and, unsurprisingly, made national news. I used this campaign image to initiate a conversation about the stereotypes we hold about one another and in particular, about Black men, and how this might impact how we treat one another.

This one image seemed to send the collective racialised fragility in the room off the Richter scale, with many in chorus saying, 'If I saw someone like that, I would want to avoid them.' I spent time inviting some of the staff to interrogate where this behaviour was coming from, asking if they would have the same fear response to white men in hoodies, and if they were able to tell the difference between actual threat or perceived threat. It got a bit lively, shall we say, and ended with one of the participants saying 'If they dress like that what do they expect?' The image and my interrogation of their compulsive reaction to avoid Black men in the street for no reason had clearly exposed some communal racist impulses they were trying to justify, and they weren't at all happy about me shedding light on that, especially in front of one another.

I then started to talk about the impact of racism and shared some studies highlighting the trauma experiencing racism can cause, not just in adults, but the terrible impact on children's mental health and self-esteem. This is usually a point in my training where people display deep sadness, concern, empathy or, in some cases, it even induces tears.

Instead, another white male senior manager raised his hand halfway through my presentation of the trauma stats and asked: 'Why haven't Black people gotten over slavery yet?'

My response? Silence.

He continued: 'I mean, Jews seem to be getting on fine and they had the Holocaust.'

I was so flummoxed by that one. This was a room full of senior managers, responsible for managing a diverse community of people. The apathy, racism and anti-Blackness was so bold that I don't even think I was able to give a coherent reply other than our experiences of trauma are not in competition with one another and have you asked every single Jew, including those who are Black, whether they have indeed 'gotten over the Holocaust'?

By the lunch break, I was wondering how I was going to get through another hour and a half. I took a moment to pause, re-resource myself and spend some time on my own. I was then approached by one of three white women in the group – the person who had booked me for the workshop. She walked up to me, sighed and then started crying. I asked her why she was crying, and she replied, 'I can see what they are doing to you.'

She could see what they were doing to me, but the power of white supremacy and white solidarity meant she was unable, or unwilling, to compromise her position and say or do anything to break that solidarity – she had remained silent for the entire workshop. This is how racism spreads like wildfire and takes hold in the workplace.

It was the most violent, racist, hostile workplace I have ever been in as a facilitator, and it was all coming from the top down. This experience was a tough learning curve: it induced trauma and knocked my confidence for months and it was also the catalyst to deciding never to collude in providing, performative one-off Inclusion workshops for companies that have no interest in learning or changing behaviour, but instead just want to tick a box and save face, again. It was the collective defensiveness, the disarming white racial power, this white fragility in the room that I want to unpack with you. It is both this fragility and its function to protect the perceived and automatic innocence of whiteness and its link to anti-Blackness that I want to explore with you in this chapter.

White fragility is defined in the *Oxford English Dictionary* as: 'discomfort and defensiveness on the part of a white person when confronted by information about racial inequality and injustice'. The term was coined in 2011 by sociologist, author and critical race theorist Dr Robin DiAngelo after decades working in Diversity and Inclusion, recognising the same defensive behaviour in white people over and over again whenever she would talk about race in her workshops. I suspect the defensive behaviour she became so skilled at identifying – she wrote an entire book on the subject – was identical to what I was experiencing in the above workshop. Except she would have been protected by her whiteness from the violence and it wouldn't have shown up in her body as racial trauma.

White fragility is an automatic reflexive response to 'protect the innocence of whiteness.' DiAngelo intentionally uses the term 'fragility' to highlight how delicate white feelings are when being confronted with race; how little it takes to provoke what I like to describe as 'spontaneous combustion' over an exchange of information about race. However, there is nothing about being on the receiving end of white fragility that is fragile, meek and delicate. In fact, some activists including Sonya Renee Taylor, author of *The Body is Not an Apology*, suggest referring to it as 'white violence'. It is toxic as hell and a very effective tool to deflect, distract, and put Black folk in their place, so that we focus on your feelings and not the actual racism. This means we subconsciously resume the racial order.

This racialised fragility can look like bullying, gaslighting, fierce denial, impulsive actions to weaponise authority like making unsubstantiated complaints, or calling the police on Black people for no apparent reason. Some of the most common ways it shows up are guilt, disengagement, belligerence, exceptionalism ('not all white people', 'racism is not as bad in Britain', 'my child is mixed race') and anger. It definitely looks a lot like apathy and it shows up in every single cross-racial conversation where conscious anti-racism work is not being actively done and it is ingrained as a protective reflex in you.

Be honest – in what ways have you tried to prove you aren't racist? Journal on it.

But here's the interesting caveat and why, after a life of experiencing racism in this body and years doing this work as an educator and activist, I believe white fragility and anti-Blackness go together. I have witnessed some of the same impulsive responses synonymous with DiAngelo's definition of white fragility, not just from white folk and people perceived to be white, but from Black folk and Non-Black People of Colour too. While in these circumstances, it doesn't function in the same way, it's very much present. Because the framework of white supremacy is powerful and widespread. We have *all* been taught to maintain 'white racial order' – especially in the West. Whether we even know it, consciously agree with it or not, we collude.

★

So, What Exactly is Anti-Blackness?

Anti-Blackness is the breeding ground of white supremacy. Anti-Blackness is not just about racism, or the specific hatred of Black people and anything synonymous with Blackness: it is about the ingrained racist belief that there is something inherently wrong with Black people. While racism affects both Black people and other Marginalised Ethnic Groups, anti-Blackness is its birthplace, explaining why, after study after study, systemic racism so often disproportionately impacts Black people.

It seeps into all of us; even Black people and anti-Blackness seems to have funded some of Unilever's wealth, who *still* sell skin whitening products in Black- and Brown-majority countries, such as the Caribbean, the Middle East, Africa and

Asia.[3] Dr Kihana Miraya Ross, Professor of African American Studies at Northwestern University defines it as 'more than just "racism against Black people". That oversimplifies and defangs it. It's a theoretical framework that illuminates society's inability to recognize our humanity – the disdain, disregard and disgust for our existence.' If you are not tackling anti-Blackness in your anti-racism work, you are not addressing racism.

Slavery existed in many communities of various ethnicities long before white Europeans made it a global enterprise. The difference? Not all were rooted in anti-Blackness. Many were directly linked to war or indentured labour, where a person is paid a low fee or agrees to work for free to pay off debt, or in exchange for mastering a trade. They were not the personal property of others, they were not deemed non-human by law and they were not enslaved because of the colour of their skin. Chattel slavery and the dehumanisation of Black bodies was at the bedrock of justifying the global money-making industry that was the Transatlantic Slave Trade. More importantly, it justified violence in the name of white supremacy, where white (the lightest skin) was placed at the top of the racial hierarchy and Black (the darkest skin) at the bottom, with everyone else somewhere in between. The existence of anti-Blackness was necessary to justify the identity and institution of white supremacy based on the fabricated belief that white people were inherently superior. It existed to protect the appearance of white innocence that Carl Linnaeus first rustled up when he stated white people are 'gentle, acute inventive and governed by law',[4] and it continues to persist. And in order to protect that presumed white innocence at all costs, it needed to concoct a nemesis: the legacy of the presumed defectiveness and guilt of Blackness.

Racialised Fragility

While I wanted to give you the definition of white fragility, I find Akala's use of 'racialised fragility'[5] is a more accurate lens for us going forward, because these impulsive reactive responses are present in anyone who is agitated by Blackness being centred, regardless of their own skin colour. Focus on observing your (and that of others) behaviour. Focus on how your body is responding. If you bring your consciousness back to that child ego state, start to recognise when it shows up and how it functions to derail or silence, rather than ignoring it and trying to bypass it. You'll be able to consciously and intentionally unpack what is going on between this abusive and dysfunctional relationship with white innocence and anti-Blackness.

Let's start by unpacking some of the common defensive racialised fragility responses I received in that staff workshop. Notice how your body responds to processing these.

'Why haven't Black people gotten over slavery yet?'

This interruption to my presentation showcasing the 'evidence' of the impact of racism was an attempt to blame the victim and derail. It exposed the fact the interrupter was unaware that British taxpayers were still paying off compensation from the abolishment of slavery, to white former slave-owning families 'for their loss of property' until 2015. Basic understanding of economics and the disproportionate wealth inherited by white elite Brits as a result of this should help those, who are genuinely interested in not being racist, understand why we haven't just 'gotten over it yet', because the impact of this period of history remains very present. I imagine the interrupter wouldn't dream of asking war veterans and their families 'why they haven't gotten over it yet.'

This response communicated that this person found it intolerable to hear about these experiences of racism and inequality. It made it difficult for them to believe me; it's far easier to blame a collective of Black children for their own suffering and presumed shortcomings than believe the stats and evidence on the screen. Why? We find comfort in blaming others; it allows us to avoid looking at our own stuff and instead alleviates our own shame and guilt. If you are also colluding with anti-Blackness, it backs up the racist belief that there is something inherently wrong with Black people.

'I'm sick and tired of staff playing the race card... My white kids are mixed race – they're Irish too… Can you lighten up the mood?'

My explanation of why the 'race card' phrase was racist, by default, exposed the interrupter's own racism and no doubt felt like an attack on his identity. Instead of responding in an honest and vulnerable way by saying, 'I didn't know that'; instead of listening and reflecting on why he had become comfortable using racist phrases, he chose to double down and defend his position. He said, 'I can't be racist because I have mixed-race white English and white Irish kids', which then manoeuvred him to victimhood, perhaps to undermine and question my integrity. Anger and reasserting authority is a common response to racialised fragility (no doubt with a whole dose of misogyny in there too) in white men. This then translated to child ego behaviour with disengagement, folded arms, lack of eye contact, arguing, victim blaming and exceptionalism, and finally, 'Can you lighten up the mood, so I feel better about my racism that you've just exposed?'

The crying statement: 'I can see what they are doing to you.'

Tears are a common response from white women to being confronted with their racism (and I am not talking about common human expressions of sadness). They often serve as an attempt to coerce or manipulate outcomes to make them the 'victim'; an attempt, most likely subconscious, to make me feel the guilt she is experiencing and place the burden of forgiveness on me, the person receiving extraordinary racism. This response communicates guilt, embarrassment and shame. It's also an attempt to make themselves an exception – 'I am not like those other white people. I am a good white person, you need to see that and you need to make me feel better about it.' It demonstrates potential fear and huge discomfort at witnessing racism and choosing the safety of white solidarity, instead of doing or saying anything about it.

> 'We seem to feel in the common culture, that if we speak hate's
> name or invoke its memory, we will suffer a grim consequence...
> The collusion of silence makes hatred unbearably dangerous.'
> KATHLEEN POGUE WHITE[6]

'If they dress like that, what do they expect?'

The attempts to continue to justify the continued criminalisation of Black men for simply wearing a leisure suit, was another classic case of victim blaming; doubling down to maintain their automatic innocence and the automatic guilt associated with Blackness.

The various faces of flushed skin communicated embarrassment and possible shame. Many felt exposed by their admission that they engage in the active avoidance of Black men and felt that their identity, their character and perhaps even their values were under attack and they needed to defend them at all costs. I imagine they were also confronted, as my dear colleague, activist and Founder of Stand For Humanity, Yazzie Min once said to me, by the fact that I, as a Black woman, know more about whiteness, than them.

Let's take an easily hidden and more coded example. Now, I have quite an aversion to needles and so does my husband. I never realised that my aversion was less about the needle, but the anxiety that builds up every time we have to have a medical procedure because more often than not, white doctors and nurses say they 'can't see our veins' and then go on a wild flesh-piercing spree.

My husband was an outpatient in hospital and needed to have a cannula fitted. The first nurse, a white woman, after some initial hacking, said, 'Oh, I can't see your veins,' and called in a colleague. The second nurse, also a white woman, after poking around and jabbing, came to the conclusion that she couldn't get the needle into his hand because, direct quote, 'Your skin is too thick.'

The racist trope that Black people have thicker skin is born out of medical racism, one that she had evidently come to believe in order to cover up her own incompetence. In disbelief and utterly humiliated, my husband was ready to say something about her racism, but chose to bite his tongue because he knew how it would 'come across' as a Black man holding a boundary with a white woman. He swallowed both her racism and her malpractice, but sadly, it didn't end there.

The third attempt was by a white male nurse. The same experimental hacking continued until my husband, vexed, bruised and bleeding, sternly told him to stop and leave him alone. Not one single medical professional was able to perform a basic procedure. Instead of apologising, they shifted the blame to preserve their innocence, whilst reinforcing the racist belief that there is something inherently wrong with Black people by blaming him for having 'thick skin'.

The Body and Racialised Fragility

Paying attention to what your body is doing and what it is trying to communicate with you will give you vital signals, even when you haven't formed the words that something needs interrogating. It could be trying to tell you that you're exhibiting both coded racism and responding to racism in a defensive, fragile and destructive state. If you are not aware of how racialised fragility shows up in your body, you will continue to inflict harm.

I asked some of my students how this racialised fragility shows up in their bodies whilst doing anti-racism work. Here were some of their responses:

- 'Shame, embarrassment, hot flushes.'
- 'It feels like a snotty nosed little child screaming "it's not fair". It comes from a very childish and immature place in my body.'
- 'It mostly crops up when I'm panicking about myself and how I look to others, rather than actually being concerned about the impact of racism.'
- 'It feels like getting into trouble as a young kid. I feel it like a crushing feeling in my chest, and a hot flush of embarrassment for being corrected. Often I get a really strong desire to explain myself, like "No, you don't get it, I meant this..." It feels like a physical challenge as well as a mental one to sit with the mistake and get past the pain of being shown up as wrong. Subsequently, when I see it in others, my go-to response is to demonstrate how right I am and how much I "know" – "Pass me a cookie."'

These examples were shared by students who are very early on in the unlearning phase of their anti-racism journey, so their reflexive response is still to defend and protect their identity and self-perception, ahead of addressing racism.

I want to share an example of a response to the same questions and what happens to advanced students on the course who are in re-learning and have developed the 'muscle' to self-enquire and then respond accordingly:

It can make me feel like I've been winded. It can blind-side me and everything prickles inside. I feel depleted, knocked down, shown up and defensive. I feel like I'm not seen, understood, recognised for who I am or what I've done. I feel it somatically first and hear myself say, "What on earth is that?!" Then I have a little joke with myself. "Ah, there you are white fragility. How I've missed you! What are you trying to tell me this time, what's this about – what do I need to see?"

This advanced student has learned how to embody the work, to go beyond the cognitive. Yes, she still has defensive impulses, but she has really learned to pay attention to the signals in her body first, then the thoughts come. She doesn't try to change or alter the feelings in the moment; she notices them and tries to explore what they are there to teach her. I encourage my students to get creative and name their inner racist (some of the names are hilarious). This helps them to provide some distance, as this student demonstrates. Doing this has helped her separate the person from the behaviour so she can add humour to it and start to interrogate from a place of curiosity, rather than beating herself up or completely shutting down.

She continues:

Sometimes my confidence drops and I feel like I'm back at square one or that I've not moved on; and I feel like I've let the cause and Black and Brown people down. Then after that little pity party is over, I realise in fact all that's happened is another layer has been revealed – I've gone deeper. And that can only be a good thing.

One of my trilingual students who had been doing this work actively for over a year described anti-racism work as like learning a new language:

> I had so much constriction and fear. Before starting this work, I could not even name myself 'white' and had such awkwardness saying out loud 'Black' and 'Brown'. If I study a language and don't practise speaking it, it's kind of useless. Learning to be actively anti-racist is the same for me.

The more you practise, the more you exercise this 'muscle', the more it removes the fear and the more able you will be to decentre whiteness. Instead, you can respond from a genuine place of active listening, empathy, respect and compassion. You'll be able to separate someone, or a collective experience of racism, from your own perceived indignation and recognise that we cannot solve social issues with personal opinions. When you can start conversations about racism from a place of curiosity and empathy, instead of defending your position, that's where the change starts to happen.

Anti-Blackness and Racialised Fragility Beyond White Bodies

Defensive and fragile, or fear-based responses to being confronted about racism, especially anti-Blackness, don't just show up in white bodies. It can show up in Black folk too. It also shows up a lot in Non-Black People of Colour, people 'perceived' to be white, and if you are perceived as white and your identity intersects with other marginalised communities, you may wear the dual hat of both benefiting from and having suffered at the hands of white supremacy. This inherent response to uphold racial order, whether you consciously believe in it or not, and to preserve the innocence of whiteness can *also* show up in you. But it doesn't always function in the same way. The difference? It can also be an instinctive reaction or even a trauma response to protect oneself from harm, to work hard and keep quiet to be a 'model minority' tied up with a survival response to assimilate. Historically, through to the present day, we have seen, learned about and, for some of us, our bodies remember, that when white folk are uncomfortable, there are devastating and often violent or tragic consequences.

In 2018, I produced a docu-film called *OTHER*, exploring what it's like to be Black and Brown in the middle of Brexit. Some confronting truths about the impact of dealing with racism were shared, especially when dealing with the coded racism from everyday well-meaning liberals. The audience at the screening was of mixed ethnicities. A number of Black peers came up to me afterwards to congratulate me, and one said something like,

Wow Nova, I felt so uncomfortable. Not because of what was being shared but because I felt so validated. It spoke to my experience so truthfully and powerfully, but I noticed how uncomfortable I was for the white people in the room. I hadn't realised how much of myself I had contorted to make them comfortable – that is painfully eye-opening for me. That needs to change.

Even I'm not immune to absorbing anti-Blackness. Once, the hubby and I got a knock at the door one early winter evening while I was cooking dinner. My husband yelled, 'Nova come to the door, it's our new neighbours.' A very sweet pair, they had come round to introduce themselves and brought us a card and chocolates. There was just one problem: I wasn't 'visitor ready'. I'd not long started wearing wigs and underneath I had canerow, a protective hairstyle to help my hair recover from a bout of hair loss. My wig was in the living room, exactly where they were standing. I froze. I could not be seen without my wig. I'd been taught from a young age that wearing your hair in canerow was an 'inside hairstyle' or for when you were in the private company of other Black people – not outside hair and definitely not for white people to see; I'd carried that hair shame and anti-Blackness well into adulthood, only feeling presentable or acceptable to the white gaze when I had a Eurocentric wig on. I panicked and didn't come out of the kitchen. It wasn't my finest moment. They left in the end with my husband flabbergasted by my rudeness and unaware of why I didn't just come out. I put my wig on and then went to knock at their door and apologise, making up some far-fetched excuse about having a cooking disaster. My default, my survival response and what had been role-modelled to me, was the importance of assimilating: to have Eurocentric hair, to be perfectly presented when in the presence of whiteness and, ultimately, to not be myself. What I had learned and experienced through racism and associated hair shame, was that being myself and failing to assimilate could be dangerous, so much so it impacted a relatively innocuous social interaction with a neighbour.

I want to share another example of how anti-Blackness manifests in Non-Black People of Colour. *Therapy Today*, a magazine for professional therapists, published a piece by a therapist of South Asian heritage, explaining why, as an avid poster on social media, she decided to remain silent on social media following George Floyd's murder. As was her prerogative. However, the therapist likened the culture to call people in to show solidarity around that time to 'verbally lynching' people.

She went on to say: 'When I have previously timidly voiced my opinion that 'all lives matter', I have been shut down and told, "yes, but this is a Black cause right now." She continues: 'I have been shamed into thinking I am not Black enough to have a voice right now. When I say I don't see colour, I see deeper than that, I am told I am in denial of my own race and colour.' She then went on to compare receiving racism as the same as receiving discrimination because of hair colour or bank balance.

As a therapist who has the skills to self-enquire or take her projections to clinical supervision for support. The fact she chose to write this response to a previous special issue in *Therapy Today* on Black trauma and why Black mental health matters, following the murder of George Floyd and that it was even published, is deeply concerning. It also signals unsafety and it explains why all-Black spaces are currently still necessary, why Black therapists are in huge demand and why the reproduction of anti-Blackness from Non-Black People of Colour is so wounding.

Her defensive response to Blackness being centred is where we see the racialised fragility show up. She centred her own experience, reframing herself as the victim for not posting about George Floyd. Her careful choice of words to describe being held accountable for her anti-Blackness as being 'verbally lynched' positions Black people as unreasonable and aggressive. Her use of the word 'lynched' speaks to the violent method of torture and brutality commonly used against Black bodies; it suggests violence, anger, whilst simultaneously using hair colour discrimination and 'all lives matter' to diminish their experiences of racism, and whilst defending her position.

This racialised fragility has the same mission, which is to de-centre Blackness. It comes from a different position on the 'race hierarchy' but it has the same impact and causes the same harm.

If you collude with anti-Blackness, you will find it difficult to empathise, automatically going to defence, suspicion and beliefs that common systemic barriers disproportionately experienced by Black people are because Black people are angry, aggressive and inherently inferior.

Maintaining the Status Quo

This inherent and historical impulse to uphold white racial order whilst colluding with anti-Blackness can also be used as a very effective and dangerous weapon for political, professional, or personal advancement.

Conservative MP and Women's and Equalities Minister Kemi Badenoch made a statement in the Commons during Black History Month 2020: 'We do not want to see teachers teaching white pupils about white privilege... teachers who present the *idea* of white privilege as fact to their students are breaking the law,' and that 'race critical theorists actually want a segregated society.'[7]

What her statement did was not only incite division, but

dismiss decades worth of pre-existing academic research, something politicians generally hold in high regard. It also exposed both her and the government's historical illiteracy and selective memory.

The response to Blackness being centred in Black History Month and the denial of our global history is just staggering and the lies that will be told to cover up and continue to deny Britain's part in history and upholding white supremacy is beyond racialised fragility and utterly ludicrous. You'd think our own Treasury's announcement in 2015 might be a bit of a memory jog. They gleefully let the public know British taxpayers had only *just* finished paying off the debt from the compensation paid out to British slave traders and owners after the abolishment in 1833 – a debt so large it took us and several generations more 182 years to pay off. The evidence of white skin privilege is not only documented in research, but in so many history books.

Badenoch's statement not only demonstrates a resistance in centring Blackness, but reveals how damaging it can be to have ill-informed Black and Brown MPs in positions of power. There, they can spout racist ideas and misinformed opinion as fact, their visibility can be interpreted as 'progress' whilst simultaneously pushing for removal of anti-racism education. This is why learning about Black History, *all* of our history is vital, for Black folk too. No. We aren't a monolith, not all Black and Brown folk are 'for' anti-racism (which I know feels like a headfuck) and yes, we are allowed to have differing views, but if we cannot even agree on basic facts and start from there, then humanity is doomed.

Home Secretary and Conservative MP of Indian heritage, Priti Patel, made comments synonymous with the denigration of Black people in the House of Commons in June 2020 and described some Black Lives Matter protestors as hooligans and mobs, stereotypes synonymous with criminalising Black men. Earlier in the year, she stated in an interview that 'if this [Britain] was a racist country, I would not be sitting where I am.'[8] This communicates her own exceptionalism; the subtext is, 'Well, I am in this role so what's everyone else complaining about?' She uses her personal advancement to diminish any claims about social issues and systemic racism, using herself as her own personal case study, implying those claiming to experience systemic racism are merely down to individuals not working hard enough.

Both of these MPs are also weaponised by the Party to further racist agendas. The Party knows it's far more powerful to have white supremacy endorsed by a minority Black or Brown voice who 'toes the line' than it is by a white person who is being challenged because it protects white innocence. It affirms racist views and delegitimises any accounts of racism that have gone before. This strategic move also makes it harder to challenge a Black person upholding racist views and leads us to question our own understanding. It's also interesting to observe, that when a majority group of Black folk speak up about racism, the default response is to assume we are 'lying', but when racist views are upheld by a Black person whose views are in the minority of other Black folk, like Badenoch, or indeed, American right-wing commentator Candace Owens, they are automatically believed. Funny that. Using one's own position in society as a weapon against others in the same or other marginalised communities who haven't reached the social mobility is individualistic and classist. Using one's position to invalidate experiences of racism and suggest anyone who hasn't reached the same heights, simply hasn't worked hard enough is bullshit. Does it mean Badenoch and Patel don't experience the dehumanising impact of racism? Of course not, *and* they also uphold anti-Blackness.

When your instinctive response to racism becomes more about denial, assuming a person's experience of racism is a lie, to victim blame, to play 'devil's advocate', centring your own experience and defending your position, you're having a racist response. The racial order you've been taught to maintain is being rocked and something in your body is telling you to either fear it or reject it and get back to the status quo. This is an invitation to interrogate.

How does racialised fragility show up in your body?

1. What feelings, sensations, temperature changes do you experience?
2. Is there any tightening in your body?
3. Does your breathing change?
4. If you're speaking, what do you notice about your tone?
5. Does your intonation pattern change?

How do these defensive responses show up in your behaviour?

1. Do you disengage by zoning out, scrolling through your phone, leaving the room, ignoring friends, unfollowing activists, and actively avoiding conversations about race?
2. Do you automatically feel guilt, implicated or apathetic?
3. Do you take control of the conversation, changing the subject to talk about something else unrelated to racism?
4. Do you focus on tone and tell people their message about

racism would be better received if it was delivered in a certain way?

5. Do you blame the victim?
6. Do you get caught up in semantics and say the reason we haven't addressed racism is because of the 'divisive language that's used'?
7. Do you delegitimise accounts of racism and make yourself an exception because you have experienced hardship or discrimination too?
8. Do you get angry and project anger onto others?

A reminder, if you need to hear it: our commonality of being hated and experiences of being discriminated against are not in competition with each other.

Using Social Location to Combat Anti-Blackness

To help us recognise and manage defensive and destructive behaviour that gets in the way of tackling racism, especially when it comes to perpetuating anti-Blackness, we have to have constant awareness of our own social location.

Our location impacts outcomes, self-perception, and our experiences. It informs our awareness (or lack thereof) to others' lived experience and it helps us to understand that our location is malleable. How we experience the intersection of societal advantage and discrimination change depending on where we are, who we are with and where we are positioned on a 'hierarchy'.

Having self-awareness and being able to take into consideration your social location in conversations about racism with trust and empathy is an antidote to those defensive impulses. It stops you centring on you and your feelings, spending unnecessary energy defending your position and instead enables you to actively listen, free from resentment or agitation, to the person who is talking about their experience of trauma.

While using a lens of social location helps all of us identify who we are, who we become and how society perceives us, when it comes to addressing anti-Blackness, it can be incredibly confronting and disorienting. Because it asks you to look at where, by default of your location, and the infusion of this 'race hierarchy', you also benefit from other people's systemic oppression.

Award-winning wedding photographer, founder of Let's Sign About and member of the Black Deaf community, Ashton-Jean Pierre, started to share more about 'white deaf supremacy' to address racism in the Deaf community where, the majority of British Sign Language (BSL) teachers are white. This might go some way to explaining why complaints have been made about many still using 'Coloured' and an old sign for 'Black person' in BSL[9] – a circular motion in front of one's face. The same circular motion is synonymous with washing or cleaning, also used to sign 'ugly' and 'Africa'. In August 2020, Let's Sign About shared a video explaining why people in the Black British Deaf community are offended by this racist sign and its suggestion that dark skin is dirty and needs cleaning. As a result, the community has requested people stop using it and use the sign for the continent of Africa instead, which is entirely different.

A common response to addressing racism, specifically anti-Blackness, from people in other marginalised communities, who also experience systemic discrimination, such as a world made for hearing and able-bodied people is to ignore race: 'This is about X so this is what we should focus on.' This ignores the social location and that of Black people who are so often identified by race first and experience racism, including in British Sign Language. Being mindful of social location helps us constantly understand where we hold societal advantages and where we don't.

I remember having a conversation about systemic racism with my sister-in-law, explaining how white people can receive individual acts of prejudice or discrimination but that white people, as a collective, do not experience systemic racism. You could see the confusion and frustration in her face. Her frown communicated to me: 'Yes we do.' She is white and Slovak. English is her second language, and she has many experiences of discrimination as a Slovak living in England and general shitty behaviour from British people who are white, Black and also Non-Black People of Colour. When you are in a hate cesspit, language might feel like semantics, because let's face it, hate feels like hate. However, racism, especially anti-Blackness, is so often unaddressed, misunderstood and lumped into one homogenous issue. It's important to have honest and accurate conversations so we can move forward and address the issue being discussed at hand. A few dialogues later, after giving space for her to have her experiences of xenophobia heard and validated and sharing more about my experiences along with some reading prompts, she understood the difference: The dehumanisation she experiences is based on her nationality and not her skin colour.

She was able to recognise that, depending on where she is, she will be a majority and sometimes, she will be an 'other'. Generally speaking, she can move through the world, go about her daily life, protected by her whiteness (until you hear the accent) and that she does not receive systemic discrimination because of the colour of her skin. It doesn't mean her experiences of xenophobia weren't real or problematic, or that our communities don't experience the commonality of being hated. It means that in the eyes of white supremacy, she both benefits and can also be seen as an 'other' – and in conversations about racism she still holds 'white skin privilege' and will be higher up that 'racial hierarchy' than Blackness.

Anti-Blackness, as we have started to explore, has been at the centre of medicine and medical racism and continues to be rife in healthcare, impacting outcomes and corroding trust. In my research I discovered pharmaceutical companies knowingly selling defective, contaminated and substandard drugs to countries in Africa, because, according to a former medical director at Ranbaxy 'Who cares, it's just blacks dying?'[10] Fast forward to April 2020 when Doctor Jean-Paul Mira, head of intensive care at Cochin Hospital in Paris, suggested vaccine studies to prove if they are effective against coronavirus should be tested on Africans first.[11] Medical experiments and anti-Blackness are not new, medical professionals used to pathologise the mental health of enslaved people who tried to escape, by claiming they were abnormal for trying to break free from being treated worse than animals and diagnosing them with an invented mental health condition called *Drapetomania* instead.[12] Today this translates as Black people being most likely to experience mental ill-health as a consequence of racism, but being less likely to be referred to psychological services and being disproportionately sectioned.[13]

One interviewee first became aware of her social location when she developed severe postnatal depression and was sectioned under the Mental Health Act 1983. Whilst in recovery she noticed, as one of the few white women on the ward, how different her care was to that of her fellow patients. She described how one of her Black peers was consistently spoken down to, in short, curt tones as though she were a nuisance. This was in contrast to the empathy my interviewee was afforded. At one point, a Black nurse presented her Black peer, who was not religious, with a Bible. None of the nurses presented my white interviewee with a Bible to 'cure' her of her mental ill-health. She was treated with respect and sensitivity throughout and was offered thorough and extensive follow-up and psychological support services at home. In contrast, her Black peer wasn't offered any home visits or counselling, and was advised to go on a parenting course (designed for parents separated from their children by social services, or those experiencing substance addiction) which she couldn't afford to attend because she had to work. My interviewee said her Black peer (and now friend) was an articulate and intelligent woman, but had been treated as if she was at risk of harming her child. She didn't need a parenting course, she needed empathy and help with her mental health. Both on the ward, both vulnerable and experiencing a period of mental ill-health, she could still see so clearly both the anti-Blackness and where she held societal advantage and how their experiences and outcomes were very different as a result.

Being aware of our own social location in anti-racism means not deviating from discussing the issue at hand to centre your own experience. It means simply listening to whoever is holding the 'metaphorical mic'. It doesn't mean one voice is more valid than the other, or that our experiences of being discriminated against are somehow in competition or conflict with one another. It just means that this is where our focus needs to be in this moment to help reduce this specific set of harms – and to be honest about how we may also have contributed to them.

★

Oppression is Not a Competition

Derailing conversations about racism and playing communities that experience social suffering off against one another conflates the seriousness of those issues and only serves to uphold white supremacy. In my experience, people who respond with questions such as, 'What about Black-on-Black violence?' or 'What about poor, working-class white people?' are generally not concerned with helping any of these communities, because if they were, they would know that crime and poverty are not synonymous with skin colour.

Anti-Blackness is right in the centre of what I call 'Yes, Buts, and Whataboutism' – the idea that you're 'just playing Devil's advocate' – to deny or explain away racism. Why? Because we have been conditioned to decentre Blackness, devaluing our humanity and silencing us. We had no voice, no rights and were often treated worse than animals, so it's little wonder that under white supremacy you too have become used to that social standing. You have become used to seeing Black bodies as disposable; you expect to see us impoverished, to see us in subservient roles, as inferior, as untrustworthy. When we start to centre our humanity and our culture, when you see us celebrating, when you see Black advancement, it agitates you.

In April 2020, English country interior stylist Paula Sutton, now fondly referred to as 'Auntie' in the virtual Black community, often uses her Instagram platform to post joyful pictures of things in her life she loves. Paula was dragged across Twitter and even called a 'cunt' for posting a picture of herself having a picnic outside her country home. One user was so triggered by Paula's evident wealth and joy, she took a screenshot of her photo on Instagram then re-posted it on Twitter with the words: 'Deleted Instagram today for the first time ever (eight years) Don't know when I'll be back, but let it be known this was the image that did it...'

When examining how racism plays out in this disproportionate response to a woman minding her own business on social media, consider these words from scholar and racial healing practitioner Sarah Bellamy:

> How does a body respond to generational expressions of racial power?... White folks must dig into your embodied racism, especially if you think it's not there. What are you carrying dormant in your body that springs up when confronted with Black joy, Black power, Black brilliance?[14]

An invitation to get curious and journal:

- How does your body respond to hate, jealousy or envy, especially when you see a Black person celebrating?
- Where does hate show up in your body?
- Where is it located? Are you tensing up?
- What does it feel like?

- What sensations or body heat changes or impulses do you notice?

Anti-racism activist and academic Rachel Cargle uses her online community to share examples of everyday racism she receives in her Instagram inbox, helping her followers learn. At times, she leaves the offending user's handle public. In one post, she responded directly to some followers who felt that sharing the abuser's name was not fair. This shows a lot of concern and empathy for the abuser, but not the same concern for the person receiving racial abuse. In her post, she asked followers to consider: if a man was being verbally sexually abusive to a woman and she held them accountable in the same way Rachel does with perpetrators of racism, would the women have the same energy and concern for the man? The answers were a resounding no. They would want them to be held accountable for their sexist behaviour.

By centring Blackness, I am not saying that white women do not experience sexism, or that other Marginalised Ethnic Groups do not experience dehumanising racism. I'm saying they experience that *and*, unless they're in the conscious process of unlearning white supremacist conditioning, they will also be benefitting from our ongoing oppression and continue to perpetuate anti-Blackness – the kind of anti-Blackness that looks like an interview I had with a British-Indian Muslim bride who had to walk down the aisle, alone, because she married a Black Nigerian man and brought 'shame' on the family. Her father refused to walk her down the aisle, or attend the ceremony.

If you benefit from proximity to whiteness, centring Blackness does not mean your experiences of classism or poverty are not valid. Centring Blackness does not mean that your experience of xenophobia, islamophobia or antisemitism aren't real, dehumanising and valid. Centring Blackness does not mean that your experiences of homophobia from heterosexual people who are Black aren't valid. Our persecution is not in competition with one another.

It's possible to experience racism *and* other 'isms' *and* to also uphold white supremacy *and* contribute to anti-Blackness. If your reductive, defensive response to the centring of Blackness is to come back with the likes of 'but Black people are homophobic and antisemitic too,' not only does it ignore, undermine and erase the intersections of Black people who are Black and Queer, Black and Jewish, or both, it is an urgent invitation to interrogate your anti-Blackness.

There is a lot of racism in the LGBTQ+ community. Research from Stonewall reveals 51 per cent of those in BME groups receive racism from within the community. Break that down further and Black people in the community receive a whopping 61 per cent.[15] Personal accounts from my interviews and the very existence of UK Black Pride, founded in 2005 by Phyll Opoku-Gyimah (who turned down an MBE due to the homophobic laws that continue to persecute and remain in many former British colonies) reinforce the fact that this is still a rampant issue. In March 2021 one of the most senior Black volunteers at Pride In London, Rhammel Afflick, came forward publicly to draw attention to the hostile environment from within and the persistent unwillingness in the leadership team to address racism. Rhammel's courage in coming forward was supported by Stonewall in a tweet, and led to the resignation of Pride In London's entire leadership team.

It has been described by campaigners as a landmark moment.[16] The presence of racism doesn't stop me from believing that all non-Black people in LGBTQ+ communities deserve to live free from abuse and live in all their humanity. My belief on that is not conditional on the entire community being perfect and sorting out their racism and other 'isms' first. This is about reducing human suffering, not adding to it.

We can hold two things to be true at once. I want to hold people in other communities that continue to dehumanise us and benefit from our discrimination and their proximity to whiteness accountable for their anti-Blackness. *And* I also want to see an end to gender discrimination, antisemitism, homophobia, transphobia, Islamophobia , ableism *and* to continue to interrogate how Black people (myself included), who may or may not also intersect with these identities, can uphold these oppressions too.

If you are using the questionable behaviour of Black individuals as leverage, to morally justify anti-Blackness, that is a direct impulse from your racialised fragility and/or internalised white supremacy. We can believe in human rights and the liberation of all, without making our commitment to do anti-racism conditional on the entire Black community being flawless, 'best-behaved' and only then deserving of liberation. To impose that condition is racist.

Challenge your racialised fragility and anti-Blackness and interrogate further:

1. Where do you hold societal advantage?
2. Where do you hold societal disadvantage? Consider age, location, where you live, class, education, skin colour,

assumed identity, gender, sex orientation, health, disability, body size.

3. How do these change depending on where you are, who you are with or your circumstances?

Acknowledging your social location doesn't take away your own experiences of struggle or discrimination. It helps you recognise your hidden spots so you can be more aware and more skilled at being actively anti-racist, to recognise where you need to further learn, listen, and probe. It helps you understand where you have power to impact your own community, influence change, build empathy, to stop reproducing anti-Blackness and racism and start to reduce harm.

★

6. Moral Monsters: Racism and Shame

'Shame corrodes the very part of us that
believes we are capable of change.'
BRENÉ BROWN[1]

At the beginning of this book, I said we need to have the courage to look and start to address what lies beneath the wound, and to rip off the plaster. Well, this is that moment.

This chapter was the hardest to write. I've tried to find ways to add lightness to it, but the reality is, our history surrounding white racial supremacy and the associated behaviour from white people past and present continues to fuel racism today. The collective shame associated with it is not pretty or light. Our history and role in systemic racism has been sanitised for too long. Many of us have spent most of our lives being ignorant to history hiding in plain sight, or worse, going to lengths to erase history. At best, we've been putting nice pink bows on shit that, quite frankly, stinks. It's time to cut to the chase, because in order to be truly anti-racist, we have to understand the root cause of that behaviour.

I have not sanitised our history in this chapter. I have depicted some historical moments of violence so please proceed with great care. The contents of this chapter may be hard to read, might churn your stomach or even induce tears. It will most definitely induce feelings of shame – but staying stuck in shame is unhealthy. It's important we move through this together to understand where the burning shame and huge feelings of being implicated for being white come from in racism. We are doing this so that we can better understand collective shame, where impulsive, defensive responses to anti-racism are coming from, and how that might be impacting your behaviour to this very day.

Pause if you need to. Visit the self-care chapter (see Chapter 8) if you need to, but come back to this chapter and come back to work. It's too important – and so is your role in no longer being an active bystander in all of this. I am an advocate of calling people in and not calling them out because I know from personal and professional experience how psychologically damaging intentionally shaming someone can be.

Understanding Shame

I started the early stages of my mental health training around fifteen years ago at the time of writing, and will always remember my first class on counselling skills was about shame. We were taught, no matter how unspeakable a client's behaviour was, how lethal intentionally shaming them could be. You know, typical dehumanising behaviour such as calling someone disgusting or telling them they should be ashamed of themselves. Calling someone out in public with the intent to humiliate, mock and 'expose' them, rather than see them grow or transform. This is shaming. We can absolutely hold people responsible for their bullshit – but without shaming them. From that place, change is much more likely to happen. You will know what it's like to feel intentionally shamed – it's not pleasant and for the most part, it's not hugely motivating.

You will most definitely feel shame in your anti-racism journey, so I must make this clear: being called in, being held accountable for your racism and experiencing feelings of shame as a by-product of that is *not* the same as me or someone else intentionally shaming you. I truly hope by the end of this chapter, you will understand the difference between the two, and also be able to start to recognise when shame related to racism is hap-pening in the moment or coming from past trauma or wounds. Shame can trigger trauma. If you have a complex relationship with shame and need assistance to help you move through past wounding, please pace yourself with this chapter and consider seeking professional support to address it.

★

I remember the sucker punch that was shame at just 7 years old.

I was quite an anxious child, hypervigilant to my surround-ings, which I have since discovered is a symptom of trauma. As a result, I used to walk quite quickly with my head down, to not make eye contact with anyone. To not be seen, almost as if I didn't look at anybody, I would somehow be invisible. Of course, growing up as a Black girl in a very white county of Hertfordshire I was anything but invisible.

Walking to school one day in my usual 'I want to be invisible' posture, I clocked a young white girl, a little younger than me, with her mother on the other side of the road. I carried on with purpose towards the school gates. I felt the staring first. You know, when eyes are so fixated on you – it's like someone is trying to examine every crevice on your body and look into your soul. I felt extremely uncomfortable, which made me look up. This young girl would not break her gaze. When you're Black, or have some kind of visible difference, you come to learn very early on the difference between someone looking at you to admire you, and when they're looking at you as if you're some kind of endangered and rarely seen species. It was the latter. My eyes catching hers didn't stop her staring either, in fact, it seemed to make her even more animated. She pointed at me and asked her mother, loud enough for me to hear, 'Mummy? Mummy? Why is that girl the same colour as poo-poo?'

And there it was. Shame.

I expect there had been many similar instances previously that I simply was too young to be able to process. Growing up in a very white area, I went on to experience constant hair touching, and white men hanging out of their white vans, ironically behaving like animals, doing monkey chants at me. This was commonplace until my early thirties. However, this question from a little white girl, a peer who evidently knew no better, was the one event that was most palpable. This one stuck like glue.

Stomach lurching, heat rising from my gut to my face, the heaviness of wanting to hide. That feeling of almost being 'outed' by my visible difference. Wanting the ground to swallow me up, feeling unclean with my 'dirtiness' in full view of everyone. I learned in that moment that my value as a human being was not the same as hers. I felt the most overwhelming feeling of unworthiness. I learned quickly the power behind the punch of being publicly shamed. I was just 7 years old.

Of course, at the time, I didn't know the feelings I was experiencing were shame. But I remember how they felt. Shame for not being the same as everyone else, shame that my hair didn't blow in the wind, shame that my 'poo-poo'-coloured skin must be abnormal, shame ultimately, that my skin was Black. To my parents' devastation, what followed were several ferocious attempts to wash my skin off because, based on that little girl's estimations and what I saw projected at me, there was no other explanation – I had to be dirty. When that didn't work, I tried dousing myself in talcum powder. I was trying, in the only way I knew how, to make my skin white. I was trying to be the same colour as the majority of people around me. I was trying to belong.

★

Shame researcher Dr Brené Brown describes shame as: 'The intensely painful feeling or experience of believing that we are flawed and therefore unworthy of love and belonging – something we've experienced, done, or failed to do makes us unworthy of connection.'[2]

I love to use Brené Brown's definition of shame because it makes the most sense to me personally and professionally. While others suggest shame comes from a consciousness of 'doing' something wrong, we can still experience intense feelings of shame, or be shamed without having 'done' anything. Seven-year-old little Nova can attest to that.

Shame is that intense, often burning sensation that feels so exposing; it tells us with a megaphone that we are bad, that we are not worthy, that we are disgusting, that we are inherently flawed, irreparable, unlovable. Recognise any of this cruel self-talk?

When we feel shame, it implies we cannot change, that we deserve what's coming to us. Guilt, which often gets mistaken for shame, centres on behaviour. With guilt, we don't carry our experience at an identity level. It centres on something we said or did that was 'wrong' or 'bad' and therefore, if we choose to, we can make some changes. It doesn't leave us with the same burning, lingering feeling of being implicated as a bad human being that shame does. As a result, most of us will avoid feeling shame at all costs.

Even the mention of that five-letter word can bring up huge feelings of shame. It can sever longstanding relationships. In fact, shame is so powerful, neuroscientists have discovered that feelings of shame can show up in the brain in the same way as physical pain.[3] However, it is also a human condition, which means that as far away as we try to get from it, it cannot be avoided. Actively avoiding shame can not only be destructive, but dehumanises us, which is the very thing we are trying to undo in anti-racism.

I invite you to learn to start to get acquainted with your feelings of shame, because anti-racism work doesn't just force us to confront individual shame, but to get curious about and confront the force of collective shame we carry too. Not addressing your shame and not knowing how this shows up in your behaviour will continue to create a toxic barrier to change, inflict further harm on yourself and others and sabotage your allyship. You'll frequently either end up withdrawing, numbing, reacting, or turning your shame into self-righteous anger, wounding other people in the process in a destructive attempt to alleviate your own unaddressed shame.

And as you can see from political characters thrust into the spotlight, such as former US president Donald Trump who believes 'no politician in history has been treated worse' than him,[4] shamed and wounded people in the world do not promote grounds for positive change. Shamed and wounded people in positions of power can, in fact, be dangerous.

Shame and Racism

The relationship between shame and racism is clear. At the root of racism is fear of the other and fear of social rejection. Social rejection is a real threat to one's sense of safety, as human beings we need connection with others to help us build a sense of belonging and improve overall wellbeing and a sense of self.[5] But that connection with one another needs to be healthy and unfortunately, we can be drawn to unhealthy connection, such as gathering and relishing in gossip and judging, and mistake it as belonging. When we gather to start collectively hating others as a means to connect, we are in dangerous territory because we dehumanise those others in the process. And it's this dehumanisation of others that is the key ingredient in every single mass genocide in human history.

White supremacy created a shared human experience and an opportunity for white people, regardless of social standing, to unite. This is indeed an example of human connection, but is it a healthy one? The absence of healthy meaningful connection and the existence of unhealthy connections with other human beings can become utterly destructive and result in ongoing human suffering and a whole load of rampant collective shame. For the social construct of white racial supremacy to exist, to be embedded in law, to form a global industry, to be backed by flawed science used to justify centuries of oppression based on skin colour, it meant another 'race' had to be inferior. For whiteness to be the benchmark for normalcy, white people *needed* to be able to look down upon another – in this case, the people at the bottom of that totally constructed hierarchy, Black people, needed to co-exist.

So what is the by-product of treating fellow human beings for centuries as worthless? Who do you have to become to torture or routinely witness the torture of another human being? Let's unpack it.

★

Britain's Shameful History

'And though she be but little, she is fierce.'
WILLIAM SHAKESPEARE[6]

I remember being interviewed for a podcast called *Three Right Turns*, hosted by a white American man called A.Ron. In his words, he's a 'man man': someone who carries a gun, a former evangelical and overtly racist thinker who became enlightened. Having realised he was being indoctrinated with bullshit, A.Ron is now dedicated to helping other white American men from a similar background confront their racism and see another way.

Just as we started the interview, A.Ron said something along the lines of, 'Up until the blow up with the Royals [Harry and Meghan], I always thought Britain didn't have a problem with racism.'

I responded, 'We hide it well.' And that we do.

We often hear retorts on TV debates, or on what I like to describe as the racist cesspit that is Twitter, that Britain is the 'least racist country'. Based on what standards and by whom? And more to the point, what competition have we entered?

I believe Britain's racism is so insidious because the most historically violent atrocities committed by the British Empire were often not done on British soil; they were sneaky with their racism like that. The British Empire was vast. According to historian Stuart Laycock, the Empire invaded all but twenty-two countries in the entire world, including its former colony the United States of America – the country that Brits like to use as a bizarre benchmark to compare 'levels' of racism. The Empire played a firm role in the Transatlantic Slave Trade for well over a century, forcibly 'shipping' around 3.1 million human beings from parts of Africa to British colonies and embedding racist laws across the globe. Slave ships regularly left Bristol, Liverpool and London, were often owned by British merchants and manned by British sailors, and even the Church of England owned plantations.

Some of the most horrendous acts of violence carried out by (and if not, certainly enabled and witnessed by) Brits have left a lasting legacy. But because most Brits are ignorant at best and unwilling at worst to even acknowledge our history, let alone discuss it, when it comes to trying to tackle racism, it most definitely shows up as collective shame. And harbouring collective shame is not the foundation for change.

During the height of the Transatlantic Slave Trade in the eighteenth and nineteenth centuries, enslaved people from what was then referred to as the British West Indies or British Caribbean islands, (read: where a lot of Brits liked to hang out under Britain's colonial rule) often endured the most horrific conditions with a high death toll of enslaved people. The island of Jamaica, where my family is from, is reported by historians to have had the most brutal of slave regimes that took the lives of 75 per cent of the 1.3 million slaves transported over there, predominantly from West Africa.[7] By no happy coincidence, the island of Jamaica was also where the British Empire made most of its wealth from slavery thanks, in part, to Europeans' insatiable appetite for sugar in beverages like tea and coffee that were, originally, made to be consumed bitter.[8]

Slave huts were overcrowded, and because of their proximity to livestock, enslaved people's water was often infested with animal waste. One in three enslaved people died within the first three months of arrival in the British Caribbean island of Jamaica – a combination of finding it hard to adjust to the horrendous conditions and many being worked to death.[9]

In her book *A Kick in The Belly: Women, Slavery and Resistance*, historian Stella Dadzie recounts a journal entry from Thomas Thistlewood, a British plantation overseer and slaver in Jamaica, who described how Black women were also routinely raped by their owners as soon as they got off of slave ships to help them to 'acclimatise' in a process referred to as 'seasoning'.[10]

Alongside frequent sexual abuse from white men, Black women also bore the brunt of the labour in gruelling conditions on sugar plantations. Working shifts between twelve to eighteen hours long, injury and violent death were common. For example, a key process of extracting juice from sugarcane was to feed the cane through an industrial roller – by hand. This was extremely dangerous, and there were many accidental deaths as a result. Those who survived had permanent disabilities, were subsequently seen as weak and discarded as a consequence. Becoming even more disposable than they were before. And if we join the dots, we can start to see ableism's intrinsic link to white supremacy as we see where perceived worth, value and superiority started being placed on able-bodied people and how much they 'produce'.

In addition to these horrific conditions, enslaved people in Jamaica also received brutal punishment from their masters. Because of the size of the island, the sheer volume of sugar plantations and increased demand for sugar, they needed a lot of labour. This meant they needed more people power and there were often hundreds of enslaved people on plantations in Jamaica, in comparison with the US plantations, which were much smaller. In theory, enslaved Black Africans significantly outnumbered their white English and Scottish planters and there was a huge climate of fear that slaves would want to seek revenge on their masters.[11] This resulted in disproportionate, legally enforced oppression and torture to 'keep them in their place' and breed a culture of fear in them.

Frequent whippings were the least of enslaved peoples'

problems. Intentional disfiguring and amputation were common methods of punishment, as well as what was often a tortuous death. This included burning alive anyone that dared to rebel.[12]

After the Abolition of Slavery

Fast forward to the abolition of slavery in British colonies in 1833 and the US in 1865. You might think that, after all of this trauma and since former enslaved people had still shown no sign of seeking mass revenge on white people for their enslavement, they would be left alone to build a life, away from abuse and shackles. To finally enjoy their freedom and live in peace. No such luck. White people's irrational fear of Black people going on murderous rampages to seek revenge on white people worsened and wreaked havoc well after the abolishment of slavery, and we can still see that playing out today.

Black basketball coach Doc Rivers was interviewed in August 2020, after an unarmed Black man, Jacob Blake, was shot in the back seven times in front of his children by the police, while reportedly attempting to de-escalate a domestic incident. In a protest against continued disproportionate police brutality against the Black community, NBA players refused to play. In a deeply moving television interview, the tenderness and utter exasperation that came out of Doc, something you don't often witness from strapping Black men who've been accustomed to hiding their pain with anger, said: 'All you keep hearing about is fear [from white people] yet we are the ones who were hanged, we are the ones being shot, we are the ones who have to talk to our kids about being careful with the police...'

This irrational fear of Black people continued to drive the oppression of Black people and, after slavery, this mutated into decades upon decades of lynching, the term describing when a mob or group of people kill someone for an alleged offence without any form of legal trial. Lynchings, which have become synonymous with the American South, were actually a practice carried across by migrants from the British Isles to colonial North America.[13] There are also ties to the origins of lynching that root back to the Irish in the fifteenth century.

Lynching has always been a method of social control and collective punishment. Solidarity would be formed from an established 'in group', or community with a similar culture and often of a higher status than the 'victim', where the group punishes an individual, usually an 'outsider' who has little to no support. In Michael J. Pfeifer's book, *The Roots of Rough Justice, Origins of American Lynching*, he explains that lynchings were often a form of vigilantism spurred on by concerns about the efficacy of formal criminal justice'.[14]

It's no coincidence that these mob lynchings gained particular momentum in the nineteenth century, particularly but not exclusively, in parts of the US from 1882 to 1940 after law change and post-abolition of slavery and the Civil War. Lynchings were a method of sadistic social control by vigilantes who felt wronged and wanted 'keep' Black people in their place and resume the 'social order' so many had become accustomed to for generations. And lynchings of the less-public kind went on until 1968. Which at the time of writing was just fifty-two years ago.

In the Jim Crow South, public lynchings were rife. They were a ritualistic and for some, patriotic, celebration that unified white people in the South in a way that transcended the ever-present gender division and class hierarchies. Families would go to church in the morning dressed up in their Sunday best and head to a public lynching when church ended, with their youngest children in tow whilst enjoying a picnic.[15] This kind of cognitive dissonance was, and still is, rife when it comes to racism and desensitising oneself from witnessing Black pain. The spectacle attracted crowds of thousands, some estimated to be up to 15,000 strong. White people would attend in droves and that didn't include the firm role the media played to not only advertise these spectacles but also to provide a resource for thousands more who wanted to hear about them in the newspaper or on the radio.[16] Even rail providers would announce when lynchings were taking place so people from out of town could visit.

According to the Tuskegee Institute in Alabama and National Association for the Advancement of Colored People (NAACP), 4,743 lynchings took place in the US from 1882 to 1968,[17] and 72.7 per cent of those lynchings were on Black bodies.[18] It's worth noting that, due to collusion from officials, the absence of law and any due process, many of the lynchings were not recorded, so it's believed the true number is far higher than documented. The remaining numbers are thought to be made up of the occasional white person for committing a crime, white immigrant Italians and some Jews,[19] and of course anti-lynching activists, often referred to as 'nigger lovers'. The culture of lynching didn't just impact people deemed to be in an 'out group'. Communal lynchings also occurred and turned inwards, punishing members of their own 'in' group if they went against their wishes.[20]

A lot of Black men and young boys were the victims of public lynchings, from the lynching of 17-year-old Henry Smith and Jesse Washington. In his autobiography, *Dusk of Dawn*, sociologist, civil rights activist and one of the founders of the NAACP W. E. B. Du Bois highlights a culture of souvenir gathering that often took place after lynchings. He remembers the time he saw the knuckles of 18-year-old Sam Hose being displayed in a grocery shop window for good measure. [21]

Black people were being lynched for anything: from Black resistance, looking at a white person in the 'wrong way' or achieving economic success, to petty crime, allegedly raping white women, and fear.[22] I write 'allegedly', because accounts of crime and rape were, more often than not, born of lies and forced confessions to justify barbaric public torture. Additionally, the more athletic and strong, the more 'superhuman' the Black body, the better the lynching 'party'.[23]

'The mob wanted the lynching to carry a significance that transcended the specific act of punishment [that] turned the act [of lynching] into a symbolic rite in which the Black victim became the representative of his race and, as such, was being disciplined for more than a single crime. The deadly act was a warning to the Black population not to challenge the supremacy of the white race,' writes historian Howard Smead.[24]

The subtext of this? 'We don't care if you are free, or if there is a growing Black middle class. You will always be a Nigger. You will always be less-than. And, in order to keep my white superiority, I need to keep all of you in your place.'

Lynchings had the engagement of local officials, from businesses and mayors, to law enforcement and press.[25] And they attracted men, women and children and unified whiteness in the most horrific way, regardless of social location or age. One account witnessed a little girl giggling at the flies feeding on the blood of a Black body.[26] Watching Black people burn slowly to death and this method of unity seemed to be quite the crowd pleaser and was a popular documented choice of lynching on Black bodies in the American South. While the practice of using burning as capital punishment was popular in colonial America, it was actually an inherited 'practice' from the English from late-medieval England era.[27]

Meanwhile, in the early twentieth century in Britain, race relations were growing increasingly tense. While segregation wasn't as prescriptive as in the Jim Crow South, colour bans across the UK were widespread and equally devastating. Racism was legal and it was perfectly acceptable to refuse work to Black people because of the colour of their skin. In fact, trade unions even backed white workers in Glasgow when they refused to work alongside former Black British colonial sailors as peers and wanted to preserve jobs for white people.[28]

The same fear of Black men either raping white women or 'taking' white women from white men seemed ever-present in the UK too. A repulsion for interracial marriages (or race mixing, as it was more commonly referred to) was palpable, often deemed to be revolting and dangerous. The media did its usual trick of colluding this narrative. One article in the *Liverpool Courier* (16 June 1919) stated that 'the average negro is closer to the animal than is the average white man and that there are women in Liverpool who had no self-respect.'[29]

Following World War I, race riots really started to take hold across the country. On 5 June 1919, Charles Wootton, a war veteran recently discharged from service, was lynched in Liverpool. Chased by a lynching mob – a crowd of over 200 people – it ended with him being stoned to death and drowned in the River Mersey, in police presence. No one has been charged with his murder. It was seemingly perfectly acceptable for members of the public to beat Black and Brown people up, at times to death, without any retribution.

Black people were depicted as the villains and aggressors of the riots – victim blaming and cognitive dissonance to justify the lynching. Black homes were regularly broken into by white mobs from Glasgow, to Liverpool to London. Thousands were dragged out, possessions set on fire, chased and beaten in the street, with many receiving regular racially aggravated attacks just for existing, and living in fear of being killed.[30] In a bid to tackle growing racial tensions, the British government took this as a cue not to attempt to prosecute those responsible for Wootton's lynching and the other racially aggravated deaths across the country, but instead issued a repatriation drive to send 'coloured' people back to where they came from.

Back in the US, around the time of Charles Wootton's lynching, the way lynchings were being reported by the media started to change. They started to expose what appeared to be a whole lot of shame, particularly surrounding the lynchings of Jesse Washington, a 17-year-old boy, in 1916 and Claude Neal in 1934. Both were pivotal moments where undercover investigators attended lynchings, on behalf of the NAACP, to expose what was really going on. In 1934, one investigator detailed and published an 'unblinking account' of the public castration of 23-year-old Neal, who was subsequently made by the lynching mob to eat his own genitalia before they killed him.[31] Prior to this, the media had gone to great lengths to depict the white mob and spectators as 'civilised' upstanding citizens of 'order and decorum'.[32] Following these accounts, this shifted to reporting that many white people in the crowd started to turn away from the horrors.[33] Around this time, there were also growing movements for anti-lynching. Southerners were being looked down on by North Americans, who themselves were also guilty of lynching Black folk, feeling implicated by their behaviour and what 'white civilization' meant. [34]

An article in the *Waco Semi-Weekly Tribune* was written in response to Washington's lynching in 1916 which drew in crowds of 15,000 people – a crowd too large for Wembley Stadium: 'Not all approved, but they looked on because they had never seen anything of the kind. No hand was raised to stop the movement, no word spoken to halt the progress of those who carried the negro to his death.'[35] An identity crisis was starting to take hold and cognitive dissonance – that inner conflict when a person's beliefs and values are at odds with their behaviour – was starting to reveal itself.

White Silence

The question remains: if so many 'spectators' were repulsed and disgusted by the dehumanisation of Black bodies, why did it go on for decades, and why was it still drawing in huge crowds? Why were so many white people still participating in it, by either watching it unfold in real time (and turning away), looking at photos, or buying postcards? Why was there still such an appetite to read about it in newspapers, or tune into hear about it on the radio? This is why white silence is often described as an act of violence – it was and it is so damaging.

In *Making Whiteness*, Grace Elizabeth Hale writes,

> W. E. B. Du Bois had boldly stated that even the deadly spectacle of African American otherness had become an amusement. And the amusement, the cultural power of spectacle lynchings lay not in the assignment of cause and of blame, the tallying of rights and wrongs, but in the looking.[36]

This demonstrates so clearly how most can vehemently and cognitively reject the notion of racism and dehumanising another human being and yet still be seduced by the power of unity and belonging and participate in it.

With the firm roots of this historical culture of lynching, brought over from British migrants, it makes me wonder whether the huge irrational and collective fear of Black people is not actually a fear of us seeking revenge, or of 'getting it wrong and saying the wrong thing', but a deep knowing that there is a cost to being antiracist. A deep fear of being ostracised, of no longer being in the 'in group'. A deep fear of no longer belonging and, even deeper, a fear of being hated and facing the same social isolation and horrific dehumanisation as Black folk. Perhaps that deep collective fear is not of Black folk at all, but a fear of other white people.

In a television interview with Kenneth Clark in 1963, titled *Perspectives: Negro and the American Promise*, James Baldwin says:

I'm terrified at the moral apathy, the death of the heart, which is happening in my country. These people have deluded themselves for so long that they really don't think I'm human. I base this on their conduct, not on what they say. And this means that they have become, in themselves, moral monsters.

When James Baldwin referred to the 'moral monster', he was talking about white liberals.

The ideology of white racial superiority that had been socially indoctrinated was starting to reveal some mighty big cracks in white liberalism. The frenzied attempts, witnessed by thousands, to cut off Black men's genitalia, to cut out organs, to cut off ears as a grotesque souvenir in front of white children who laughed, was essentially showing up white liberals too. The liberals who looked away, the liberals who may not have been present, but still wanted to read about it the paper. Was this culture really an honest reflection of superior beings? Or nothing but some ugly projections exposing the violence justified under white supremacy that implicated everyone with white skin, including silent liberals, who were also complicit?

Breathe. Take a beat. An invitation to notice what is going on in your body right now.

Humans are not built to actively want to participate in barbaric behaviour like this while eating a nice ham sandwich. It's learned. All who benefitted from the social construct of white superiority and Black inferiority had to remove what caused them dissonance. In other words, in the height of oppression and lynchings, in order to participate in, and benefit from, white supremacy, you had to lose empathy towards our suffering, you had to dehumanise us. Unless you're a sociopath, it is just not possible to torture another human being without making them less human. To come up with a reason why Black people deserve this treatment made them feel better about the horrors they were participating in. You can start to see how the culture of victim blaming has become a firm fixture when it comes to racism.

When you start to reconcile that, what replaces the victim blaming and the moral justification?

Shame.

Is any of this your fault? Absolutely not. Are you personally responsible for slavery and what your ancestors did? Absolutely not. However, it is this barbaric history, these acts of dehumanisation and consciously, wilfully and continuously not challenging these events that have contributed to white superiority, which remains a social issue. Which you will, by default, because of what you have inherited, continue to benefit from. Without question, this realisation will lead to deep-rooted feelings of individual and collective shame.

It's this unspoken realisation, this deep visceral shame that makes white people feel implicated and shame just by looking at Black folk and it's what makes conversations with white people about racism so hard. However, it's not addressing this shame that keeps racism alive today. Understanding the essence of what white racial superiority meant, and still means today, also means acknowledging what had to occur. It means acknowledging who our relatives and ancestors had to become. The trauma inflicted that is now in our DNA and has barely even been acknowledged, let alone reconciled.

To be anti-racist is to address this deep-rooted shame. It is an invitation to make contact with the pain of shame and, most importantly, to make contact with the parts of yourself that you have discarded because you dislike them – the parts of yourself that disgust you, or perhaps you even hate – and to start to claim all parts of your humanity and reconcile them once and for all.

Trauma Epigenetics and Racism

Dr Joy DeGruy, racism and trauma researcher and author of *Post Traumatic Slave Syndrome*, discusses how we can experience PTSD directly and indirectly. She recounts how a person in Brazil, who was nowhere near the Twin Towers when they came crashing down, witnessed the events of 9/11 unfold on TV and was no longer able to get on a plane. They needed therapy for PTSD.

In her research, DeGruy regularly talks about the long-lasting impact of transgenerational trauma and how trauma from chattel slavery impacts Black people to this very day. What I find most revealing about the depths of systemic racism, through nearly three years of my research for this book, is that given the global significance of slavery and the centuries of elongated violent trauma on Black bodies, there are very few studies about the impact of African enslavement and the persistent transgenerational harm inflicted upon us through white supremacy.

Nonetheless, through research and epigenetics, there are studies we can draw parallels from. Studies exploring the impact of singular events like 9/11 show pregnant 9/11 survivors passed on trauma to their children.[37] A 2015 study on Jewish children of Holocaust survivors showed altered stress hormones in both children and parents, suggesting that trauma can be passed down through generations. Our bodies adapt to survive and this can change the entire expression of our DNA.[38] Another scientific study has found trauma can be passed down from up to fourteen generations.[39] Our bodies absolutely remember that experiencing racism is an attack on our humanity and a threat to our life.

Trauma expert and author of *My Grandmother's Hands*, Resmaa Menakem explained to me that trauma stays stuck in the body until it is addressed. So this research shines a spotlight on the enormity of what we are dealing with. It explains why a simple 'change in law' doesn't magically undo layers of trauma or change behaviour. It may even explain to those who declare that 'slavery ended a long time ago, get over it' that, even though the majority of Black folk living in the West haven't directly experienced the horrors of lynching, the body remembers. We are so interconnected that when a Black person like George Floyd, a stranger out of billions, died, Black people felt it so viscerally because it triggered deep-rooted historical trauma we were not even witness to. In May 2020, that inherited trauma, passed down through my ancestry, triggered so much historical and transgenerational trauma that my hair started coming out in clumps.

If transgenerational trauma exists for people who have been birthed from survivors of 9/11 or the Holocaust; if it can express itself in adaptive survival behaviours, in historical and transgenerational trauma in Black bodies, what is the impact in white bodies? Based on the essence of these studies, intergenerational trauma as a result of experiencing, participating in and witnessing the violence born out of white supremacy must also exist in some way in people who are racialised as white, because this violent shared history belongs to all of us, it is all of ours.

★

The Normalisation of Black Pain

'While we see anger and violence in the streets of our country, the real battlefield is inside our bodies. If we are to survive as a country, it is inside our bodies where this conflict will need to be resolved.'
RESMAA MENAKEM[40]

What is the cost, for white people, of becoming so accustomed to witnessing the deaths of, and inflicting torture on, Black human beings?

The cost is an 'All Lives Matter'-type shame reflex. One that, for example, shows more outrage at and empathy for a statue of slave trader Edward Colston – a piece of metal – being torn down in Bristol, than for Black lives being violently taken by police officers.

The cost is an automatic fear reflex so powerful that US police officers instinctively shoot an unarmed Black man, like Jacob Blake, in the back seven times leading to his paralysis, and the predictable public responses of, 'Well, what did he do?' and, 'He shouldn't have run.'

The cost is inherent racist behaviour that leads to the type of cognitive dissonance that emboldened British police and immigration officers to break into the home of Joy Gardner, a Black mother and child of the Windrush generation, while she was asleep in North London in 1993, restrain her with handcuffs and leather straps and tie thirteen feet of tape around her mouth to stop her screaming. She collapsed and died of brain damage due to asphyxia in front of her 5-year-old son. To this day, no one in law enforcement has been prosecuted for her murder.

The cost is a continued irrational fear of Black people.

A few years ago, I spoke at a conference dedicated to women in business. There were around 300 women in attendance – I was one of two Black people and the only Black panellist. (I subsequently found out other speakers were paid and I wasn't, but I'll park that for now.) I had been asked to speak about my identity as a woman in business. When I started curating my talk, I quickly realised I cannot separate my identity of being a woman from my race – but I felt huge pressure to 'tone down the race aspect'.

On the day of my talk. I was the only Black person in the room. Were they going to 'get it'? I doubted it. A few hours before my talk, I attempted to change it, to delete the 'race stuff' that might make the white majority audience feel bad. But ultimately, it was my truth. Though sharing it in a sea of white faces made me feel extremely vulnerable, I decided to leave it in.

I spoke about navigating life and entrepreneurship as a Black woman, not feeling good enough as a little girl and some of my experiences of racism that I had overcome to do the work that I do now. My talk reduced some audience members to tears.

It was then followed by the final panellist, a white, Russian woman. I remember her, not only because of what happened next, but because of her striking beauty. I felt a palpable energy shift and discomfort when she took to the stage. She had just started to present her recent trip to Kilimanjaro with a relative when she stopped mid-sentence. She turned to thank me for my talk and said: 'I feel I need to be honest with you.'

We had never met before that moment.

'The reason we were visiting Kilimanjaro was not to conquer the mountain in Tanzania,' she continued, 'but it was to confront our fear of Black people.'

I can't remember what else she said, but I remember my silence. I did not know what to say. I wanted the ground to swallow me up. I was in a room full of white people. I was hyper-aware of how I would be perceived if I reacted. Just my presence and hearing the pain of experiencing racism triggered shame she was carrying; shame so powerful that she felt she needed to abandon her talk altogether and use that moment to centre herself and confess to me. The teacher in me now certainly admires her courage. But the shame and embarrassment I felt then, being exposed on that stage, was insurmountable.

She then asked me for a hug.

It was a strange moment and the most awkward exchange, I remember sweating profusely. She encroached my personal space, arms extended, and I didn't feel able to say no. I was acutely aware of being the only Black person in the room and how I would be perceived, so I obliged.

★

In November 2017, a few months after the Grenfell Tower fire in West London, which took the lives of seventy-two people, camera footage emerged of white Brits gathering together in their garden to have a 'party' creating a cardboard version of the Grenfell Tower with cut-outs of Black and Brown people, including one wearing a hijab and screaming for help from the mock windows. They set it on fire. Laughing their heads off, they stated that this is what happens when they don't pay their rent.

On 2 June 2020, just days after the graphic video of the murder of George Floyd started circulating, swathes of white men, including teenagers in the UK, created a 'George Floyd Knee challenge' – proudly taking pictures of themselves with their knee on a pal's neck, uploading and sharing images around the internet with big grins on their faces.

In August 2020, the BBC made the decision to issue a prime-time news report using the word 'nigger' to report on a violent racist attack against a Black NHS worker in Bristol by white men using their car as a weapon. The use of the word in the news report sparked 18,600 complaints to Ofcom. Instead of accepting responsibility that the decision caused a lot of harm and apologise for a 'judgement error', the BBC chose to double down and justify their use of the word. I can't recall another example in my living memory where a leading broadcaster has used racist, inflammatory language to describe any other racially marginalised group in a news report. I mean, the word 'fuck' isn't allowed to be broadcast, but as far as the BBC is concerned, 'nigger' is fair game.

Don't underestimate the ease with which you can become desensitised to Black trauma, with which you might be able to scroll down your social media timeline, see a Black person dying and carry on with your day. This is learned behaviour, and the residue of centuries of white supremacy.

The real cost? This learned behaviour, devoid of empathy, makes us a little less human.

*

Addressing Shame

It is this – the barbaric culture of violence that can be linked back to medieval England; the persistent acts of dehumanisation; the wilful unchallenging of these events; the collusion of officials and media; this passive and active participation for centuries – that maintains the illusion of white superiority and the white skin privilege that you now hold. This history, even if you don't know the depths of it cognitively, you feel it in your body viscerally. Your body remembers and that, without question, leads, not only to feeling automatically implicated but also, to feeling deep-rooted individual and collective shame. It is this complex relationship with racism and shame we must be aware of, acknowledge, speak about and, finally, address.

I know this has not been easy to digest; we have been poking around right in the centre of the wound. This is why I describe my anti-racism work as collective healing: *we* have to heal from our wounding to embed sustainable change. When slavery was abolished, no opportunity for healing was offered. Instead, in an attempt to re-assert white superiority, further trauma was inflicted on Black bodies through lynchings, continued rape, violence, segregation, further dehumanisation and of course, legal and structural inequity.

If we don't address the root of what triggers a primal shame response in us, we will continue projecting our bullshit onto one another. We, and yes, I mean white folk too, won't ever heal from the trauma of white supremacy if we continue to skirt round the edges, picking scabs and periodically changing dirty old plasters without exposing the wound. Outcomes will not change.

Some common responses to shame:

- Lack of empathy
- Disengagement/numbing (which can also look like addiction)
- Feeling anxious
- Overcompensation/people-pleasing
- Seeking perfectionism
- Anger
- Increased judging and blaming others
- Shaming others
- Low self-esteem/confidence
- Defensiveness and denial
- Feeling exposed
- Lying
- Feeling unworthy

Sarah Bellamy, practitioner of racial healing, writes: 'White people may not realise it, but white supremacy causes disruptions between their psyches and their bodies. These disconnections are both literal and metaphorical. When white people are racially triggered they have reported numbness, experienced ringing ears, tunnel vision, a faster heartbeat.'[41]

Some common physical sensations in response to shame:

- Overheating
- Sweating
- Stomach lurching
- Palpitations
- Freezing
- Increased heartbeat
- Shallow breathing
- Dry mouth

These common physical responses are linked to a stress response and what is known as an 'amygdala hijack'. As explored earlier, this is where your thinking brain goes 'offline' and the body automatically tries to protect you because it thinks it is under attack. This is why slowing everything down and practising self-awareness is key. Ask yourself: is this a perceived threat or an actual threat? Do not confuse the discomfort you feel in anti-racism, because you haven't yet developed the mental agility to talk about racism without having a shame spiral, as actual danger.

Check in with yourself and journal.

1. Do you recognise any of these common responses in you?
2. How does shame show up in your body and your behaviour?

Trauma in Black people and People of Colour caused by racial violence can trigger shame and can also show up as what psychologist Guilaine Kinouani describes as 'epistemic homelessness.'[42] This is 'the subjective experience of becoming unanchored from one's truth base...it leaves the person of colour feeling unsure about their perceptions of reality.[43] Not trusting our judgement about reality is a direct impact of being shamed through years of gaslighting from well-meaning white peers who had their own shame reflexes triggered. Instead of tending to their shame, these white peers continuously invalidate our experiences of racism with words like, 'It was just a joke,' 'Maybe you misheard?' and, 'Not everything is about race.'

Not addressing your shame responses related to racism inflicts further trauma on us.

★

Building Shame Resilience

You are, by the very nature of being racialised as white in a society that still centres and favours whiteness, going to have your shame triggered in this work over and over again. That's where the importance of shame resilience comes in.

Much like building general resilience, building shame resilience doesn't mean we won't experience shame, but that we become more able to deal with shame when it arises. We can recover from shame more quickly, attend to any trauma wounds that need our attention and, of course, be more useful in allyship.

To do this, we first need to recognise how shame shows up for us individually. What triggers an extreme shame and subsequent trauma response in one person, might be mild embarrassment or completely benign for another. And because anti-racism invites you to move out of your comfort zone, it's important not to conflate discomfort with an actual trauma response.

I invite you to get curious with your shame. Instead of fearing it try to welcome it. How does shame feel in your body? What happens? Journal on it.

1. Any changes in body temperature?
2. Any tension is your body?
3. Is there contracting, numbness or nausea?

Pay attention to what your body is trying to communicate with you. Is this feeling familiar or brand new? Our bodies are wise. If you are having a disproportionate response to being called in, or to an everyday interaction about racism, that's a sign that what you are experiencing is more likely to be historical. A shame response to racism you may have inherited.

Acknowledge shame

Don't try to bat the feelings away – acknowledge feelings of shame and name them.

1. Say, 'I am feeling shame right now.'
2. Slow your nervous system down.
3. Breathe in for 3 counts and exhale for 5.

Repeat until that unbearable shame wave has passed or lessened in intensity. Naming shame reduces confusion, helps us process and brings awareness to our behaviour. Whilst it doesn't feel like it in the moment, it always passes.

Get back in your body

Notice if your heart is racing, notice how the weight of your body feels in your chair, notice how the soles of your feet connect with the ground. Yawn, or blink. Remind yourself you are safe. Being present and aware of what is going on in our bodies helps us recognise shame triggers that are present; it helps us to regulate emotions.

Don't make any decisions or try to engage in anti-racism discussions while you're in a shame spiral. It will probably be disastrous. Your ability to process information and think clearly will shut down because your body thinks it's under attack. Take a beat, if you have hurt someone in the moment, apologise, let it pass and then re-engage in a meaningful way when you have returned to a more useful state.

When experiencing shame related to racism try completing these sentence stems:

- I am sensing X; I am experiencing X; I am feeling X; I am experiencing all of these things; I know they will pass and I am safe.

This affirmation, created by one of my students, helps her to move through shame:

- 'Shame is something I work through. Shame is not something I use against others.'

Own your shame

One of my anti-racism students got so stuck in her own tango between guilt and shame that it took her nearly a year to return to the work. The longer it took her to return, the more she would beat herself up and the more shame she felt for not being a 'good white person'.

When the reality of another student's racism hit her during the summer of 2020 in the height of despair of so many Black lives publicly wiped out by law enforcement, it triggered shame that she found unbearable. Within twenty-four hours she had sent reams of messages about how ashamed she was, multiple voice notes and several emails all trying to explain her position – while my own trauma had been triggered by the horrific events. She wanted to have her shame soothed and taken away by the closest Black person to her, which at that time, happened to be me.

Around the same time, a colleague who I hadn't heard from in over a year messaged out of the blue to express his shame at allowing a client to call a member of staff a 'nigger'. This shame response happens a lot and I had to hold some firm boundaries over that period.

It's not Black people's role to comfort you for your racism. Professing how ashamed you are to be white in an attempt to connect with Black folk actually ends up causing further disconnection. It is also an act of racial violence that centres you as 'the victim' and leaves those affected by racism in a position of having to manage your feelings. 'I am ashamed to be white' confessions centre on your shame of racism with an intention to prove you're one of 'the good ones' and be comfortable again, rather than supporting the people experiencing the trauma of racism. We end up sending resources to soothe and comfort your temporary feelings of shame, instead of tackling the actual racism itself and holding space for those actually impacted by it. It's a bit like a pedestrian getting knocked over by a car and everyone running to the car – leaving the pedestrian bleeding on the ground.

No one, least of all Black folk, want you to feel shame for being white. Feeling shame for the colour of your skin, for who you cannot help but be, is not justified, it is not healthy, and more to the point, it is not a useful state for responsive action and change. The dehumanisation of Black people was, and is, utterly shameful, so experiencing shame is a normal human response, especially in anti-racism. So you need to become shame-resilient because staying stuck in shame is destructive. To be anti-racist means moving through shame to start to make conscious and intentional steps towards change. It means taking responsibility for your words and behaviour to dismantle learned racism within yourself and not continue to wilfully benefit from the systems of oppression built off the back of Black exploitation and genocide. You feeling shame about being white doesn't help. Action, change and atonement does.

Speak on it

It's so important to talk about what is making you feel shame. It takes away its power. I say this with a caveat: I wouldn't rec-ommend speaking about this with random strangers or people who are not safe because they may, in turn, shame you. Unless you have crystal-clear boundaries and explicit permission from peers, don't speak about the shame you feel because of your racism with a Black person or a Person of Colour. It can trigger further racial trauma, it places the burden of forgiveness of your racial violence on them and your racism is not their burden or responsibility.

Speak about shame with people who have the capacity to empathise with your experience and, even better, are also on their anti-racism journey. Sometimes if my husband says or does something that triggers a shame response in me, I name it. I tell him I am feeling shame and he can hold space for me and, if necessary, we revisit the discussion later when I've done some self-soothing and have better capacity to listen.

Reconnect with yourself

It's important to pay attention to how shame manifests, not only in your body, but also in your behaviour. Continue to revisit the common response to shame we explored earlier. Once you've been able to calm your nervous system down and are no longer in a state of fight or flight, then get curious about why those feelings of shame might be coming up. Why was I experiencing shame in this moment? What is it teaching me? What have I learned? What more is there to learn? What I can I do next?

One student is now able to recognise her shame spirals and identifies that her behaviour related to racism looks like over-performing. It looks like wanting to be perfect, going through bursts of intense periods of study at surface level only so she can just 'get it done' and tick it off a list to temporarily relieve the guilt that the shame has triggered, getting buried in the superficial and performative 'busy-ness' of the work to cover up and bypass her shame, leading to burnout and difficulty re-engaging and feeling further shame as a result. She now knows when this happens, she needs to slow down, get in her body, seek support, revisit the areas she is glossing over and own her shame.

Building Empathy

You're going to need to practise a whole heap of self-compassion to start building empathy and your shame resilience. Dr Kristin Neff, an expert in self-compassion, has some great free resources online and books to help you start to mindfully cultivate self-compassion.

For obvious reasons, I had and, to an extent, still have, a complex relationship with shame. When I first started teaching anti-racism, I found I had a profound capacity to hold compassion for white people and other non-Black people exhibiting anti-Blackness and a complete lack of compassion for myself. But I had gotten really good at shaming myself as a response to being shamed.

Instead of the abusive shame talk ('I am disgusting', 'I am such an idiot', 'I am bad'), start to self-parent and relate to yourself in a healthier way. When you start experiencing debilitating shame, acknowledge this is a symptom of some kind of suffering. Talk to yourself like your struggling 7-year-old self would need you to, with understanding, compassion and empathy. Swap shame and judgment for curiosity. Remember empathy is the kryptonite to tackling shame. We know what it feels like when we're in the middle of a shame spiral and we are met with empathy rather than further shaming. It validates, it soothes, and it lessens the intensity until it passes. Remember it is not OK to seek soothing and validation from the person you have harmed with your racism. Go to your support network or therapist for that.

If the opposite of shame is empathy, and if the cost of white supremacy and persistent racism for white folk is a loss of, or a complete lack of empathy to trauma on Black bodies, then it is going to be vital for you to consciously cultivate empathy. This starts firstly with yourself, and secondly, by learning to believe and empathise with experiences of racism without a 'yes but' or Oppression-Olympics shame reflex.

Learning something new can help build resilience. It helps you to be present with 'not knowing and getting it wrong' and to build trust in your ability to grow. Anti-racism isn't about perfectionism and getting everything right. That is a function of white supremacy. It is about being more interested in making a meaningful connection and finding out more about an experience that is different to your own, rather than remembering stats and data or obtaining a certificate.

A vital part of building empathy is learning how to actively and deeply listen. So often our voices are not heard when it comes to trying to address racism and we are presumed to be lying or deemed to be incapable of recognising our own experiences of trauma. Start listening to hear, rather than listening to react and defend your position. You must be able to empathise with others who could be great allies, but are not as far along on this journey as you. Instead of judging, hold compassion for them as I do for you, and call them in on the journey. Racism has kept us disconnected from all of our humanity for too long. Building empathy is a vital ingredient to increase our ability to meaningfully connect with one another.

Acknowledgement and Accountability

Though far from perfect, what the German government has done that Britain has failed to do is acknowledge their part in history and the horrors their ancestors inflicted in Nazi Germany – who, incidentally, learned some of their finest torture techniques from what was used on Black bodies during African enslavement. Race science continued to spill into the twentieth century and their Final Solution methods, used for the mass genocide of six million European Jews, were actually developed by British eugenicist Francis Galton from a London lab at University College London in 1904.[44] Galton was yet another scientist obsessed with racial purity, who used pseudo-science to justify violence under white supremacy. Angela Saini, science journalist and author of *Superior*, writes:

> Galton's seductive promise was of a bold new world filled only with beautiful, intelligent, productive people. The scientists in its thrall claimed this could be achieved by controlling reproduction, policing borders to prevent certain types of immigrants, and locking away 'undesirables', including disabled people.[45]

Acknowledgement of Nazi Germany's past is not to suggest living Germans are personally responsible for what their ancestors got up to, but they speak about it, they acknowledge how they benefit, they educate the next generation and it's taught in schools. It's not hidden away like some dirty little secret we all know about but pretend isn't there. They have also, since 1952, paid and continue to pay reparations equating to over €71 billion to surviving family members of the Holocaust.[46] That, of course, will never undo the horrors of the mass murder and the transgenerational trauma inflicted on Jews, nor does it mean they are immune to poverty or miraculously live free from anti-Semitism. However, it provides acknowledgement as a bare minimum and groundwork for change and atonement. One of the biggest counters to shame is to speak about it and, if there has been wrongdoing, to take accountability that leads to some form of atonement. Britain, though quick to point the finger at other nations for their barbaric behaviour, conveniently forgets its orchestration in all of it and has shamefully and arrogantly done neither.

In confronting the absolute horrors of our collective history I think it's vital to reinforce: Black people are not victims of racism. They are extraordinary survivors of racism.

This work is about collective healing, and any kind of healing brings responsibility and accountability. It's easier to judge and project blame onto others than to address our own shit. Holding up a mirror to behaviour can be painful, but on the other side of that, it is powerfully liberating; and how you show up in the world transforms, because our lives are bound up in each other's.

Black Buddhist Rev. angel Kyodo williams once shared in a meditation class I was attending that, 'There is no liberation without the liberation of all. There is no liberation that does not include the wholeness of each of us.'

You cannot go through your anti-racism journey, nor life itself, without experiencing shame, nor would I want you to. As history has taught us, numbing parts of ourselves, actively avoiding experiencing feelings, including shame or anything we label as 'bad' or 'negative' makes us a little bit less human. You can't experience the full range of joy without experiencing sadness. And you definitely can't experience feelings of worthiness without experiencing shame.

'I have great respect for the past. If you don't know where you come from you don't know where you're going. I have respect for the past, but I am a person of the moment. I'm here and I do my best to be completely centred at the place I am at, then I go forward to the next place'
MAYA ANGELOU[47]

★

7. Black Women Are Divine

'It is relatively new that you, Black women, have any dominion or stewardship over your own bodies. For most of our history the white body has had full unfettered access to our bodies. Every orifice, every idea, every understanding. White bodies expect to have access.'

RESMAA MENAKEM

1 June 2020.

I felt like I was being eaten alive by a pack of wolves.

40,000 hits to my website – 4900 per cent more than my average month – just shy of 2000 emails in a month. An insurmountable sense of entitlement over me after the murder of George Floyd and a very apparent collective and global white guilt.

I had been doing anti-racism work long before this, so I didn't understand why, increased volume aside, some of these interactions felt so different to the usual business enquiries I receive. I felt there was such a sense of ownership over me, my time, my words, what I should talk about and when. And, I'm afraid to say, the repeat offenders were white women. The more boundaries I put up, the more they would trample over them. Not only was I receiving huge volumes of emails and requests to 'quickly pick my brain', there were rampant WhatsApp and text messages from friends and colleagues (some I hadn't heard from in years). But they weren't checking in to see how I was. They were using me as a chess move. It was like the digital lynching of George Floyd suddenly morphed me into a Catholic priest at confession, to whom they could start excavating their own sins and shame about racism. I've never experienced anything quite like it.

The demands for my attention were most curious. When one white woman didn't get an immediate response from me, her tone mutated from the previous 'with love and light' sign-off to written abuse telling me my activism was 'bullshit'. Another turned to flooding my Instagram DMs (my following quadrupled in days) to 'find out' if I had received her email even though I had a clear out of office on. When she didn't get an immediate reply there either, she did some online 'detective work' by going through my 'followers' list and contacted a mutual Brown colleague, asking if she could tell me to expedite her non-urgent email.

This was under the backdrop of insomnia, a heightened state of anxiety and deep-rooted grief. From friends and peers assuaging their guilt, to complete strangers using me as a pawn. All of this after many Black people had started to speak up publicly about the health implications of experiencing racism and the collective trauma being experienced around the world. BBC Radio presenters, such as Clara Amfo, were dedicating entire music sets to civil rights and Black Lives Matter, radio DJs were breaking down on air, TV broadcasters were putting out statements in solidarity for Black lives, and dedicating entire sections to Black Lives Matter in their programming. It was everywhere.

The sense of entitlement over me was way too familiar. Even though their reason for contacting me was clear – they wanted to be (or at least be seen to be) anti-racist – their behaviour was, ironically, racist. In those moments, they still could not see nor treat me as a full human being. 'What can you do for me? How can you serve me? How can I weaponise you to soothe my discomfort and prove that I'm not racist?' There was a distinct and clear difference between the intention behind these kinds of interactions and the usual enquiries: these were self-serving. I knew I was being extracted from, but my usual self-care go-to tips to re-resource were barely scratching the surface. I felt the difference so viscerally, I felt grief so insurmountable that I knew that the weight of what I was experiencing had to be historical, but I did not fully understand the essence of this until I heard the quote that opened this chapter, from racial trauma expert and healer Resmaa Menakem, during a divinely timed trauma workshop for Black women.

★

Estranged Friendships

'If Black lives matter, why am I losing friends over it?' I remember reading an article of this title by Funmi Olutoye in the *Independent* about the impact of racism in friendships.[1] It deeply resonated, discussing the pain and the grief of witnessing decades-old friendships, where so many life events have been shared, dissipating, with one single exchange.

The tumultuous summer of 2020 highlighted the hard reality of trying to navigate cross-racial friendships, specifically with white women. I am contacted a lot by my Black and Brown peers in despair and exasperation about how to navigate racism in friendships. In fact, in one of the workshops I led on navigating everyday microaggressions, the idea of even role-playing confronting friends about their racism caused so much anxiety, it induced panic attacks in three of my participants.

In May 2020, I ran a poll on Instagram asking my Black and Brown followers to share how speaking up about how racism in white friendship groups was impacting them. 91 per cent said giving feedback on friends' racism was having a negative impact on relationships, with many not surviving. A lot of cross-racial relationships either deepened in that summer, or exposed their fragility and how surface-level so many of these relationships are, particularly between Black women and white women.

Some of the messages I received from Black women around this time included:

- 'I'm emotionally, physically and mentally exhausted. I don't even have the energy to talk about it anymore.'
- 'It feels harder to navigate these relationships now than it did before the "Black squares", as if just acknowledging racism is enough work.'
- 'I recently ended a relationship with a person who was constantly bringing trauma into my mental space by wanting to talk about the latest act of aggression towards Black and Brown lives. It took me a while to figure out that she is a trauma/racism-porn addict and she was using my pain as a way to feel better about her life.'

- 'I've had to let go of a friend who did not want to do the real work in addressing their complicit silence. I accepted they weren't ready and that our relationship didn't mean enough to them as a motivating factor. I've learned the loss of friendship is part of the cost of wanting a more humane and just society for non-whites.'
- 'Having to repeat conversations, or points of conversations and keeping calm when they're screaming in your face, or belittling you for even attempting to hold them accountable...and then unravelling the mindfuck of having someone who you thought loves you not really even trying to learn anything new.'

One person shared that she left an entire middle-class liberal friendship group after speaking with a close friend about their racist behaviour: 'After several months of silence, I agreed to meet. They told me I was wrong for the way I felt, and that the things they said were not racist – she did not apologise.' It took the friend several months to re-engage with the relationship, only to reinforce her position and status as a 'victim'. Needless to say, that was the end of that relationship group. They added: 'I felt like I was grieving without support. I was depressed. They inflicted so much harm that I didn't fully recognise at the time. I have now been able to flourish without their oppressive weight and my life is so much brighter.'

You will come to understand as we move through this chapter that the wounds you can inflict with your silence and disengagement with Black friends on matters of racism are collective, historical and traumatic experiences from our ancestry and can have harmful consequences. As some white friends took a step back from Black friends during this time, there was a shift, for what sounds like the first time for many. Certainly in my own case, I consciously chose not to step forward towards white friends.

Being Black is not all that we are but it's a huge part of our identity, our community and our culture. If you are white, reading this and thinking that everything is cushty because your best friend who is Black never brings up race to you, that is not something to celebrate. It's more than likely that they are not bringing this up with you because they do not feel safe around you.

I will never forget when I first heard shame researcher and author Brené Brown explain that one of the biggest forms of betrayal is disconnection. It's no surprise really because, as living beings, we have an innate need for connection – it serves our emotional and psychological wellbeing. The very function of disconnection threatens that primal need to belong, which can also trigger shame. This makes so much sense in terms of anti-racism because so much of it is about belonging. The feelings of betrayal that come up in many cross-racial relationships explain why white silence and disengagement relating to racism can be so damaging.

Every moment we have with another human being is an opportunity to deepen our connection with them, or disconnect; to build trust or break it. The more we disconnect from close relationships, the more powerful feelings of betrayal build and the more we lose trust. This is why, in some friendships, deep down it can feel like something catastrophic has happened even though nothing outwardly significant has. You can't quite put your finger on why you no longer feel safe, why you no longer trust this person or why your relationship has seemingly become dysfunctional. This is because there have been multiple occurrences of disconnection and they all contribute to feelings of shame and a lack of trust, which can feel especially destructive in relationships between white women and Black women.

Because I understand human behaviour and do this work, one might imagine I would be unscathed from experiencing racism from white friends, have a friendship circle filled with anti-racist allies and have become flawless at calling friends in so that every exchange ends with us running off into the sunset doing cartwheels. Nope, nope and nope. Sadly, because of their proximity to me, many white friends think they are exempt from doing anti-racism work, because 'I'm their mate'. So, whilst I have some incredible, courageous friends leaning in with full gusto, I am not immune to the sting in the tail when it comes to navigating these topics with pals. It's hard.

That same fateful week in June, I found myself in a position where I needed to hold a firm boundary with a close friend and give them feedback on how their racism, which I often swallowed and in doing so, enabled, had and continued to hurt and impact me. I knew giving that feedback and holding that boundary would either transform our relationship or end it, but I was prepared to take the risk.

In the weeks prior, it had become public knowledge that Black, Asian and people in Ethnic Minority groups were disproportionately being impacted by COVID. The deaths of Belly Mujinga, Breonna Taylor and Ahmaud Arbery had just reached mainstream news. After many failed attempts at contact, I hadn't heard from this friend in months until she texted out of the blue to ask how I was. Thanks to COVID, I was no longer invested in having soulless robotic, 'Fine thanks, how are you?' exchanges with anyone. I was having a tough day, so I replied, after the usual pleasantries, with honesty. Something along the lines of: 'With everything going on, I've been having a difficult time. I'm really hurting right now. I appreciate it's a tough time for so many, equally it would have been really lovely to have heard from you.' No response. Not a phone call. Not a message in response to say, *Sorry you're hurting.*

I received nothing in response to this message for four weeks until George Floyd's murder hit the news and it was impossible to continue to ignore rampant racism and my Blackness anymore. Four weeks of chosen silence. It was excruciatingly painful.

So why did seemingly small incidents feel like such big betrayals between all of these Black women and white women; relationships synonymous with nurture, solace and sisterhood? Where does the conflict and this uncoordinated tango between 'just be kind' disconnection and a sense of entitlement over Black women really come from?

We need to pull apart and detangle the complex relationship between Black women and white women. It goes without saying, by unpacking some of the historical and present damage caused by white women and their unaddressed, internalised white supremacy, this does not mean all white women are bad human beings or that all Black women are inherently morally superior. None of us are free from human flaws. However, we need to first uncover how white women have been protected from being held accountable for their racist actions and understand the powerful and painful role white women played in the oppression of Black people, Black children and especially Black women, which has contributed to where we are today.

White Women and Black Women

My experience of being a woman has been so eclipsed by racism, it's become almost impossible for me to decipher if what I am receiving is racism, sexism, or in fact the ugly combination of both. Misogynoir. A term coined by African American feminist and scholar Moya Bailey, describes the specific set of discrimination on the intersection of sexism and racism that Black women experience, 'more corrosive than racism or sexism alone.'[2]

I have a vested interest in equality of all genders, but I've never truly identified with being a feminist and I definitely don't engage with feminism that isn't intersectional – a term coined in 1989 by another Black woman, Professor Kimberlé Crenshaw. Crenshaw describes it as the interconnected ways our identities overlap with one another, by highlighting dynamics within discrimination law that were not being taken into account by the courts. In her paper, 'Demarginalizing the Intersection of Race and Sex', Crenshaw highlights that by treating Black women only as women, or only Black, you ignore a very specific set of challenges and discrimination that Black women and other women of colour face.[3] It's been wildly misinterpreted and oddly co-opted to stop us talking about the intersections of race ever since.[4]

When feminism is not intersectional, to quote academic and activist Rachel Cargle, it's just 'white supremacy in heels,'[5] I suspect some of these struggles I have with how feminism is expressed are the same as those that led author of *The Color Purple*, Alice Walker to coin the term 'womanist' in 1979 as an alternative that respects the intersections of race, gender, and class. I've experienced some of the most emotionally violent racism from liberal feminists, one of whom exclaimed in irritation, 'We're not talking about race today, we're talking about gender.' Since I can't separate my race from my gender, I quickly learned feminist spaces were really only preserved for middle-class white women.

In one of my interviews with author, colleague and psychologist Binna Kandola OBE, we ended up discussing common stereotypes associated with women being sympathetic, caring, and empathetic. When you unpack these stereotypes further, it quickly becomes apparent these stereotypes are generously applied to white women only. The stereotypes of Black women being 'angry' and 'aggressive' are anything but those things. 'If white women are that sympathetic, caring and empathetic you would expect them to be less racist than men and they are not,' Binna explained.

These stereotypes of white women are embedded historically. It served white men to have helpless damsels in distress on their arms in order to justify patriarchy and assert a large part of their role, their identity, their purpose, their 'manhood' on being a rescuer and provider. What this narrative ignores, or conveniently bypasses, is a sadistic collusion that took place. Yes, while white women experienced the dehumanising oppression of patriarchy, and being treated less-than because of their gender. But they also shared racial power, which, by default, enabled patriarchy. If white men are at the top of that racial hierarchy, white women are right underneath them in second place. This might go some way to explaining why 47 per cent of white women in 2016,[6] and 55 per cent in 2020 voted for an openly sexist and racist son of a Klansman aka President Trump.[7] It is access to that shared racial power that was, and still is, deadly. The perception that white women were passive and innocent during the height of slavery and post-abolition is nothing but a big white lie.

Hurt People Hurt People

The intersection of sexism and racism was ever-present during the height of slavery in the eighteenth and nineteenth centuries. Under patriarchy, white men had continuously maintained that women were not equal to them, that they were inferior and therefore unable to do jobs equal to men. Slavery somewhat exposed this level of nonsense as there were, in plain sight, Black enslaved women working equally to Black enslaved men – in fact, more often than not, working even harder. However, this did not mean Black women were given any respite, fewer manual roles or softer punishment. Quite the contrary. They were all for gender equality on plantations, it would seem.

The abuse and conditions that Black women endured, particularly in the British West Indies, would be inconceivable to most of us today, and were as severe as those for Black men.[8] At times, worse. To morally justify yet another big contradiction, this was the start of treating Black women as though they were both superhuman and subnormal, not 'true' human beings like white women. Gruelling shifts, whippings and physical abuse equal to those of Black men became commonplace. On top of that, Black women were prey to the continued sexual advances of white men (and yes, sadly, some enslaved Black men too) at the end of an eighteen-hour day. The regular sexual violations inflicted on Black mothers, daughters, sisters and loved ones was often in full view of Black men and boys too – imagine the ripple effects of witnessing Black women being treated this way.

During this period, the role of white women in white supremacy and their relationship to Black women was complex and, more often than not, rooted in jealousy and violence. While white women were being oppressed by white men, they were unleashing their frustration by controlling and abusing Black bodies, including Black children. While white women were under the domination of white men, with no access to property or land, enslaved people, especially Black women, were often gifted or indeed inherited to white women by parents, in place of land.[9] In short, enslaved people were their vehicle to wealth and social and economic power. With all of this in mind, we can confidently assume some of the toxic jealousy Black women received from white women was born out of the sexual 'relations' and objectification of Black women whose bodies were regularly at the mercy of their white male masters and their friends. Whilst also being forced, by white mistresses, to breastfeed white children at the expense of providing nourishment for their own children. Their bodies were not their own.

Black women were so often seen and treated as sexual objects, they were believed to be inherently 'promiscuous'. Thomas Thistlewood, a British overseer in Jamaica, shares in his diary of having sexual intercourse with eleven out of eighteen enslaved young 'newly arrived African girls' in a two-year period.[10] They weren't seen as women and as such, the free access to Black women's and girls' bodies by white men wasn't even treated as rape. In fact the law justified it, stating that 'no white could ever rape a slave woman.'[11]

Evidently, legalised rape meant any concern for Black women being raped by white men was non-existent. It didn't warrant the same concern that just the mere idea of enslaved Black men going on rampages to rape white women in large volumes, did.

Even the clergy colluded with the rape of Black women. In his diary, British merchant and Reverend John Newton described enslaved people as 'lesser creatures without Christian souls and thus are not destined for the next world.'[12] As a captain on slave ships trafficking human beings between West Africa and the British West Indies, he used this thought process to justify having access to Black enslaved women at his own free will. It's worth noting that Newton is probably most famous for helping Wilberforce abolish slavery, as well as writing the hymn we've all come to know, love and sing with glee and wilful ignorance at weddings, funerals and school assemblies: 'Amazing Grace'.

The part of his story that is so often conveniently forgotten in mainstream narratives is that this hymn is autobiographical. Newton wrote it in 1772 when he finally came to understand the impact of his role in regularly raping Black women and physically abusing Black people. Suddenly, the guilt and horrors of his actions caught up with him and the song was written as a confession of his own sins. We often hear about his 'enlighten-ment' and grace from God, but not of the horrors he inflicted on Black women. It's also worth noting that, contrary to what most whitewashed resources will tell you, Newton found evangelical

Christianity nearly three decades prior to this epiphany. Adam Hochschild's *Bury the Chains* describes how, for decades prior, Newton didn't think anything was wrong with slavery until other people pointed it out to him and he grew a conscience.[13]

Yes, Newton, played a role in the abolition of slavery, but it wasn't the only role he had. Placing him as a saviour is not only factually inaccurate but it conveniently erases the numerous slave rebellions and the role of Black women – who had more than enough incentive to play a part in both larger and less-obvious rebellions. For example, according to Dr Joy DeGruy by the mid-nineteenth century, there were approximately 600,000 mixed-race babies being birthed in the US alone.[14] While some of these births will have been a result of consensual relations, given the era and that miscegenation laws were in full swing – interracial relationships were illegal – many will have been a result of abuse.

There would have been more births, but accounts of Black women show many used self-inflicted abortion (which sometimes led to their own deaths) as a method of rebellion, to prevent them from birthing more human beings into a life of oppression and further enabling slavery. This had a direct correlation to the dwindling 'slave stock' planters were berated about in the British Caribbean and the French West Indies. In fact, it caused so much noticeable concern, it got debated in the House of Commons in 1789. At one point to address this 'problem' in Jamaica, Black women were even given 'incentives' to fall pregnant by being excused from labour if they had six children or more. Their slavers were also given a tax break for successful delivery if their baby lived for at least two weeks.[15] Even their wombs were not their own. From this, we can start to understand where the policing of

Black women's bodies started to take hold, from being forbidden from breastfeeding (because there were more false beliefs that breastfeeding prevented pregnancy) and not being allowed to name their own children, to wet nursing, to forcibly being used as subjects for gynaecological experimentation to prolong fertility.

The obsession with Black women's gynaecology continued well into the nineteenth century when the 'Father of Gynaecology' and inventor of the vaginal speculum, James Marion Sims was at his peak. Non-consensual surgical experiments carried out on Black women's genitalia without anaesthesia (because he believed 'Blacks did not feel pain in the same way as whites'[16]) helped Sims find cures to gynaecological complaints that were also present in white women. After four years of Sims perfecting 'experiments' such as the vesicovaginal fistula repair on Black women, he performed surgery on white women to fix their conditions, fully anaesthetised.

In bell hooks' *Ain't I A Woman?*, hooks shares diary entries dated 1861 from a wealthy white American mistress and author named Mary Boykin Chesnut who showed no empathy for the sexual abuse inflicted on Black women. Instead, she described Black enslaved women as 'prostitutes'.

'Under slavery we live surrounded by prostitutes...Our men live all in one house with their wives and their concubines; and the mulattoes one sees in every family partly resemble the white children... My disgust sometimes is boiling over...'[17]

Black women and, indeed, their young 'offspring' were seen as loose, 'innately morally depraved' and somehow complicit, making them therefore deserving of centuries of violation and sexual abuse.[18] The pent-up rage depicted in Chesnut's account must not only have been a wider expression of her own oppression, but a reflection of the wider beliefs held about Black women and their perceived promiscuity with the men of white 'ladies'. This rage and jealousy lying in wait was clearly demonstrated by the treatment white women unleashed, not just on Black women, but their babies too.

OK. Breathe.

Notice what feelings and sensations are coming up for you. What is your body communicating with you in this moment? Don't edit, journal on it. This inhumane treatment inflicted by humans on humans is in no way easy to write, and I know, will not be easy to read, so please pace yourself.

In *They Were Her Property*, historian Stephanie E. Jones-Rogers gives a unique perspective away from the lens of the oppressor, sharing accounts from people who survived the brutality of enslavement. Jones-Rogers uncovers their experiences of how they were treated, especially by mistresses who owned slaves and their children too, who were essentially being 'groomed' to become planters and slavers. One story, by former labourer Mary Armstrong, recounts a mistress called Old Polly who she referred to as 'the devil' for beating Mary's little sister, just nine-months old, to death, because she wouldn't stop crying.[19]

In 1857 in Georgia, three sisters, Catherine, Sarah and Mary Martin, regularly watched their father, Godfry, and brother, Greene, inflict violence on enslaved people, which resulted in them beating a 12 or 13-year-old Black boy called Alfred, to death. A death that was so brutal, even though law allowed for 'corrections' (violence against the enslaved to keep them in order) someone reported it to authorities and the Martins' ended up in court. The girls, one of a similar age to Alfred, had to testify and it became quickly apparent that they had become so desensitised to witnessing violence on Black bodies, they had convinced themselves Alfred deserved it. Even though they had witnessed the abuse and saw him lying dead and naked in the mud, nothing made them want to intervene. It wasn't fear. They simply didn't want to; their father and brother were 'behaving in ways they deemed normal and acceptable' and that they 'acted as they usually did.'[20]

The story of Henrietta King is one I share with my anti-racism students that still plagues me ever since I first discovered it.[21] King recounts being around 7 or 8 years old, daily tempted and, indeed, tested by her mistress who would deliberately leave a sweet in a chamber pot that she was responsible for cleaning. Which child wouldn't be tempted by sweets today? What made the allure of that sweet even more tempting and evidently cruel was that domestic slaves in the home were operating in a state of near starvation. She left it for days, but finally succumbed to the temptation. What followed was horrendous child abuse.

Henrietta was whipped and because, as one would expect, the young girl wouldn't stop writhing around and just 'take it', her mistress went to great lengths to place her head under a rocking chair and proceeded to rock back and forth on her head while instructing her white daughter to continue whipping Henrietta – her daughter who, up until that point, had also been her playmate. The abuse she suffered was life-altering; her face was completely mutilated, and she was unable to eat solid foods ever again. After inflicting a permanent disability on Henrietta, they got rid of her in the end. All of this for eating a sweet sadistically used as bait by an adult – a far cry from the benign role played by white women, so often depicted as innocent, caring, sympathetic and empathetic in the stereotypes so carefully painted by white men.

Let's be clear, there were many enslaved people who didn't take beatings lying down, would be insubordinate, or even retaliate, including a 10-year-old Mary Armstrong who, rageful at her mistress for murdering her little baby sister, smashed a rock in her mistress's eye. Miraculously, Mary was never corrected by Polly's daughter, Olive, who was now her mistress. After witnessing her mum's violence for years, she obviously chose not to follow in her footsteps. But sadly, more often than not, there was a culture of immense fear that kept enslaved people controlled and 'in their place'. White mistresses were heavily represented in the British Caribbean, often in isolation, away from their husbands on plantations in Caribbean islands such as Jamaica and Barbados and they were notoriously spiteful.[22] They successfully bred a culture of fear, disproportionate scrutiny and torture towards Black women.

If you think pregnant Black women were spared this harsh treatment, think again – some were even lashed for having miscarriages. In her book, *A Kick In The Belly: Women, Slavery and Resistance*, historian Stella Dadzie shares one account of an enslaved woman named Hetty being stripped naked and whipped so severely because one of the cows she had fastened with a rope came away from its stake. Her naked, bloody, pregnant body was so severely abused, it induced early labour and her baby was stillborn.[23]

We know through human epigenetics and the earlier studies shared that trauma can be passed down from womb to womb, from generation to generation. So just imagine for a moment the impact of the continued exposure to direct and indirect daily trauma from both white men and white women; the impact of prolonged anticipation of receiving physical abuse for making a misstep, or being regularly 'set up' by mistresses as a means to justify violence for centuries. Imagine what this does to the insides of so many generations of Black women who were incentivised to have children, whose children then went on to have children, in continued hostile environments without having any opportunity to heal. Imagine what that does to your genetics, your mental and physical health, or how it mutates into behaviour and cultural norms? It's unimaginable for you, isn't it?

*

No Room for Error

We cannot underestimate the impact of continued trauma, for Black people, especially Black women: carrying around this low-level anxiety of getting 'caught' and being punished for doing something miniscule. The enormity of carrying this all-encompassing daily fear of making a misstep, of 'doing something wrong' and facing an almighty wrath if we dare to make a mistake is historical, with utterly devastating consequences today.

Understand what this does to psychological wellbeing and self-esteem: it leaves an imprint so deeply ingrained, creating an automatic reflex to 'people-please'. For some, seeking validation from whiteness becomes normalised. We dissect every interaction to the nth degree, spend vital resources managing how others perceive us, overwork until we experience regular bouts of burnout to prove worth, whilst simultaneously denying joy and wellness in the pursuit of perfection to avoid persecution. Conversely, some of us may become fiercely over-independent as a method of survival until we are unable or unwilling to ask for help, seeing that as a character flaw and a sign of weakness, to our detriment. Do not underestimate the impact of what carrying this inherited fear and hypervigilance can do to one's ability to simply get up out of bed every day, let alone expand, create, innovate and thrive. These traits are often just normalised or accepted as personality when they are, in fact, adaptive behaviours in response to inherited transgenerational and historical and persistent exposure to trauma.

Black women are not held to the same standards – we never have been. Generally speaking, people who face abuse or systemic discrimination from a dominant group often aren't. For Black women, we are held to infinitely higher standards, to jump hoops and show receipts to prove our validity and credibility.

One of my anti-racism students, a white educational psychologist, was approached to deliver paid anti-racism training. At the time, she had attended just one three-hour masterclass with me and was instantly seen as an authority and anti-racism expert; she had automatic credibility. Simultaneously I was approached by a teacher keen to do my online course and have it paid for by her local authority. They wanted everything but a vial of blood to prove my credibility and did not agree to fund her place because it was not 'accredited' by a body. The irony, that they wanted my course to be accredited by a body that is not anti-racist, is not lost on me. My years of experience in the industry, my background in human behaviour, my anti-racism courses, testimonials from other students including teachers, my

TED Talk, my TV appearances and the reams of articles I have written or featured as an expert from CNN through to *Metro* was not enough 'evidence' of my credibility.

Consider this:

- In what ways might you undermine, disbelieve and struggle to take leadership or authority from Black women?

We have to straddle this strange tension between being held to higher standards and having to overcome such low expectations of our validity and ability to achieve. Simultaneously, when we surpass expectations, we are either met with surprise, indifference or loathing, whilst mediocrity in whiteness is celebrated.

'I don't have the luxury of being mediocre, or the luxury of people assuming my opinion is valid because of the package I come in.'
JUNE SARPONG[24]

We've all seen it on mainstream TV – where Black female excellence and confidence wipes the floor with the other contestants, only for them to either get voted out early on, or, for those that do cling on, for vitriolic comments such as 'bitchy', 'arrogant', 'I just don't like her, she's aggressive' from the public take their toll. It is no coincidence that characteristics that are often celebrated in men as the bedrock of success, such as confidence, assertiveness, and self-assurance are traditionally incompatible with the sexist and racist, meek, subservient roles and stereotypes that have been handed to us.

Don't think that your negative opinions about Black women you have never met are not being influenced by white supremacy and all that intersects with it, either. Alexandra Burke on *Strictly Come Dancing* in 2017 springs to mind, with her high kicks and electric moves: even the judges, who were giving her the highest possible scores, couldn't understand why the public were not seeing what they saw and she repeatedly ended up in dance-offs. She was dragged online, described as 'unlikeable', 'fake' and 'so full or herself'.[25] Burke eventually broke down and asked, 'Why does everyone hate me?' Similar incessant public character assassinations contributed to driving Meghan Markle out of the UK.[26] This may also explain why a study into online abuse by Amnesty International reports Black women are disproportionately targeted and 84 per cent more likely to receive online hate on Twitter than white women.[27]

Disproportionate sanctions for missteps by Black women (or, a lot of times, no missteps at all) from white people are a historical residue of our relationships with one another and are regular problematic occurrences that lead to persecution we experience to this very day.

One such example is the consistent public annihilation of Cambridge graduate and the first Black female MP, Diane Abbott, who according to research by Amnesty International, single-handedly receives eight times more online abuse than any other female MP. In the six-month run-up to the 2017 elections, she received half of all online hate directed at MPs.[28] She was also dragged online, shamed and deemed as untrustworthy when she misspoke and gave an incorrect financial figure in an interview about police funding budgets, even though the figure was corrected. [29] How many MPs regularly make blunders on TV?

Chancellor Phillip Hammond, in charge of Britain's spending at the time, made a financial blunder about the cost of a high-speed railway to the tune of £20 billion around the same time as Abbot, which barely made the news.[30] Boris Johnson has made too many to count. In 2017 he said British-Iranian journalist Nazanin Zaghari-Ratcliffe (detained in Iran at the time) was somehow training journalists in the area. Fellow cabinet colleague Liam Fox, said people 'should not overreact to slips of the tongue.'[31] This 'slip of the tongue' resulted in Zaghari-Ratcliffe being summoned into an Iranian court and threatened with her sentence doubling. This generosity wasn't extended to Diane's slip, and it transpired that Diane Abbott was also having a hypo (when blood sugar levels become dangerously low) after recently being diagnosed with type 2 diabetes, which can cause confusion. In August of the same year, a 69-year-old pensioner who described Abbot as 'Black vermin' sent a letter to the House of Commons calling for her to be burned alive. He was fined a whopping £85.[32] Imagine trying to do your job and live your life whilst navigating that level of bullshit and trying to serve the country you love.

In 2018, world tennis leader Serena Williams lost the US Open against Naomi Osaka and received a fine equivalent to £13,000 for a coaching violation, calling the umpire a 'thief' and breaking her tennis racket.[33] Her responses were no different to how other top champions, such as John McEnroe, behave when in the heat of the moment. Sure, it wasn't her finest hour, but she was clearly 'corrected' and disproportionately punished for displaying 'anger' and accused the umpire of sexism. She was subsequently dehumanised by a cartoonist for Australia's *Herald Sun* who depicted her as a supersized, monstrous animal-like figure, with big lips, mouth and nose jumping up and down. It had an uncanny resemblance to centuries-old British racist cartoons of Black women being depicted as ugly, masculine and subhuman to breed fear about interracial procreating with Black women.[34] Williams, an exceptional, world-class athlete, is regularly compared to a gorilla, a man and accused of being on drugs. God forbid a Black woman could just be exceptional due to talent and hard work.

During interviews I carried out, these same issues came up again and again in the midwifery field. One NHS midwife shared that she would often have to do eight-hour shifts without being given a lunch break, unlike her white peers. Because she is Black and Muslim, she would be asked if she could work though her lunch break since she was 'fasting' during Ramadan. The nit-picking slowly started to chip away at her confidence. She would repeatedly ask superiors for feedback when they made complaints about her practice, and would be told it was just her 'attitude'. She was demoted and underwent a disciplinary procedure for a commonplace and non-life-threatening clinical mistake. She felt that she was being punished, while often observing white peers who made clinical mistakes involving drug miscalculations with life-threatening consequences were not demoted or sanctioned, but instead asked to write a 'reflective' journal.

We are not given the benefit of the doubt when mistakes are made. It was programmed for us to be disbelieved, disproportionately sanctioned, punished, or indeed, entirely wiped out. There is no room for error or woe betide us.

Expecting Black women to be perfect, to be held responsible for our entire 'race' if we, or another Black individual makes a misstep, is not only inherited, it is learned. It is historical and it is racist. To make a mistake, or to simply just be human, has serious retribution for us. To not be allowed to have human flaws is anti-human.

Speaking from personal experience, the pressure to be perfect almost always leads to ill-health. To constantly manage our perception and 'appearance' to tone police our language leads to high-functioning anxiety, overextending and unhealthy people-pleasing. To always be exceptional is one expectation that sets anyone up to fail. It's also steeped in white supremacy and does nothing other than continue to dehumanise all of us. Being anti-racist means taking Black women off the temporary pedestals you like to place us on, only so you can tear us down, like the sweet used as bait, and metaphorically whip us when we make a poor choice, or just simply, exist. If you, instinctively, in your body, feel justified and entitled in punishing Black women and 'putting us back in our place' or to envy our advancement, because we're getting 'too big for our boots', this is an urgent invitation to address your anti-Blackness.

There is no collective of human beings in the world that is perfect. We're not either good or bad with nothing in between: we're all of it. People can intentionally and unintentionally do or say really shitty things. My doing this work is testament to that. On a daily basis, I hold space for, and hear accounts of, questionable behaviour from white folk who continue to cause harm through their unaddressed racism. We're not searching for perfectionism in anti-racism; we're searching for being better human beings and that means inevitably getting things wrong, taking responsibility, accountability and atoning. If I approached this work with the same contempt, dehumanisation and expectation for perfection, and if I were to cancel you when you do or say something racist, without any compassion or capacity for forgiveness, you wouldn't have even bothered to pick up this book.

> *'You either want people to be better, or you don't.'*
> MUNROE BERGDORF

Being anti-racist is being able to hold Black people and Black women to equal standards, without abuse and anti-Blackness layered on top as justification for further abuse. There is a difference between holding someone accountable and dehumanising them: to be anti-racist is to recognise the difference *and* explore where the impulse to 'correct' us is coming from. This is historical behaviour. Interrogate it.

★

A Threat to Patriarchy

The sexual abuse and hypersexualisation of Black women didn't just miraculously stop after the abolishment of slavery. In bell hooks' *Ain't I a Woman*, one account from a Black woman and servant describes they were regularly accosted by white women seeking mistresses for their husbands.[35] The reality was that sexual 'needs' were not typically met by their white wives because they were framed as 'ladies'. In contrast, enslaved women were portrayed as 'sexually loose, morally depraved' and 'prostitutes'.[36] There was a fear in the post-abolition era that if men's 'extramarital urges' did not continue to be met, they might stray with other white women – so this strange kind of 'pimping' took place. To have an 'arrangement' with a Black woman, who was evidently of a lower social ranking to them, was clearly less threatening and far more bearable.[37]

Leading newspapers perpetuated this perception of Black women. bell hooks writes: 'They [journalists] convinced white readers they would not want to live as social equals with Black people by arguing that contact with the loose morals of Blacks (and particularly those of Black women) would lead to a breakdown of all moral values'.[38] Rather than elicit outrage for the continued sexual abuse of Black women by white men, the media and the white public justified it and blamed Black women for 'inviting it'.

This draws me back to a personal memory of being hypersexualised. It was a rare sunny day in West London and I had just delivered a workshop on race inclusion. I was enjoying my lunch outside on the grass when I was approached by a white man, perhaps in his late sixties, in a suit, who asked if he could sit beside me. He was pretty ordinary and friendly until he just came out with it – he asked if he could take pictures of my feet, which were in sandals. He also asked if he could pay for me to accompany him around Oxford Street so he could watch and take photos of me trying on shoes. He was so emboldened! I remember feeling completely discombobulated because he was so polite with his ask in the light of day. I declined and he thanked me for taking the time to talk to him. Off he went, with his suit and briefcase. I rang my husband and made a joke out of it at first, but when I ended the call, it didn't take long for me to feel sick to my stomach.

The hypersexualised perception of Black women and desensitisation to centuries of sexual trauma may go some way to explain why two-decades' worth of complaints of alleged abuse by popular RnB singer R. Kelly remained unaddressed for so many years, even though it was widely reported that he married singer Aaliyah when she was 15 years old.[39] Given the intersections of patriarchy, sexism, misogyny, and Kelly's own personal experience of being sexually abused, society has been conditioned for so many centuries to view Black women and pre-pubescent Black girls as promiscuous – so it's little wonder that it was pretty much ignored. Where was the outrage? Abuse towards Black women and girls has always been and remains prolific – that's why the #MeToo movement was started (not that you would believe it by the movement's erasure of Black women), and was founded by a Black woman, Tarana Burke, precisely for this reason.

★

Black women were (and still are) consistently seen as a threat to patriarchy. If white women's position in the 'race hierarchy' – both beneath and fiercely protected by white men – was intrinsically linked to white men being protectors of white women, then where did Black women fall? Under patriarchy, right beneath Black men. At the bottom.

Despite historical fears about 'race mixing' and the racist abuse that many interracial couples endured, it eventually became commonplace to see Black men and white women together in the twentieth century. However, it seemed less common (certainly according to the limited marriage statistics gathered about inter-racial marriage) to see Black women with white men. Black women were – and still are – plagued by centuries of negative stereotypes absorbed about Black women being 'less desirable'.

In the State of Kentucky, one former slaver who devel-oped a relationship with one of his former enslaved Black women, wanted to marry her. It went to court and the judge was asked to rule insanity.[40] And today? One of my colleagues, a dark-skinned Black woman, shared her online dating experiences and how she was often fetishised. One boyfriend never even wanted to be seen with her in public: she was his dirty little secret.

This brings to mind the true story of Dido Elizabeth Belle, the mixed-race daughter of a white British aristocrat and Navy Captain Sir John Lindsay and Maria Belle, an enslaved African in the British West Indies in eighteenth-century England. Hiding 'mulattoes' (a derogatory term for a mixed-race person with a white parent and a Black parent) out of sight from guests was a regular occurrence for aristocratic families. They were seen as not 'pure'. When her mother died, her father took Dido to live with his Uncle William Murray who was also the Lord Chief Justice of England and Wales and played an important role in the abolition of slavery. The family had great love for Dido and, even though she had inherited wealth from her father, she was still treated as someone with lower social ranking due to her race – she was made to dine separately from the rest of the family and was regularly fetishised by guests.[41]

Under patriarchy, white women marrying Black men did not pose a threat to economic power or to the existing social order and hierarchy. Of course, without question, these relationships posed a threat in terms of ideas of racial purity, but they didn't pose the same threat to social hierarchy, because in marriage, a white woman's social ranking would be lowered to that of the Black man she was marrying.

bell hooks writes: '…slavery ended and whites declared that no Black woman regardless of her class, status or skin colour could ever be a "lady".'[42] Unless, of course, if Black women married white men.

If Black women were to marry white men in volumes equal to the regular 'relations' on plantations, their social ranking would, in theory, increase and pose a real threat to both patriarchy *and* white racial power. The continued dehumanisation of Black women was no coincidence, it was a form of prolonged social control. As a result, we've been socialised *not* to see Black women, especially dark–skinned, Black women as fully human, credible, or desirable.

The Erasure of Black Women

From who we see on magazine covers, to who is depicted as the love interest or protagonist in films and books, to the adverts we consume on TV, the erasure of Black women is still playing out today in popular culture and beyond. Who is deemed as credible?

Who is seen as automatically trustworthy; as a leader? Whose work is regularly plagiarised? Whose ideas at work are claimed by others? Even in the anti-racism movement, so much of my content is lifted and passed off as the work of others. There have been so many Black women activists who have sparked enormous change, including in the law itself, who we don't hear about in the same way. We hear about Dr Martin Luther King Jr, Malcom X and rightly so, but what about their wives, Coretta Scott King, Betty Shabazz? Do we hear enough about their activism? Or over in the UK, what about Olive Morris, Dame Jocelyn Barrow, Stella Dadzie or Jessica Huntley?

In the world of climate-change activism, it is well known that it is previously colonised countries who are most impacted by the climate crisis. Those communities, who contribute to climate change the least, have been campaigning for years after experiencing catastrophe after catastrophe as a result of colonial exploitation of resources, long before it became trendy in the West. While the spotlight was being firmly shone on climate activist Greta Thunberg in Sweden, it seemed to miss Black and Brown activists such as 'water warrior' and First Nation activist Autumn Peltier, who at just 16 years of age has for years been trailblazing and advocating for clean drinking water for Indigenous people across the world.

In January 2020 it emerged that Ugandan Activist and Black woman Vanessa Nakate was strategically edited out of a picture taken at a climate change conference by AP News.[43] It instead featured fellow white activists including Greta Thunberg. The story leaked after Vanessa recorded a video on social media. She was devastated. I understood, not only the historical significance of her being erased, but also how important the press would have been in helping her raise awareness of and gain support for urgent climate issues being faced in Uganda. She said not only did they erase her, but they erased an entire continent from the discussion.

The year prior, I had been booked to host and curate a panel about activism on how we can all become change makers for an exciting event for International Women's Day. I had been reluctantly convinced to take part without payment and was told participants were donating their fee. I was experiencing income poverty at the time, so genuinely did not know how I was going to afford to even get there. I was promised expenses and accommodation so as not to be out of pocket. They also promised video footage to use for my showreel and promo as an extra incentive. It was a great event and something I was passionate about, so I agreed. The panel was a success; I was congratulated for curating a dynamic session and it was where I first met my colleague, Gina Martin, who campaigned to make up-skirting illegal. The video arrived a day or so later and, lo and behold, I had been completely erased. The video and all the subsequent press said Gina hosted the panel. Not only that, I subsequently found out that other speakers involved with the event, had, in fact, been paid. I have never felt so exploited.

Attribution is so important in anti-racism work. So many of the contributions of Black women in history have been erased. Many records of our humanity as a community have been lost or never captured in the first place. It is so important to do so, not only to credit and acknowledge the labour that goes into creating anti-racist resources, but because it leaves a much-needed paper trail. It also respects all that has been endured by those who have gone before to get us where we are today. Anti-racism is all of our work, but to witness or participate in the erasure of Black women's contributions in any arena is to uphold white supremacy.

★

There's also a long-standing history of erasing Black women in media and beauty industries. When I got engaged in 2011, I looked through several wedding magazines, each with over 300 pages, and didn't find one Black woman. In fact, it's what spurred me on to start my wedding business and was the beginning of my work in anti-racism. Upon challenging magazines for their lack of racial diversity, I was told by the magazine editors and publishers that 'Black doesn't sell'. Or, my personal favourite: 'White women won't want to buy a magazine with a Black girl on the cover.'

The title at the time, the now-defunct Condé Nast *Brides* magazine in the UK, had just celebrated sixty years in publishing by sharing every single front cover of their issues. They obviously included not a single Black woman. I found it curious that they were clinging onto their racism so boldly in front of me, not just because I was a Black woman and they seemed to have no problem saying these things to my face, but because by sharing every cover, they exposed their own institutionalised racism. The evidence was there in plain sight. How could they know 'Black didn't sell' if they had never even attempted it?

Around the time of the Brexit vote in 2016, I noticed a visible effort being made to provide more on-screen diversity in television adverts. One Christmas, I started to notice a pattern. Whilst there was much-welcomed ethnic diversity, all of the multicultural families had something in common. The father figure was almost always Black and the mother role was almost always played by a white woman, or, occasionally, a light-skinned Brown woman – something that the mainstream evidently appeared to find much more palatable in representing 'Blackness'. There was not a dark-skinned Black woman in sight, and presumably two Black people celebrating the festivities on screen would have caused a cardiac arrest. The blatant colourism was palpable. I remember remonstrating about this with my husband. His response was an unsympathetic and exasperated one: 'Oh, come on, there's diversity – what more do you all want?'

I let rip. I explained how racism shows up differently for Black men and Black women and, as a Black man, he is used to seeing himself represented in everyday settings such as this. Black men are painted as desirable and socially acceptable in mainstream media – not being represented is not an issue. Fetishisation and negative stereotyping was and still is present for Black men too, but generally speaking, they are not regularly dehumanised for their looks, they do not have their bodies constantly policed by white folk, other Black folk and Non-Black People of Colour to the same extent as Black women. I can't imagine any industry where there would never have been a Black man on the front cover of a magazine over a sixty-year tenure.

In 2016, homeware store John Lewis made the headlines after a Twitter user shared a screenshot of her complaint: that a rare advert featuring a Black family (but mainly a dog and other animals jumping on a trampoline) was 'too Black'. 'We White Brits are *still* the majority in the UK… Very disappointing that you seem to be unaware of the resentment building in the

UK, much of it due to adverts like this… how I grieve for my country and culture.'[44] It's worth noting that the mother figure that John Lewis cast was a light-skinned Black woman and it still sent bastions of the Great British public wild. If my dark Black skin and I had been cast, perhaps there would have been riots.

Let's trace it back.

The ugliness of Anti-Blackness has been breeding and lying in wait in Britain and its colonies for centuries. There was a well-established type of 'informal' segregation running rampant across Britain, from Manchester and Glasgow to Bristol and London, referred to as the 'colour bar', where it was entirely legal to discriminate against someone because of the colour of their skin. The colour bar discriminated against Black and Brown folk, typically West Indian and South Asian communities, who had full rights of entry and settlement under the British Nationality Act on settling in Britain from other British Colonies. [45] The British government, oddly, weren't best pleased about the 'influx' of Black and Brown people that had been invited from the British Commonwealth, and in 1955 the prime minister at the time, Winston Churchill suggested 'Keep England White' might be a good slogan.[46]

As far-right activity and disdain towards Blackness grew, Claudia Jones founded Britain's first Black newspaper, the *West Indian Gazette* in 1957 and in 1959 set up the Notting Hill Carnival. This was not just in direct response to the Notting Hill Race Riots which arose after the racially motivated murder of Kelso Cochrane and growing hostility towards Afro-Caribbean communities who had settled in Britain post-Second World War.[47] In its original conception, the Notting Hill Carnival was, in fact, a Caribbean beauty pageant.[48] It was devised as an indoor event specifically to promote and celebrate Black beauty and counteract negative programming, whilst simultaneously raising funds to help the young Black men who had been unfairly arrested by the police.[49]

Meanwhile, colour bars prevented Black people from getting jobs, denied them equal access to housing[50] (unless you paid a premium or 'Black tax' as it was informally referred to, to live in squalor at three times the price white tenants were charged),[51] substandard education[52], you name it. The colour bar even made its way to the shops of Oxford Street and was rife in the early 60s. If you were Black and seeking retail work, you were refused employment or, at best, you were paid a pittance and forbidden from front-facing roles, relegated to work in the basement or out back.[53] In a 2017 interview with the late Dame Jocelyn Barrow DBE, the activist recalls this as a time when many white people didn't even want Black people to touch their patients in hospital, let alone the clothes in stores.[54]

Dame Barrow was one of the founders of 1964 CARD (Campaign Against Racial Discrimination) in Britain who campaigned tirelessly, for race equality. Having the Oxford Street colour bar overturned was among CARD's successes, and it was responsible for influencing a change in law and the passing of the 1968 Race Relations Act.[55] In a 2017 film project called *1000 Londoners*, Dame Barrow spoke about how, in order to get Black women employed in stores on Oxford Street, she needed buy-in and the first shop that offered to support the campaign, Marks & Spencer, told her they would help, with a caveat: only if they sent 'pretty West Indian' girls.[56]

Exposure to centuries of this type of socialisation that depicted Black women as being ugly, undesirable and morally depraved doesn't just impact perceptions of other communities – it is so powerful it even conjures up anti-Blackness in oneself and in one's own community too. The type of negative perceptions that drove a Black man to call into a BBC radio show hosted by Vanessa Feltz to berate Black women live on air in 2008. I remember listening to this unfold live. The caller was masking anti-Blackness as his dating preference and made no secret of the fact he found Black women repulsive. He compared Black women to horses, with large heads and said all Black women were bitter. After giving a small pass to Halle Berry and Beyoncé, he delivered his parting words: 'Black women are repulsive… I don't find them attractive, in general, my friends don't find them attractive in general and I think a lot of Black men don't find them attractive.'[57]

All of these examples are the collective by-product of centuries of socialised conditioning to normalise both the dehumanisation (and, as bell hooks aptly names it) the devaluation of Black women and is reflected in society to this very day.

*

On 13 March 2020 in Louisville, USA, 26-year-old Breonna Taylor, an emergency medical technician, was sleeping in her bed at midnight with her partner when plain-clothed law enforcement forced entry into her home. Unsurprisingly, their unannounced visit startled him, and he fired a single shot, thinking they were intruders. The officers retaliated by firing a whopping thirty-two rounds. Breonna died in her own hallway. No officers have been charged with her death, but one was charged for 'wanton endangerment' for firing into a neighbour's apartment. Her life was worth less than a bullet in a neighbour's wall.

News of Breonna's death broke a few weeks before George Floyds and there have been questions as to why her death at the hands of law enforcement generally commanded a lot less press and public attention. The answer? The devaluation of Black women.

Govia Thameslink railway employee Belly Mujinga had serious health conditions and was concerned about catching COVID-19, given the disproportionate number of Black, Asian and other ethnic minorities dying from this virus in key worker roles. She raised a formal race discrimination grievance about her supervisor on 10 February 2020 which, according to her solicitors, senior managers did not respond to.[58]

On 21 March, Belly was assaulted. She was not on rota to be on the concourse and should have been in the office, however, she had been forced by her supervisor, knowing she had health conditions, to work in a public-facing role without PPE. That day, she said a man spat in her face and told her he had COVID. She reported the incident to her supervisor straight away. Govia did not call the police and instead, Belly was made to continue to work on the concourse after she begged not to.[59] She fell ill a few days later and was diagnosed with COVID and died on 5 April. Because her employer did not report the incident until it made mainstream news several weeks later, police had little to no DNA evidence to make a conviction and closed her case. She was 47 years old and left behind a husband and an 11-year-old daughter. The devaluation of Black women.

On 3 March 2021 Sarah Everard, a white woman, went missing in London. On 12 March, horrendous headlines hit. Sarah

Everard's body had been found dismembered, in Kent woodlands, and a Metropolitan Police officer was swiftly arrested on suspicion of her kidnap and murder.[60] Her death and police involvement understandably, sparked a wave of fury, support, financial contributions, calls for accountability from the police, debate about women's safety and a vigil where thousands attended, including the Duchess of Cambridge.[61] But the response felt different.

Questions on social media started to arise about the response to Sarah's murder. People started to highlight indifference towards the treatment of Black and Brown people who regularly go missing. People like Blessing Olusegun, a Black woman who, until March 2021, was relatively unknown to most and also had gone missing after a walk. Her body was found on 18 September 2020.[62] Her family maintain on their GoFundMe page that they were told by Sussex Police that her death was not being treated as suspicious and were not doing enough to investigate. There was also a glaring difference between the response to Everard's murder and those of sisters Nicole Smallman and Bibaa Henry, two Black women who were murdered in Wembley Park in June 2020. Two Metropolitan Police officers were subsequently charged with offences based on alleged taking of selfies with the women's lifeless bodies at the murder scene.[63] This story didn't achieve the same press attention, highlighting reporting disparities concerning Black women. And publicly, it did not appear to receive the same moral outrage and collective empathy, highlighting how desensitised to the suffering of Black women so many are. Even in death, we are not treated the same and don't seem to warrant the same basic human dignity.

This behaviour from white men and those in power is not

new. It leaves me wondering, had accounts of sexual abuse by white men to Black women and the persistent mistreatment of Black bodies by police been treated with this level of interest from the white-majority public and media, could more lives have been spared? Would more women be safe? Would there have been a reform? Would there be more understanding of what 'defund the police' actually means and would actions to redistribute money into services such as social work, therapy and preventative measures have been implemented instead?

Take a moment to check in: what's showing up for you?

Let's start to bring the conscious to the forefront. Be honest about all the ways you may have contributed to the devaluation of Black women. Journal on it, and notice any physical sensations or bodily responses to these prompts:

1. In what ways have you tried to police or touch Black bodies (including hair) without invitation?
2. What negative stereotypes and perceptions have you inherited and perpetuated about Black women, about us being 'angry and bitter'? About us being 'promiscuous'? What have you come to believe?
3. In what ways have you believed that Black women would be more likeable or receptive to others if we just changed our 'tone'?
4. In what ways have you weaponised your tears to take on the role of the 'damsel in distress' to gain sympathy when being confronted by your racism by a Black woman or to get your own way?
5. In what ways do you regularly appropriate Blackness?

6. In what ways have you copied the work or ideas of Black women and passed them off as your own?

7. In what ways have you personally (or have you witnessed white women) assert racial power over Black people to manipulate an outcome?

★

The Path to Building Trust

If you are a white woman, you will have experienced systemic oppression, been persecuted and discriminated against based on who you cannot help but be. It will form a large part of your identity, and you will have become accustomed to the role of the victim. You may have even absorbed and perhaps embodied those stereotypes of the caring, empathetic, sympathetic woman which is why you are probably only just coming to anti-racism work now. To then be confronted by a Black person, especially a Black woman, who you have been conditioned to devalue, someone who historically fell well 'beneath you' in that racial hierarchy, to have them 'dare' highlight your racism, what does that trigger in you? How do you respond? For a Black woman to call you in, it can feel exposing because it suggests that, at times, you have been none of those above stereotypes. You have, in fact, been the opposite: an 'oppressor'. For many, it will, at best, leave you in an identity crisis. At worst, you may find yourself scorned, envious and wanting to reclaim your position at all costs.

This is why trying to find a rhythm in cross-racial friendships with white women who aren't doing the work can be so tough.

For me? The situation with my friend who ignored my message (I know you are keen to find out what happened next) came to a head in that first week of June. She could no longer brush aside me nor the 'inconvenience' that is racism anymore and she called. I shared how deeply painful it was to have been ignored by her when I told her I was hurting. She said she never considered how her choice not to contact me would make me feel. Honest, yes, but that packed a punch.

In reality, our friendship had not been in a good place for a number of years, namely due to me stepping back to avoid the 'casual' racism or frequent instances of disconnection. On the rare occasions when I did talk about personal experiences of racism, I was shut down and gaslighted. It made me recoil and no longer feel safe so, of course, that would impact the flow of any relationship. I also didn't have the courage or desire to address it then. But in the height of a BLM resurgence, my own trauma being triggered, I knew I had to have a hard conversation with her and could no longer pretend everything was OK.

Her phone call also coincided with my hosting a five-day anti-racism class for seventy white women to excavate their racism. It was an extraordinarily difficult week. I was drained, but I was rooted. I knew holding her accountable for her behaviour would trigger her fragility, so remembered telling her more than once that I loved her. She responded with, 'But I've been nothing but supportive,' as if somehow, previous instances of support absolved her of racism and that I should be grateful. It is possible to love people whilst simultaneously holding them accountable for their behaviour – we do that on a regular basis with children. It's also possible to love people and hurt them.

She asked what she could do to help. My response (as it always is to this question) was, 'If you really want to help, start to unlearn your inherent racism.' I even offered her a complimentary place on my anti-racism course which, judging by the sharp change in her tone and how swiftly the call ended afterwards, she found completely and utterly offensive.

I could tell very little had gone in and she was in a state of defending her position and character throughout. I'm not suggesting that it's easy being called in, but the trouble is, when you are in a state of defence about your racism, you shut down, zone out and may as well have put your fingers in your ears. You no longer have the capacity to listen. You disconnect, causing mistrust and even further wounding, which is exactly what happened. It really did reinforce how those closest to us are capable of causing us the most harm.

In the last few minutes of the conversation, I received some 'I am sorry you feel that way' apologies. (If you've been on the receiving end of these, you will know these are not meaningful. Anyone that that starts with 'I'm sorry you…' fails to take any responsibility for their own behaviour and the harm their actions have caused, and places blame on you and your hurt feelings.) After which, she offered to speak again soon and the call ended. And that was the end of that. We never spoke again. A promise to do better and again, absolutely no change in behaviour, leading to further disconnection.

Holding boundaries in friendships where you haven't before and the potential risk of them ending can feel like a grieving process. It can be excruciating – it was painful enough for me to take it to therapy. We all play roles in our relationships and when we grow and hold boundaries, those roles can shift or take on new forms, so friendships will either evolve or become redundant because your roles have changed. For example, if one person plays the role of the saviour and the other the role of needing to be rescued, whilst these 'fixed roles' will absolutely serve both of you at times, the function of the relationship will have its limitations when one of you steps out of it, as was the case for my friend and I. She liked the version of Nova who had excruciatingly low self-esteem and preferred to swallow racism to keep the peace and maintain equilibrium. But as my self-esteem and my capacity to hold boundaries grew, I didn't need rescuing anymore and our relationship altered. I realised that what I used to tolerate meant I wasn't able to be my full self in our relationship. That was no longer tolerable. I have since made peace with the fact if we are meant to circle back and be in one another's lives, we will and if that ship has sailed, it's sailed. I will not abandon myself and tolerate any friend gaslighting my experiences of racism to the point where I question my own sanity again.

At a time when most would have expected solace, nurture and support through sisterhood, so many Black women were left devastated by 'all lives mattering'. Denial, or worse still, complete avoidance can be catastrophic. Direct avoidance and disconnection from those closest to you, when they've revealed personal trauma they've experienced, can sadly, also lead to more trauma. Embarrassment related to inherent racism can be so profound, you centre your own discomfort and in doing so, you forget how to treat your Black friends as human beings in the process. In a time of sadness, turn towards them to offer support. Say 'I love you and I am so sorry this continues to happen to Black people.' Or when words don't come, just be there to listen and see Black people in their humanity. Instead of showing compassion and acknowledgement of their pain, so many chose to turn away from their Black friends, causing disconnection and further pain, which can lead to feelings of betrayal.

Don't underestimate the wounding power of your silence. To be anti-racist is to consciously build trust, especially with Black women for all of the reasons we have explored in this chapter. A reminder, anti-racism provides us with an opportunity to re-build trust, and re-connect.

Cross-racial sisterhood is possible, but it requires honesty, vulnerability, a willingness to get it wrong and to be able to withstand receiving feedback on your racism. One white anti-racism student said to me:

> You have changed the life of many Black women in my life as I have been able to show up for them in ways I just didn't know how to before. They've been able to lean on me for support in ways they hadn't been able to and didn't know they could before. While she tells me I have never shown her explicit racism or bias, I have previously failed to see her full experience as a Black woman and have at times invited her into unsafe spaces and failed to support. I had previously failed to check in on her as well or as often as I could, especially with COVID, the violence against and murder of Black lives as and when they are in the news. I could have just checked in more this year and just asked how she's doing.

She added:

I have acknowledged this, apologised and asked her to lean on me more when she needs to, and to call me out/ in when I fluff up again. We now have a channel of communication that is more open, more honest and more effective. She knows I'm doing anti-racism training and she now says she can say things to me about racism in ways she didn't use to.

Some Black women shared with me the impact of white friends doing this work:

'They treat me like a human being and the relationship is more reciprocal and less transactional.'

'I don't feel like I have to perform or walk on eggshells. The more I see white friends engage in this way the more it makes me examine the relationships with folks who don't. It makes it crystal clear where to set the boundary around who to let in and who to let go.'

Understand the healing power of a meaningful apology, not because you 'feel like you should' or because you want to go back to how it was, but because you genuinely care about the person you have hurt. Being vulnerable and apologising doesn't incriminate you, or mean you're a bad human being. It means you did or said something that caused harm. Approach it with integrity. We don't expect you to know what to say all the time and just be frank about that. All it takes is 'I find this really hard and that means I don't always know what to do or say. I'm sorry I hurt you. But I am here, and I am listening.' Contrary to bizarre popular belief, giving a meaningful apology doesn't make the other person lose respect for you, it does the opposite.

It builds respect. It reconnects, it builds trust and provides healing *if* there is an accompanied change in behaviour.

So, here's an important prompt for you: Which Black women do you owe a meaningful apology to?

★

An Ode to Black Women

In the documentary film, *(In)Visible Portraits* by Oge Egbuonu, Black women were asked to describe Black women in three words. Unsurprisingly, what has so often been bestowed upon us, came up as an adjective again and again and again: strong. However, one word floored me. One word made my body temperature change, my heart pound and provoked spontaneous tears: 'Divine.'

This interviewee paused and, with such congruence, said, 'Black women are divine. I think that Black women are the closest that there is on this earth to God.' She then paused and became completely overcome. Tears started to fall as she continued: 'We submit, we are vessels, we're filled.'

I am not religious, I don't go to worship or believe in any one God, but I am spiritual and believe in something greater than all of us, so I had no idea why these words moved me so deeply in a way that felt almost otherworldly. It was only until I discovered something six months later, which turned out to be not only healing, but reaffirming.

In 1997, Mother Nature had big plans. Extreme and prolonged rainfall in the Northern Rift Valley in Ethiopia caused part of the ground to quite literally wash away, exposing several fossils.[64] Scientists, including Dr Berhane Asfaw and palaeontologist Tim White, discovered a human skull, thought to be the oldest Homo sapiens to date, which they called 'Idaltu', meaning 'the first'.

Years of cleaning and study by scientists and anthropologists revealed something quite magnificent. Based on the discovery of these fossils, these new scientific breakthroughs and archaeological evidence tie all of us, every single modern human being, together. Evidence reveals humans were on earth a lot earlier than first thought and that we share a direct maternal ancestral DNA originated approximately 160,000 years ago from an African woman known as 'Mitochondrial Eve'. The DNA was successfully passed down for so many generations from mother to daughter that the Mitochondrial DNA survived of which we now carry in our cells. This ground-breaking evidence shows that all of us, no matter what we look like today, descended from a common ancestor in Africa. A Black woman.[65]

I had known on a surface level, but it didn't land with any congruence until I heard it, in a trauma workshop with Resmaa Menakem. It was like being cradled and rocked. Throughout my existence, I have received and been exposed to so much negative programming, so much of which I absorbed, and at times, to my shame, turned inwards. For years, I used chemicals linked to causing cancer in my hair, chemicals that left scabs on my scalp all to conform to Eurocentric white beauty standards. I swallowed the racist bile and came to believe the myth of the Black people being inferior and the even bigger myths of the inferiority of dark-skinned Black women, about our 'place' in the world, violations on our bodies, commandeering of our wombs, policing of our hair, attacks on the essence of who we are, our beauty, our capability and our intrinsic worth.

In discovering more about my own ancestry, the hidden histories about the horrors of what Black women were subjected to at the height of slavery and far beyond it, and then this 'Mitochondrial Eve' – there is something to be said and acknowledged about what we endured and continue to endure, and thrive in spite of. There is something to be said about what we resist, smash through, swallow or tolerate in order to maintain equilibrium. There is something to be said about the vessels we become in order to survive, in order to love, and protect – fiercely – what seems to me to be, all of our humanity.

Black women, I wrote this chapter for you and to 7-year-old little Nova, who believed the myth that she was worthless. Black women are divine.

★

8. Armour Up: Self-Care and Advocacy

'Anyone who is interested in making change in the world also has to learn how to take care of herself, himself, theirselves… it means that we are able to bring our entire selves into the movement.'

ANGELA DAVIS[1]

What makes social justice seekers and human beings like you great at anti-racism work is your capacity for empathy. It's our superpower. But it's also our kryptonite. We absorb so much that it can sometimes leave us feeling like we are carrying the entire burden of injustice around the world on our shoulders, leading to regularly experiencing exhaustion, stress, and burnout.

If we do not intentionally and consistently prioritise our well-being in anti-racism work, it can have a detrimental impact on our emotional, physical and psychological health. Looking after yourself, practising self-care beyond bath bombs and building resilience is vital in any type of advocacy. It is critical in making your anti-racism work sustainable.

You will be more perceptive to injustice than you have been before. You will be coming up against more resistance and belligerence than you have before, having to repeat yourself over and over again while facing parts of yourself that might not feel great. This can lead to overwhelm, shame, apathy or complete disengagement, so it is important you operate from a resourced place.

It's easy to end up operating from a worn-out, beaten-up, martyred version of yourself, but dragging yourself along is really no good to anyone, no matter how well you've taught yourself to function through stress or adversity. Trust me: I learned this the hard way.

Working in wellbeing, I remember feeling guilty about not being at work. Despite being in an environment where I lost count of the daily microaggressions I received, despite the fact I was regularly experiencing extreme physiological reactions to stress, I continued to convince myself it was just an upset stomach, *every* Sunday evening for years. It took the culmination of a family bereavement, a house move, gastroenteritis and a high-speed motorway accident within days of each other to slow me down and to jolt me into a lifestyle change, taking better care of myself and kickstarting my ancestral healing journey.

★

Activism and Anxiety

Audre Lorde was not playing around when she said: 'Caring for myself is not self-indulgence, it is self-preservation, and that is an act of political warfare.'[2]

The system of white supremacy wants everyone engaged in racial justice to be burned out, tired and worn down. It wants us to be consistently sad and angry, so that we give in and continue to maintain the status quo. It's far easier (and perhaps even a bit enjoyable) to be carried along with the powerful undercurrent, than to waste vital energy swimming in the opposite direction.

This work is about resistance. Resisting most of what we have become accustomed to, noticing it, questioning it and challenging it. The latter will bring great opposition. Being able to withstand this force will support you in doing this work. So, let's armour up.

You will have already discovered this work can be hugely anxiety-inducing. We're tribal beings and the urge to belong and be in the 'in group' cannot be overstated. The urge to get it right only intensifies this. When I talk about anxiety, I am not talking about clinical anxiety which can be incredibly debilitating, but instead, the everyday anxiety that we all experience as part of being human. Just the hint of racism can generate huge feelings of anxiety, we often lose our cognitive ability to be able to cope. Anxiety often makes us freeze in our anti-racism work, makes us want to fight or take flight, people-please, withdraw, or completely abandon ship.

It's important to be aware of how anxiety related to anti-racism shows up for you, and to be mindful of when you have the capacity to meaningfully engage, or not. There is a balance to strike. Being honest and aware of your own wellbeing and when you may need relief and when avoidance might be creeping in is key, so that you don't use past trauma or anxiety related to racism as an excuse not to engage at all. The fact is that racism waits for no one. There are plenty of people living with life challenges, infertility, loneliness, divorce, bereavement, and poor mental health or physical health, and they're still dealing with racism on top.

When we feel anxious or stressed, the first thing we do is withdraw, and drop our natural coping strategies such as creating, exercising, socialising, talking and eating well. These are things that bring us joy or peace of mind and can actually help us. When we are engaged in advocacy, we actually need to be inviting more of these natural coping strategies into our life. This work – doing our part to leave the world in a better state than when we entered it – can be all-consuming and, if we're not mindful, lead to burnout.

Anxiety means we are in a heightened state of alert, as a result of increased stress, or perceived threat. Often in matters of racism, fear takes us off into an alternative reality and our thoughts and feelings become so overwhelming that we can mistake them as fact. But perceived threat is not the same as actual threat. Discomfort you may experience by being asked to move out of your comfort zone is not the same as distress.

Anxiety, everyday stress and feelings of worry are indeed part of being human, but when we exist in a constant state of fight or flight and experience anxiety for prolonged periods of time it can compromise our immune systems and lead to serious illness such as anxiety disorders, depression and can also seriously impact physical health. Being aware and having tools to recognise when you are being triggered is going to be crucial to helping you manage. Our bodies are wise; they often give us signs. Becoming more self-aware is key to recognising them.

Get curious with me: what are the signs you may be experiencing early stages of anxiety? How does it show up in your body or behaviour? What do you experience?

1. Irritability and nail biting?
2. Loss of, or increased, appetite?
3. Upset stomach?
4. Disrupted sleep or sleeping more?
5. Overworking?
6. Withdrawal from exercise, over-exercising or self-isolation?

What else happens?

Get intimate with your body. Be mindful of what it is trying to communicate with you. Consider these questions:

1. What sensations am I experiencing?
2. What am I feeling anxious about?
3. Is this thought or fact?
4. Do I need to pause?
5. How is my anxiety related to anti-racism impacting my allyship and my ability to process information?
6. What do I need in this moment?
7. What can I do to feel less anxious at this moment?
8. Who, or what, can I turn to for support?

When we get into anxious states, we are so used to bypassing our emotions and responding to simple questions like, 'How are you?' with a superficial 'OK' or 'fine' that we often end up disconnecting with ourselves and our bodies. One student became so overwhelmed with the state of the world, she had stopped meeting her most basic needs and had forgotten to eat and take care of herself. Being able to name our emotions and pay attention to bodily sensations means it is far easier to ascertain what we need so that we are resourced and able to work, think, respond and act from a place of rejuvenation or empowerment rather than disconnection.

★

Challenge Your Perception Over Reality

Our minds love drama and can trick us into thinking that there is danger where there isn't any. It likes to play out full-scale theatrical productions of all of the things that could happen but haven't and, more so, probably won't, which doesn't serve us and most definitely doesn't serve the bigger cause. If fear of the unknown and getting things wrong, saying the wrong thing or general catastrophising starts taking over and getting in the way of being effective in your anti-racism work, ask yourself:

1. What are the things that could go well?
2. What else could the outcome be?
3. What actually happened and what did I make it mean?

Most of the time those are two entirely different things.

Our minds going into overdrive is something that happens to us all. Don't beat yourself up. Offer yourself some compassion. Thank your brain for its vigilance and for doing what it is designed to do – to try to protect you – and then when you realise you are not in any actual danger, and that all is well, tell it to calm the fuck down.

A key part to looking after our overall wellbeing and being effective in anti-racism work is building resilience. Resilience is something that is acquired through experience, allowing us to successfully bounce back from challenging and traumatic events. It does not mean we are never going to be vulnerable, scared, or need support, it is simply about our individual capacity to cope with adversity and recover.

The most robust definition of overall wellbeing and resilience I came across was during some training with mental health charity YoungMinds. The definition was conceived by the Department for Environment, Food and Rural Affairs (DEFRA) in 2010 and approved by the World Health Organization.[3] It has since been adapted, but I still prefer to use it because it remains the most robust and takes into consideration social influences that impact our overall wellbeing and resilience.

A positive physical, social and mental state: it is not just the absence of pain, discomfort or incapacity. It requires that basic needs are met, that individuals have a sense of purpose, that they feel able to achieve important personal goals and participate in society. It is enhanced by conditions that include supportive personal relationships, strong and inclusive communities, good health, financial and personal security, rewarding employment and a healthy and attractive environment.

Look at all of the components required for overall wellbeing and to support us in building resilience in all of us. Now think about all of the components required to boost wellbeing and build resilience for those of us who are Black or belong in other marginalised and intersecting identities. Note how much is required, and how often our basic human needs are not met. You can quickly see why I refer to racism as a public health issue. Understand how wellbeing and our capacity to build resilience are compromised because so many spaces are not safe, and our opportunities to participate in society without abuse are so often encroached upon.

★

Building Resilience

Firstly, yes, we absolutely need to set higher standards to tackle racism, but please stop seeking perfection in your anti-racism. Perfectionism is a function of white supremacy. It is not human to know everything and never get things wrong. Where is the joy in learning if you know everything? You build resilience by risking failure. You are going to get things wrong over and over again in your anti-racism journey. You learn by doing, building resilience along the way. So instead of trying to cling on for dear life, relinquish some control and enjoy the feeling of free-falling.

Set boundaries

Boundaries are a vital way to look after our wellbeing, boost resilience, and heal and meet our basic needs. So often we either fail to set and communicate our boundaries, or fail to enforce them, especially with family and friends, and it can compromise our wellbeing and sense of self. It also depletes our energy, and we need as much energy as possible for ourselves, those dear to us and our advocacy.

I would not be able to do this work if I didn't have healthy boundaries. In fact, I am certain I would be very unwell. That doesn't mean my boundaries aren't constantly being tested, that I don't drop them sometimes (and then re-learn the hard way why they are necessary) or need to review them. It's important to keep ourselves resourced and sometimes that means learning to say no. Saying no doesn't mean you're an arsehole. Only we are responsible for setting healthy boundaries, communicating them and enforcing them.

Setting clear boundaries about what is and isn't acceptable to you, especially in relationships, isn't always met with gratitude and respect from friends and family who have been able to take advantage of your bendy boundaries in the past. They will probably struggle with it, maybe even think you're unreasonable, but the boundaries are there for you and your wellbeing.

Try this when the racist behaviour of someone you love is becoming problematic: 'When you do or say X it makes me feel Y. It makes it hard for me to be around you. I want to spend time with you and if you continue to do X I can no longer be around you. I care about you and I love you and this is important to me.'

People learn very quickly how to treat you by the way they see you treat yourself. For example, if someone emails you a work query at midnight and you reply straight away, you've set the tone — 'You can have access to me at any time of day.'

In the height of the Black Lives Matter resurgence in summer 2020, my website leapt from its usual 800 hits a month to 40,000 overnight (no wonder it kept crashing) and, in addition, it was a profoundly difficult period.

I eventually removed my email address and instead

added a contact form and a clear message about my availability, letting people know when they would receive a response. That didn't stop people disrespecting that boundary by sliding into my DMs, contacting mutual colleagues, to give me a nudge. The pressure to bow was real. I do not know how many times I had to repeat myself and re-enforce boundaries during this time – I am not available. It started to sink in about seven weeks later, but if I had folded to pressure and started to respond outside of my own boundaries, not only would I have communicated a lack of trust – I don't do what I say – but most importantly, being all things to all people when my own trauma had been triggered would have done me nor them any favours. Asserting boundaries also helps others learn to manage and meet their unmet needs.

If I did not hold boundaries, I would spend every working hour responding to emails and messages on Instagram; giving free advice would be my full-time job. I would spend every minute fire-fighting every incident of racism online. Not only would that quickly make me incredibly ill, but it's also not an effective use of my time, nor is it a fair exchange of energy. I would not be giving the best and most powerful version of myself. When we do things we don't want to, or are under-resourced, we can start acting from a place of resentment (yup, I know you've been there – muttering under your breath as you do whatever task you agreed to do) which isn't useful.

Question this: Do your boundaries reflect your behaviour? Are you communicating a boundary then doing the complete opposite? Stop saying yes to things you mean to say no to. If your impulsive default is to people-please (like me) it's OK to pause. I once heard author, founder of Baggage Reclaim and relationship expert Natalie Lue say: 'Know the power in the pause. How do I really feel? What's my current capacity? What's my current energy level?'

Try it: 'Thank you for thinking of me. Can I think about this and get back to you by X?'

Or, if like me, you are susceptible to respond with a reflexive yes, you can always go back and say that you have changed your mind and it no longer works for you. You are allowed to change your mind. Setting boundaries can also extend to what you won't tolerate if family start trying to get you to collude with or excuse their racism. 'I have a firm boundary with racism. This is not OK for me. I care about people. Please stop'.

You can also set boundaries around what you consume. If one of the first things you do is reach for your mobile phone when you wake up in the morning and easily get sucked into online hate, consider removing social media apps from your phone and only logging on in controlled bursts, perhaps via a desktop computer. This also stops the mindless scrolling. You could even completely remove the temptation. If your phone is your alarm, consider buying an old-fashioned clock or alarm instead and keep your mobile phone in a separate room altogether. It's much nicer waking up to your own thoughts, to some of your favourite music on the radio, with a book or meditation than online bile or the noise of WhatsApp groups. Be boundaried. We have limited energy, especially in anti-racism. You are in control of where, who and what you give your energy to.

Boosting wellbeing and practising joy

These are important tools to help make sure you are balancing your day with general self-care. Ask yourself: what can I do today to support my wellbeing?

This could be anything, from reading a book or listening to a wellness podcast, to crafting or having a mindful cup of tea with no interruptions. Try something new like learning to cook a new cuisine by taking part in an online cooking class. Learn a new language. Learning something new boosts wellbeing and our confidence and trust in our own ability. And while it might sound obvious, stay nourished. When I am immersed in this work, I can easily treat my body like a machine and forget to drink water or skip meals, so keep hydrated and be mindful of what you consume – explore foods that boost mood, give you energy and increase concentration.

My students hear me talking about joy a lot. Find every opportunity to practise joy daily. It is vital for wellbeing and is an act of resistance as a consequence and makes this work sustainable. I could not do this work without practising regular joy. We need the light and shadow; we need our rain and rainbows. Joy and pain can and do co-exist. If you think that denying your joy somehow means that you are expressing empathy to others who are suffering, then newsflash: that's not empathy. We can show empathy for others without suppressing our joy. And we can feel sad without wanting those who are shining their light around us to dim theirs.

Create a power playlist – music can be an automatic healer. Let it soothe or energise you. Sing and play with little ones. Volunteer, roller-skate, be outside in nature, play with your pet, dance, wear bright colours, paint, knit, do some gardening in the local community, buy or grow your own flowers, connect with friends who resource you. Whatever it is, cultivate joy every damn day.

Self-compassion

Keep coming back to this one. It is so vital to practise self-compassion in your anti-racism, especially if you're having a shame spiral where the negative 'I'm disgusted with myself' self-talk keeps cropping up.

Get curious: What is the relationship you have with yourself? How do you speak about yourself, especially when you feel like you have done something wrong, or when you uncover things you did or said that have caused harm? Is it with a commitment to do better and an understanding that you were doing the best you could at the time with the resources you had available or are you beating yourself up?

Speak to yourself with love, respect and kindness. We say things to ourselves we would never say to others. You don't need to punish yourself on this journey. Don't confuse punishment with accountability. A great way to practise self-compassion is to write a letter to your younger self. If they weren't feeling good enough, what advice would they need to hear? What words of affirmation can you use?

Sometimes it's helpful to just surrender to how you are feeling by naming it, being honest and accepting things as they are. Say to yourself:

'This work is hard for me right now and I am feeling X.'

'Even though I said or did X, I am still worthy of love and

belonging and I remain committed to reducing racist harm and doing better.'

It sounds, simple but sometimes all we need to do in a challenging moment in anti-racism is breathe. Slow the nervous system down, remind yourself you are safe, get your thinking brain back online so you can respond.

1. Breathe in slowly for 3 counts.
2. Release for 5 counts.
3. Repeat until you feel your heart rate return to normal, or a shame spiral dissipate.

There are lots of breathing apps and guided meditations online to support you with this. See what works for you. And remember, here I am talking about the general everyday anxiety we all experience as part of being human. If you find yourself in frequent and prolonged states of anxiety, please connect with a medical expert.

Practise gratitude

I used to struggle with gratitude. I had learned to measure my worth by productivity, an ugly gift handed down through my ancestry; a reminder that my ancestors had no value or worth unless they were working, without compensation, often to death. If I was having a shitty day where I didn't feel I had adequately 'produced' or 'performed', coupled with that feeling of, 'What have I got to complain about? My ancestors had it worse,' I did not feel deserving of reward, let alone that I had anything to be grateful for.

On 11 September 2019, I lost one of my very best friends. She was loved by many and also happened to be one of the most exceptional hip-hop dancers in the UK, dancing for Rihanna, Kylie Minogue and even Nelson Mandela. She was mesmerising on stage. In fact, when I watched her dance, I would often catch myself holding my breath. She literally took my breath away. Her name was Teneisha Bonner, nicknamed Tin Tin by those who loved her. She was a phenomenal human being and the gap she leaves behind in this world is colossal. She was a woman of faith and would often talk about gratitude – we'd regularly chuckle when I was having a rant about something that happened. As I was getting animated, she'd always lovingly call me in, saying 'Grace, Nova. Grace.'

She taught me so much about grace and gratitude, because she role-modelled them. She practised gratitude throughout her three-year battle with breast cancer. Even in her final moments, when, no doubt as a woman of deep faith, she knew the hand she had been dealt, she still found things to be grateful for and entered them into her journal without fail.

That was all the inspiration I needed to kick-start practising gratitude regularly. I cannot do this work sustainably without it and I often found myself thanking her and others who have gone before me before I start to write or teach each day.

Practising gratitude does not mean bypassing our pain or reality. It simply means being grateful, wherever we are in that moment because we are, quite simply, still here. Not only does practising gratitude support resilience, cultivate empathy, compassion and give our immune systems a boost – it brings us hope.

The effects from much of the advocacy we are doing now will

not come to pass in our lifetimes; we will not see the benefit of all of it and sometimes the reality and disillusionment weighs heavy. But you, right now, are involved in monumental societal change and that kind of seismic shift takes time. Every intentional action you take has a ripple effect. Sustaining yourself is crucial to having a greater impact in the world and passing on the baton so that when we are gone, the work not only continues, but it expands. Believing in the process and trusting that change is already happening is all the hope you need.

'Hope and fear cannot occupy the same space
at the same time. Invite one to stay'.
MAYA ANGELOU

★

9. Raising the Next Generation

'Each child belongs to all of us and they will bring us a tomorrow
in direct relation to the responsibility we have shown them.'
MAYA ANGELOU

I'll never forget the exposing feeling of burning shame of watching a clip doing the rounds on the internet from a documentary film called *Dark Girls*, aired on the Oprah Winfrey Network and produced by D. Channsin Berry and Bill Duke, back in December 2011. The clip featured a white child psychologist sharing pictures of cartoon characters of little children that all looked the same, except for a sliding scale of melanin to determine their difference, with the darkest shade at one end and the lightest skin tone at the other.

The psychologist asks a Black girl, around 4 or 5 years old, to point to the 'smartest' child. The little Black girl points to the cartoon character with the lightest skin at one end of the scale. Next, she asks the little Black girl to point to the 'dumbest' child and she points to opposite end of the scale where the Black cartoon character is. The psychologist then asks the little girl which one is the 'bad' child. She points to the same character.

When asked why, she responds, 'Because she is Black.' Asked by the psychologist to point out the 'good' one, her finger goes to the white character. The psychologist asked her why, and the little girl responds, 'Because she is white.'

This exercise was part of a pioneering study called the 'Clark Doll Project', also known as the 'Doll Test', founded by social psychologists and husband-wife duo Drs Kenneth and Mamie Clark in the 1940s. It was used to observe children's bias and racial perception between the ages of 3 and 7 and the psychological effects of segregation in the US in African American children. The test revealed many of the children, including white children, associated positive attributes with white and negative attributes with Black.[1]

In a 1985 PBS TV interview called 'Eyes on the Prize', Dr Kenneth Clark recalled that the majority of African American children who took part in the study would often reject the Black doll and when told to show the doll that most looked like them, many became incredibly distraught, and even left the room when they realised they identified with the doll they had just rejected.[2]

These psychological tests not only expose the self-hate and internalised racism some Black children experience, but also how widespread anti-Blackness – and indeed, colourism – are. Both anti-Blackness and colourism are by-products of white supremacy and a painfully revealing example of how damaging racism is to children.

The results from the Clark Doll Project were astonishing, but perhaps unsurprising. This study and the Clarks's testimonies played a monumental role in the 1954 *Brown vs Board of Education* Topeka Supreme Court case which proved that systemic racism in schools was widespread and that prejudice, discrimination and segregation were negatively and psychologically impacting children. Findings like these led to the abolishment of segregation in schools in the US. It was ruled unanimously that segregation promoted a feeling of unworthiness and, in the words of Dr Kenneth Clark, a feeling 'some Black children may never get over... These children saw themselves as inferior and they accepted the inferiority as part of reality.'[3] This doll test has subsequently been used to determine racial bias in children all over the world, including the UK, with children of varying backgrounds and skin tones yielding similar results.

In 1970s Britain, 'Educationally Subnormal schools' (ESNs) were a firm fixture. Before that they were called MSNs, which meant schools for the Mentally Subnormal. Observe how this language influenced and continues to influence the dehumanisation of people with differing needs. We would probably translate these as Special Educational Needs schools (SENs) today. They were where Black working-class children, regardless of their individual academic and cognitive abilities, would be 'dumped' with other children with severe learning difficulties, just because they were Black. This was commonly referred to as the 'Black Children Dump.'[4]

'Bussing out' policies also took place in the 60s and 70s in places like Bradford, Haringey and Southall. In response to protests by white parents, a number of Local Education Authorities took it upon themselves to introduce a 30 per cent upper limit of Black African, Caribbean or South Asian children in their schools.[5] Buses would be sent to take out these 'excess' Black and Brown children from one school and dump them in a neighbouring borough, pandering to racist fears from white parents that there were 'too many' Black and Brown kids in one area and that their mere presence would hold white children back.[6] Students on these buses, often called 'Immigrant' or 'Paki' buses, became the target of dehumanisation abuse and racist attacks. One attack was so horrific that it resulted in the murder of Shakil Malik who was bottled to death in 1974 in Ealing while getting on one of these buses.[7] The Black Children Dump and 'bussing out' continued until 1976 in London (and until 1980 in Bradford).

After tireless campaigning from the Black and other ethnic minority communities in London, a new court ruling in 1975 (under the 1968 Race Relations Act) deemed 'Bussing Out', in fact, racist and therefore against the law. It makes you wonder, with the 1968 Race Relations Act in force for the seven years prior, how this was able to continue for so long before being ruled illegal. This type of targeted social exclusion corrodes self-esteem, self-perception and sense of belonging and safety. Without a doubt, it also impacts mental health, social behaviour, classroom engagement and academic achievement. For some of these children, they were also dealing with culture shock, homesickness and separation anxiety from being away from family still living in another part of the Commonwealth. Caribbean people had been led to believe Britain would be 'a promised land with streets paved in gold'.[8] In reality, they met a bomb-damaged UK and a racially hostile environment – not exactly a nurturing environment for learning.

In an attempt to expose and address the impact of systemic racism, in 1971 Bernard Coard published, *How the West Indian Child is made Educationally Subnormal in the British School System* to make Black parents aware of the horrendous ways British schools were consistently failing Black children, in particular, Caribbean children who had migrated to join their parents. Unsurprisingly, traditional publishing houses refused to publish the book and it was independent Black-owned publishers New Beacon Books and L'Ouverture Publications that published it. It gained national press attention and all initial 10,000 copies sold out. The book exposed racist policies and discriminatory behaviour, racism in the curriculum, teacher bias, lack of parental involvement and general low expectations from teachers, contributing to poor self-image and self-esteem in the children.[9] It was around this time that the British Black Panthers were also formed. Members including Olive Morris, Beverley Bryan and Altheia Jones-LeCointe led community activism, to help tackle racial discrimination in Britain and the sub-standard education Black children were getting and to encourage a positive sense of self. It also provided Saturday schools to supplement education and a free child-care service.[10]

Watching *Dark Girls* and discovering more about the Doll Test was a sobering reminder of how easily children pick up societal cues and perceptions that they learn from adults. It's also a reminder of how powerful the system of white supremacy and, in these particular cases, anti-Blackness is. It reveals how so many of these children have already started internalising either white supremacy or racism.

We can confidently assume that none of the white children in these tests were little Neo-Nazi extremists secretly plotting Black genocide. We can confidently assume none of these children or their parents, who gave permission for their participation, were on a quest to hurt one another. They were just children, unfiltered and honest, already learning racism from the world around them.

Fast forward to March 2020. A clip of a 4-year-old Black girl called Ariyonna stunned the internet when she was captured on camera telling her Atlanta-based hairdresser, 'I am so ugly' before breaking down and crying.[11] It received 10 million views, broke the hearts of many globally and prompted many celebs, including Michelle Obama, to send their love and positive affirmations to Ariyonna. However, the positive affirmations alone sadly don't stop discrimination in either society or the playground.

In 2019, an investigation from UK charity the National Society for the Prevention of Cruelty to Children (NSPCC) stated that racist bullying had gone up by a fifth since 2016. It revealed children were receiving racist abuse every hour and more than 10,500 racist incidents were reported to the police in 2018, many of which involved babies and toddlers. The NSPCC also reported that many children were keeping their experience of racism a secret from parents. The same report revealed that some children, as young as ten, made calls to UK charity Childline stating they were using makeup to lighten their skin to avoid racial bullying.[12]

A few months after the results of this investigation were published, I was contacted by a friend in despair saying they caught their 3-year-old Black son trying to wash his skin off in the bath because he was being bullied at school; children didn't want to play with him because he was 'dirty'.

We have to do better than this. We are repeating cycles and patterns of behaviour. Racism is learned behaviour. We have to unlearn it, at the very least for the sake of our children.

Our Children are Watching

Children start expressing racial bias and picking playmates based on race as young as 3 years old.[13] According to a study by the University of Washington, some children can start to express bias based on race as early as 16 months old.[14] So, whether we intentionally decide to talk to children about race or not, they are learning from our social cues. While I imagine most who read this book are not consciously teaching children overt racism, the silent code of cultural norms, lack of intentional positive representation, programming and the perceived social hierarchy still seeps into children by osmosis, and they learn racism pretty quickly. So much so, they are already picking up on who is valued in society, who isn't, and more so, where they belong within that spectrum.

When 7-year-old little Nova was compared to faeces by another little girl, never would I imagine such an experience would stick like superglue, shape who I am and be the driving force for the work I do now. To many who don't experience racism, perhaps even you, that girl's moment of curiosity about the colour of my skin might seem like an innocent and harmless exchange. But like the clarity of a fake diamond under a microscope, it exposed the flaws and rigidness of the good vs bad person 'rules' that adults like to use to demonstrate who is and isn't racist. What became magnified at warp speed was how early racism can be learned and how damaging it can be.

> 'If we care about the health and wellbeing of all our children, we have to take steps to address racism'.
> AMERICAN ACADEMY OF PAEDIATRICS[15]

I intentionally use examples of racism in children in my teaching, not because it almost always brings forth tears and much-needed empathy, or because it moves us out of the juvenile 'good vs bad' binary. But because it exposes and accurately frames racism as a public health issue. While we continue to live in a racist society, it shows how this stuff seeps into our conscious and subconscious. It reveals how easily these innocent little beings learn and then exhibit racial bias; Until we start to intentionally tackle racism, unlearn, relearn and most importantly, actually follow through and role-model change, it will continue.

As someone who is childless, I am writing this chapter with all of us in mind who influence young people in our sphere. From parents and caregivers, to teachers and elders in our extended families, places of worship and local communities, every single one of us plays a role in influencing and raising socially conscious and curious children, raising them to leave the world in a better state then when we entered it. We need to feel less clumsy in talking about race, find ways to start to reduce harm and stop passing on our unaddressed bullshit to the next generation.

Having courageous conversations with children during their early years' formation is vital. The question is no longer whether or not to talk to children about race and racism. It's when. So, let's start.

The Talk

When it comes to talking about race, so many white adults centre their own discomfort that they avoid it like the plague. It means many children are not starting the track event at the same time. Some are stuck in their starting blocks, some have finished, some are lapping others, and many haven't even turned up for the event at all.

Many, not all, Black children and non-Black children of colour have already had racism brought to their door. Perhaps they have already been given 'the talk' by a parent or caregiver preparing them for how to navigate experiencing racism.

One parent I interviewed in West London recounts one devastating moment when her daughter was just 5 years old, having just gone to visit McDonald's as a treat with her grandmother. It was fairly busy and there were no free tables, so the little girl and her grandmother went to sit with a single lady on a bigger table with several free seats. The lady responded with words to the effect of, 'No you can't sit there, I don't want you and your lot sitting here.' It led the little girl to ask, 'Why was the lady mean to me? Why didn't the lady want to sit with us? Why were adults shouting and why did Grandma get so sad and upset?'

The parent went onto explain to me:

We had already started to talk to our daughter about race and skin colour and to have age-appropriate conversations to explain that there are some people in the world who don't like others because of the colour of their skin. Never did I imagine I would need to talk to her about her own experience of racism so soon. It made me angry that a 5-year-old was a victim of a racist attack from an adult. Nothing prepares you for that, and as a parent you feel angry and helpless and that, regardless of the groundwork we laid for her, nothing can really prepare her. Now we're waiting for the next incident. It left my daughter upset, sad and confused and she couldn't understand why an adult was being mean to her and her grandma because they're Brown. It didn't make any sense to her.

One Black parent I spoke to, who is raising two boys in Birmingham, wanted to approach 'the talk' without making it a 'big deal'. 'Let's face it, having to explain that there are people out there who won't like them, or will treat my sons differently solely because of the colour of their skin is bullshit,' they shared. 'I felt like I wanted to throw up when I had the first talk. But I have to prepare them. My youngest was 8. I have to take the lead; I've been in a interracial relationship for eighteen years and I am still educating, not only my kids, but my partner. I need back up!'

The Trouble with 'We're Colour-blind'

These kinds of intergenerational pep talks have, sadly, been present for centuries in Black communities. From Black enslaved women teaching their daughters how to relax and numb their bodies to help prepare them for the torture of rape,[16] to parents teaching Black boys their rights during a stop and search and how to protect themselves from being harmed by the police. Explaining that some won't like them because of the colour of their skin, or that they have to work twice as hard as their peers has been commonplace within many Black and Brown families.

In contrast, many children being raised by white caregivers either do not discuss race at all or they are brought up being told 'we don't see colour' or 'we're colour-blind'. Of course, not only are these well-meaning statements, in fact, microaggressions, but neither of these things are true, unless you have an actual visual impairment. Even then, there have been studies involving white people, who are blind, that have revealed even blind people exhibit racism just like sighted people.[17]

Unless you have a visual impairment, of course you see colour, just as you see other obvious identifiers in people, such as hair colour or the other social construct that is gender. The question is: why is it so important for you *not* to see it – to bypass such a huge part of someone's identity and culture?

In an interview with clinical psychologist and paediatric psychologist Dr Martha Deiros Collado, she explained how children of colour often notice race sooner; they think about their race and the things that they are singled out for such as hair colour or skin. She told me: 'We have to move away from colour-blindness. We do see colour and we need to see colour. Claiming that we do not see colour belittles and dismisses individuals' history, cultural heritage and the future. If we don't see colour, we are saying we are all the same and we all have the same experiences – which is not true.'

Research also shows that teaching children the 'colour-blind' tactic of 'not seeing race', a tactic mostly adopted by well-meaning white liberals, not only perpetuates everyday racism, but in fact, has the opposite effect.[18] They do see race and it teaches children that talking about race is bad and that there is a stigma surrounding skin colour, making children less able to recognise discrimination.

In 2016, the American Psychological Association shared results of a child experiment they undertook. Researchers read children aged between 8 and 11 story books that either 'downplayed' racial differences or centred race and the value of diversity.

The results showed that the stories that featured examples of racial bias that were read by children with the 'colour-blind' books were 'less likely to recognise bias'. The children who intentionally learned about diversity were better at identifying examples of racial bias and discrimination.[19]

I have lost count of the number of white people who say, with a sense of pride, that their children just don't even see race. I have to stifle my eye rolls. Just because a child is not explicitly mentioning race does not mean they don't notice it. Evidence shows that it is more likely that white children, or children with primary caregivers who are not anti-racist, won't 'see' race because they have already learned that they aren't supposed to see, let alone mention it, rather than because they are somehow entirely free from racial bias, don't see colour and see everyone around them with translucent skin.

I had a strange experience with a white mother and colleague in her 40s who once almost seemed to have regressed back to childhood and kept whispering the word 'Black' to me, like it was a swear word, every time she said it. I found myself reassuring her that Black was not a dirty word and that she could say it; that being Black is positive and in fact, in her case, just a descriptive word. She'd been raised with a colour-blind approach.

A parent and anti-racism student once said to me, 'We make so much of everybody's race and we make nothing of our own.' By teaching children about race, and normalising talking to children about their own skin colour as a simple part of their identity, we are helping them to not only understand who they are, but to better understand, hold empathy and compassion for others.

Another thing to consider is that children and adults can have difficulty in identifying faces of races different to their own, especially those who are not integrated in multicultural environments. This is something called the Cross-Race Effect or the Other Race Effect.[20] This seems to happen a lot in British journalism where Black people are regularly misidentified by journalists. According to research by City University London, journalism is an industry that is 94 per cent white.[21] In September 2020, the world's fastest man, and the most famous athlete of the twenty-first century, Usain Bolt, was misidentified by NBC as another well-known Black man, comedian Kevin Hart. In January 2020, the BBC were reporting on the death of basketball superstar Kobe Bryant who died with his daughter and seven others in a tragic helicopter accident. Instead of showing footage of Kobe Bryant on screen they showed footage of basketball player LeBron James – who was alive and well. A few journalistic errors seem harmless – it can happen to anyone, right? But imagine what the impact of the Cross-Race Effect can look like in eyewitness testimonies and criminal justice systems.

On 27 March 2020, Michael 'Mike' Boateng, former footballer and former *Love Island* contestant published an interview on YouTube with hosts Ben and Emmanuel Tedeku, discussing his experiences of signing up to join Greater Manchester Police back in 2017. He explained how, on the second day of his police training, he was called in to the sergeant's office. Upon discovering that Mike used to be a professional footballer, suspicion clearly set in and the sergeant had felt the need to Google him. On doing so, he'd discovered another footballer, who was also Black with the same name, who had been arrested for match fixing.

The sergeant pulled up an image of the other Michael and

oddly surmised that, despite the extensive vetting and legal checks required to join the force, Mike, and the other person were one and the same. The sergeant even called in a colleague to also look at the picture on the screen and they were equally convinced they had the right man. They then asked Mike to bring in his passport to prove that he was not the same person. Mike complied – and subsequently made formal complaints. Needless to say, Mike no longer works for the police force.

Research shows for some children, the Cross-Race Effect may never even develop if they regularly see and interact with people of different races and for those that struggle, it can also be reversed.[22] Bronson and Merryman's studies show that 'explicitly talking about race to 5–7-year-olds can dramatically *improve or inform* racial attitudes in as little as a week'.[23]

The Work Begins at Home

White parents and caregivers are far less likely to introduce conversations about skin colour or have an open dialogue about racial issues with children than parents and caregivers in ethnic minority families. This is often because race is ignored, not perceived to be an issue, taken for granted and ultimately, not directly impacting their lives; therefore, it is easily overlooked and fear of broaching the subject seeps in.

Common fears I hear from parents about talking to their children about race are:

Fear of destroying their child's innocence

I find this is an interesting signifier of racialised fragility in itself, that just the conscious mention of 'race' is somehow going to destroy a child's innocence. Why is it that the automatic response to even discussing the very colour of our skin, not even racism, is one that is so negative and anxiety-inducing?

Fear of making an 'issue' out of it

The impact of racism and not talking to your children about race is *already* an issue. Not talking about race does not and, evidently, has never ended racism.

Avoidance and not knowing what to say

Tapping out and choosing not to have conversations with your children about race because you feel awkward is, in fact, a privilege.

A reflective prompt for you:

1. What are your triggers around conversations about race with children?
2. Where is any resistance or discomfort truly coming from?

Many parents and caregivers often express that because they don't know enough, they don't talk about it. I also observe a common expectation that parents, in particular, need to be the oracle and know everything, that they need to have read all the books and to be a critical race theorist before they approach discussions about race with children. However, fear of not knowing what to say is a big driver of racial illiteracy. That fear of 'getting things wrong' not only blocks progress and attempts to learn, but it reproduces racism, prevents us from raising children to have more empathy and understanding for difference, so as to better recognise and stand up against discrimination, and it also teaches children that not knowing something is something to fear – that not knowing something is scary.

One of the most empowering things we can do for children and young people is teach them that it is OK to not know. By role-modelling that adults, especially parents, should know everything, we are not only preventing ourselves from being human and putting ourselves on some bizarre pedestal, but setting ourselves up to fail. We are definitely not role-modelling honesty and vulnerability.

I remember asking one interviewee if she had started talking to her 4-year-old daughter about race. She said no, because she didn't know much about race, didn't 'really like history' and that she would be teaching her about race and racism based on her own opinion. It's worth noting this interviewee was still using words like 'coloured' in her vocabulary.

We do not and will never know everything. Winging it and trying to teach children about race based on your opinion and not fact is more than likely going to do a disservice, pass on more 'isms' and continue to leave them completely misinformed. There is always an opportunity to do something about not knowing and to continue learning in a way that suits your learning style. Learning something new also builds resilience, and that's definitely something worth role-modelling.

Another interviewee, who is co-parenting two white children aged 7 and 8 in South East London with her partner, started to talk about race, when one of the girls started to demonstrate avoidance behaviour when they hired a cleaner. She said she didn't like the cleaner because she was Brown. She said she didn't like the look of her, because Brown people are scary, and that she didn't want to play with Brown people.

It emerged that she was learning this from her stepdad, who would often exhibit xenophobic and racist rants about 'immigrants' and the Brown people next door. To counteract this rhetoric, my interviewee and her partner are trying to reassure her and introduce programmes with positive representation of Black and Brown characters, reminding her of the Brown dolls she likes to play with and of her Brown friends. Up until this point they had no prior conversations about race or racism.

Another interviewee based in Surrey – a white woman married to a Black man with three mixed-race girls between the ages of 4 and 10, explained to me how they tried to broach age-appropriate conversations about race at home as soon as the children started to notice the different skin tones present in their own family unit. They actively wanted to encourage curious conversations by taking the lead from their children.

Their youngest wanted to understand why she wasn't the same colour as her mummy or daddy, so they chose a creative way to help. They decided to use painting as an abstract way for their daughter to understand what happens when you mix different colours together. She understood, in age-appropriate terms.

When her eldest daughter saw a photo of her mum as a child and asked if she would have preferred to have white children with a white husband, she took that as a cue to invite further curiosity and asked her why she was asking. The mother intentionally created a relaxed and neutral space in the home where the children could come, lie down and ask any questions they wanted to without judgement or shaming.

> I try not to bring too much emotion into it and keep to fact and I will make sure my answer is backed up by books, websites, other sources, experiences or even draw parallels with some Bible stories. If they ask me questions that I don't know the answer to, I will say "I don't know – why don't we look together?" and we spend some time searching together.

This interviewee demonstrated the importance of normalising not knowing and sharing the fun, creativity and curiosity of learning that can come from discovering something new and seeking out the truth together.

★

The Power of Racism and Non-verbal Communication

Aside from conversing with my Black peers, some of the most uncomplicated and refreshingly honest conversations I have had about race are, in fact, with children. Adults overcomplicate conversations about race by bringing their own unaddressed stuff into the arena. Often the fears and anxiety you hold about talking about race with children, are not actually coming from them, but from your own 'isms', projections and embarrassment.

I remember having a chat with a very curious 6-year-old who wanted to show me a book she had been reading. In sharing what she had learned, she referred to me as a 'coloured' person. Her mother, who was also in the room at the time, was visibly embarrassed. I asked the little girl what colour my skin was, and she said, 'brown'. I explained to her that it was okay to describe my skin as brown and that 'coloured' was a word used in the olden days that wasn't very nice anymore. She acknowledged it and then carried on telling me about what she had learned and about the other exciting Brown characters. That was the end of it. Lesson learned. No drama.

Children are incredibly sophisticated at picking up on our non-verbal cues. It's how we all first learn how to communicate. From the sudden tightening of a grip, to sweaty palms, a parent's increased heart rate, or even a change in tone. They notice our discomfort at talking about race.

With the beauty of hindsight, what I came to understand about what made my experience of 'the poo-poo incident' so harmful, was not the little girl's curiosity at seeing someone with brown skin who didn't look like her. It wasn't even that her only association with the colour brown was something dirty and negative. Rather, it was her mother's response. I looked to her mother, as an adult, for reassurance and, instead, got the most powerful non-verbal cue that confirmed everything her daughter verbalised: with one look and one swift move, she ushered her child as far away from me as possible, like I was contagious.

With emotional intelligence, education and time, I, of course, now understand that the mother's response was likely down to her own embarrassment, or even shame. What the mother could have done, which would have led to less confusion, perhaps less shame and a lot more empathy and understanding, was, instead of reacting to her own embarrassment, to respond to her child:

- 'Yes she has brown skin, what are some nice things you can think of that are brown?'
- 'What other things can you notice about her?'
- 'That girl looks very nice and kind to me and calling her poo-poo is not kind.'

In an interview with child and adolescent therapist Oluwakemi Omijeh, she explained to me that children can read and understand basic non-verbal cues and pick up on certain social cues from as young as 7 months. Not years. Months.

She went on to share a story from a white man who remembers walking through Brixton market in London, at the time a predominantly Black area (pre-gentrification), holding hands with his mother. He noticed his mother tighten her grip so hard it has left an imprint in his memory which still reverberates into his adulthood. That grip in that moment communicated that this area and these people are not safe, creating an unconscious anxiety about Black people and perpetuating the narrative that Black people are to be feared.

Not discussing, explaining or guiding children when it comes to questions about racial difference can leave children confused. It provides a dangerous opportunity to start forming reality based on their thoughts and their imaginations. This can lead to them learning what is being role-modelled, in this case, that Black people are bad, scary, dirty, or all of the above, which can lead to unconscious anxiety and engaging in avoidance and anti-social behaviours. This lack of guidance and space to ask questions and satisfy that curiosity can also lead to forming an obsession with the 'other' – otherwise known as fetishisation.

As Omijeh explains: 'Like adults, children react to fear differently. A child who hasn't been given the opportunity to explore and learn about the world beyond their small world will become an adult who sees the world in a very black-and-white way.'

In a bid to promote equality, well-meaning adults often teach children, who already start to develop a strong sense of fairness and moral sense of justice at around 7, that we are all the same – when they can clearly see, not only are we not clones, but that we are not all treated the same. Children naturally learn about who they are and where they belong by noticing both the similarities and also the differences in themselves and others. Of course, we are all human and there are many similarities, but we should get into the habit of celebrating differences, not ignoring them.

Good Hair, Bad Hair

One of the biggest targets for othering and discrimination for Black children is their hair.

In October 2019, I read an article in *Cornwall Live* about 8-year-old Finley who lives in Par, Cornwall,[24] Finley was not only subjected to unwanted hair touching and physical and verbal racist attacks from children, but from adults too. You'd think an article about the racial abuse of an 8-year-old at the hands of adults would generate some kind of empathy in the comments section. Sadly not. I read a number of comments blaming Finley for his own persecution, but one comment stood out, stating that maybe he wouldn't be bullied if he had 'normal' (subtext: straight white European) hair. Classic victim blaming. In some part of their mind, they believed his Afro hair, which was in a common protective hairstyle, was somehow to blame for adults behaving like Neanderthals and bullying children.

One of my interviewees, who identified as mixed race, was adopted by white parents and recounts not knowing what to do with her hair growing up in Bedfordshire:

> My mum kept my hair short because she didn't know what to do with it. I had short hair until I was nine and remember being called a boy a lot. I wanted to grow it long, but I didn't know what to do with it and would have plastic combs that would just end up ripping my hair out. I didn't know how to manage it and I had no access to Afro textured hair products and would instead just use coconut oil from the Body Shop. I can't remember a time when my hair was not touched.

Years of feeling like a zoo animal and having children and adults refer to her hair as 'pubes' took a toll on this interviewee: 'As an adult, people still try to touch mine and my child's hair. So now I touch theirs. It catches them off guard, you can see them processing they are discombobulated, and they stop.'

One of my white anti-racism students asked me for help to address the continued hair touching of her mixed-heritage Black daughter who was getting increasingly upset by constant unwelcome hair touching, not just from children, but once again, adults who cannot keep their hands to themselves. The hair touching would happen several times daily and she would ask them not to touch her daughter's hair. They even had T-shirts printed for her to wear saying 'Don't touch my hair' but it didn't seem to be working, as people responding with, 'But it's so nice' would continue putting their hands in it. This obsession over Black hair and hair touching is something too many Black children have to contend with and it all comes down to what we are teaching children about difference and basic consent.

Of course, we can trace back this behaviour to when human zoos were commonplace and Black and Indigenous people were paraded around like animals for white Europeans to grope and prod and poke. This behaviour is all too familiar, and this sense of entitlement over Black girls' bodies from complete strangers is, without a doubt, learned behaviour. It is also in no way accept-able – it never was.

When I re-framed the scenario as a matter of consent and that this was a violation on her daughter's body, this automatically changed things for my student. Now, seeing her mum say 'no' without apology or pandering to white feelings has empowered her daughter to learn to say 'no' when her mother is not with her. They have since started to work on some 'scripts' to help her feel able and more confident to address the constant hair touching from younger peers.

★

A month or so after the resurgence of Black Lives Matter, a parent shared an incident with me that occurred when her 5-year-old

Black daughter had a playdate with her white friend, aged 4. Unbeknownst to the adults, the two little girls started to have their own little, but very grown-up, private conversation about their favourite book about Rosa Parks. The 4-year-old surmised the book as being about 'a lady who wanted to sit on the bus because she was tired, and the police made her get off and put her in jail.'

The 5-year-old said, 'That's not what it's about. It was about the Black lady on the bus and in the olden days, white people were mean to Black people and Black people weren't allowed to sit at the front of the bus, and she did, so they put her in jail.'

Her friend didn't say anything because she didn't hear her. The 5-year-old Black girl then got upset that her friend didn't know the truth of the story but didn't say anything about being upset because she didn't want her white friend to feel sad about the fact that she is white. This little Black girl had already learned at the tender age of 5 to maintain white dominance and to place white feelings above her own.

★

Children are literal: meet them where they are at and keep it simple. See this as an opportunity to help them think and understand someone who is different to them. Normalise and affirm difference and their observations, rather than being embarrassed by them.

For example:

Child: Look at that boy, he's a different colour. Why does that boy have hair like that?

Adult: Yes, good observation. It's really nice you are interested in that little boy. He is Black and Black people have different hair.

Child: But his skin is brown, not black.

Adult: Yes, you're right. What colour is your skin?

Child: Creamy.

Adult: Sometimes, even though our skin is creamy, we call ourselves white and sometimes even though that little boy has brown skin, we call him Black.

This honest exchange validates what the child is observing and normalises different identities, whilst also helping them to think about their own identity. Child psychologist Martha Deiros Collado suggests if a child's curiosity causes you embarrassment in public, you should breathe, pause and, if possible, get down to the child's level to communicate. Remember, by slowing everything down it gives you an opportunity to respond and not react.

Another example:

Child: Look! They're brown like poo!

Adult: That was not kind, was it?

Child: No.

Adult: Poo is not very nice, and that little girl is nice. Shall we say hello, and then have a talk about colour and nice things that are brown when we get home?

Think about the message you want to portray as an adult: panic and fear? Or empathy and compassion?

Racism in the Family

One of the reasons I centre my anti-racism work on helping people address racism in their social circles, with people they generally like, love and respect, is because that is where we have the most power to influence change. It's also because a lot of racism happens from within family units.

White supremacy does not conveniently excuse itself from the table in families; some find the notion that our own flesh and blood can be racist to us completely unfathomable. Yet more often than not, it's the people closest to us who can cause us the most harm.

'How can I be racist? I've got Black kids! My partner is Black.' Your personal proximity to Blackness does not prove you aren't racist – that's like maintaining you can't be sexist because you have a mum. No logic.

Anyone who spends energy 'proving' that they aren't racist always is – and red flags automatically go up whenever white people start a conversation by weaponising Black people closest to them to make themselves look good. Besides, history has also shown us that it's quite possible for white men to demonstrate how commonplace it was to be incredibly racist and still have no problem whatsoever having sexual 'relations' with Black women.

In one interview, a mixed Black, transracially adopted woman shared with me that, even though she had a positive adoptive experience full of love and opportunity, it left her unprepared to deal with the impact of racism.

My white parents did not have a clue about race. They had no tools to address it and I didn't always feel safe as a result. There was no talk, no positive affirmations. I never felt prepared to navigate racism. I had a lot more insight into whiteness and how that operates and was always out of sync with my own cultural identity, which I still feel today. I lived a childhood full of gaslighting from others, including my parents and, as a result, I didn't share as much with them about the frequent racism I experienced because I was worried it would go over their heads, so I just swallowed it.

She added:

Tremendous harm can be caused, and the adoption process is also one that is riddled with systemic racism that needs interrogating. But additionally, there needs to be more awareness and support for those who are transracially adopting Black children and children of colour to help give them the language to talk about race but also to ensure they themselves are actively anti-racist and 'safe'.

Another white interviewee in South West England reflected on the influence of racism from elders in the family towards her Black husband and children. Her white mother, in her 70s, still uses phrases like 'I don't see colour' and 'half-caste' (the word caste, derives from the Latin word *castus* – it literally translates as half-pure) and is not all that enthused with her anti-racism. 'She thinks we shouldn't talk to our dual-heritage children about race and that we are opening up their lives to be more difficult by talking about race, and that we should all treat each other equally, because we all bleed the same blood.'

For this interviewee, this was the moment the penny dropped. She realised her mother's words don't match her behaviour, as she's not treating her Black husband and Brown girls the same. On first meeting her husband, my interviewee's mother asked if he'd ever eaten spaghetti bolognese before. She regularly allows strangers to touch her granddaughter's hair when my interviewee is not there, resulting in her daughter not wanting to wear her hair 'out' and have braids instead, because they look more like 'normal' hair.

Another interviewee, who identified as mixed-race was raised in a single-parent home recounted:

> It was a nightmare growing up mixed race in South East London with a white mother. People almost want you to choose a side. My Black friends would constantly call me 'lightee' and say I don't understand about racism because I look racially ambiguous. I was regularly asked, 'Well, are you Black or white?' I am both.

She continued:

> My mum was always making racist comments about Black people. She hated my husband because he was Black and middle class. She couldn't believe Black people could be middle class and when we were dating, she used to call him a golliwog and me Barbie. She was jealous of our relationship, so she kicked me out of home when I was eighteen and didn't speak to me for six months. I had no money. When we got pregnant with our first baby, instead of congratulations, my mum's response was: 'I bet they're going to be ugly and have nigger hair. You better hope that baby looks like you'.

Despite all that she endured with her mother, my interviewee wanted to let me know she still loves her mum and, in fact, feels stronger now, no longer tolerates the abuse and even demonstrates empathy towards her mother.

> She was horrible to me. But I know that her behaviour comes from her own experience of being hated by her own family for getting with a Black man – they kicked her out for having a Brown baby and being a 'race traitor' in 60s and 70s Britain. And then on top of that experiencing physical, verbal and psychological abuse from her ex-husband, who was Black, for over a decade. She'll never change, that's just how she is.

When I asked her what the worst racism she had received was, she said, 'I've honestly never received racism from a white person.' Her natural protectiveness towards her mother, and perhaps her own trauma response and learned allegiance to whiteness, meant she was unable to recognise that by very definition of what she had been recounting in our interview, she had indeed experienced racism from a white person: her own mother.

★

Racism in Schools

We can see from the earlier report from the NSPCC and the Doll Test (see pages 260 and 263) that the impact of systemic and overt racism is wide-reaching in children across the UK and the globe, from nursery to school and beyond. I've heard accounts of nursery staff ignoring and leaving Black babies in dirty nappies for hours, social exclusion from white children refusing to play with Black and Brown children in the playground, to predicted grades for Black children being disproportionately marked down and teachers disproportionately putting Black students in lower sets.

In January 2020, it was reported that primary school exclusions for racism in England had increased by more than 40 per cent in just over ten years[25] and the YMCA's Young and Black study released in October 2020 confirms 95 per cent of Black young people have witnessed racist language in schools.[26] It's this persistent exposure of racism in schools that is a direct reflection of wider society. We can be lulled into a false sense of security that taking a zero-tolerance stance to racism, by simply excluding or firing the perpetrators, the few 'bad apples', will solve the problem. It doesn't and hasn't. Well, at least not in the long term. Exclusions in school might be the correct intervention in some cases, but that alone, without education, engaging children, staff and caregivers to address their behaviour, while also developing a place of belonging and keeping recipients of racism safe, will never be enough.

The stereotype that Black children of Caribbean heritage (especially boys) are just lazy and 'underachievers' because of their 'culture', stems from the discriminatory 'dumping' of Black children, predominantly of parents from the Windrush generation, that took place in ESN schools until 1980. But it didn't stop then. In his book, *Natives: Race and Class in the Ruins of Empire*, Akala recounts his own experience in the 90s of being 'dumped', without his mother's knowledge or consent, into an SEN class alongside children with extreme learning difficulties at the age of 7. [27] It would seem his clear appetite for learning and intelligence, instead of making his teachers at the time proud and inspired to nurture his gift, seemed to wind them up, to the point where one teacher in particular no longer wanted Akala in her class. In addition, in a lecture about racial discrimination in schools by Neil Mayers, author of *Gifted at Primary and Failing at Secondary*, I learned that if your child is a Black boy on free school meals with a Special Educational Need (such as dyslexia or autism) and/or Disability (SEND), they are currently 168 times more likely to be excluded from schools than their fellow white British girl without an SEND, rather than be given the actual support that they need. [28]

The exposure to racism can start when children are babies and the accumulative impacts of racism lead to social suffering. This impacts mental health, truancy, ability to contribute in the classroom, non-compliance or overcompliance ('the model minority' or 'the good Black person'). Instead of addressing possible roots of disruptive behaviour in Black boys who may be experiencing continued exposure to racial trauma, we're quick to socially exclude. They're set apart instead of teachers investigating how a learning environment may be adverse and building a safe classroom to study without exposure to social suffering. As such, the impact of discrimination in the 60s and 70s still plagues Black children into young adulthood, with Black Caribbean pupils permanently excluded at three times the rate of white British pupils. And students excluded from school by the age of 12 are four times more likely to be imprisoned by the time they are 24.

★

In 2017, students at St Winefride's Catholic Primary School in East London were asked to come to school wearing dirty worn-out, tea-stained clothes to dress up as slaves for a 'special' Black History Month assembly. This reveals how the regular depictions of Black people throughout our diverse history are limited to us either being dead, in poverty or experiencing trauma. Yes, we need to hear all parts of history, but there needs to be balance. This school could have chosen to share exciting Black History featuring their local area, inventors, or the incredible contributions of nurses or engineers from the Windrush Generation. If they had wanted to centre this history of slavery, how about the incredible resilience of Black enslaved people, of warrior women and abolitionists like Nanny of the Maroons? We are continuously dehumanised when there is no balance, and it continues to communicate that we are victims and less than. More to the point, imagine for a moment the impact this shame-inducing activity could have on Black children in the school.

Shaming activities don't just exist in primary schools. In May 2020, a parent alerted me to the fact her son had been asked by his Bedfordshire senior school to debate that there is no racism in the UK and to do a PowerPoint presentation on it. Debate suggests there is more than one possible outcome. There isn't. Racism is a form of trauma. It's hard to imagine teachers would have the audacity to ask young people to debate any other kind of persistent trauma rooted in physical, verbal and systematic abuse. Imagine the impact this would have on impressionable Black and non-Black students who experience racism? This is another example of the by-product of white people being historically desensitised to Black pain.

A Black couple in Luton shared with me how they travel thirty miles to take their 2-year-old Black boy to a Black-run Montessori nursery with skilled and nurturing teachers. Their son was previously at a private school and was told he had behavioural problems. Thanks to my research and interviews, I can tell you that this is not an isolated incident. With some time and nurturing at the Montessori school, it turned out their little boy had a mild speech delay and is now getting on well and speaking in full sentences. As it turns out, schools in the couple's borough have shocking outcomes for Black boys.

I interviewed a father raising two Black boys and he shared about the number of times staff butcher his sons' names or muddle them up with the only other two Black children in their class. How can you feel included if your teacher of a number of years still hasn't taken the time to learn your name, or can't even identify you? Names are important, and you must understand the historical significance of enslaved Black people having their names taken and anglicised by slavers. Understand the significance of having to anglicise one's name in order to assimilate. To have to change your name to avoid the humiliation of having to consistently correct it, or have it shortened by teachers or managers for their comfort.

How children feel and are made to feel about themselves in educational settings has a direct impact on their behaviour, attainment and ability to succeed. If a child is in a nurturing environment, they are much more able to thrive. Shame resilience expert Adéwale Adenije spoke to me about the importance of belonging:

'All humans are wired for connection. We need it to survive, and children are hypersensitive to belonging and connection.

It's so important to teach children that being different does not mean otherness.'

For early years formation, celebrating children's identity and what makes them unique is vital. Improving representation in toys and books is the bare minimum we should be doing to help children feel like they belong in their educational settings. From intentionally seeking out books for home and libraries where the protagonists are Black in stories that aren't just about racism and trauma, to ensuring crayons, and plasters in your first aid kit are also 'flesh-coloured' for Black and Brown children too.

Interrogate what is being taught and who is being celebrated in the histories your child is learning. Get involved, especially if you have a child at an Academy School, because Academy Schools are publicly funded, independent schools and, in theory, there is more freedom over curricula. Ask what is being taught on the curriculum, challenge it and make recommendations for holistic and inclusive changes. Demand and seek out better representation of teaching staff that is reflective of wider society. Teaching children to celebrate difference over sameness is also vital. How can you bring in food or music to do this?

Educating yourself and inviting parents and caregivers into anti-racism work is key to making schools a safe place where all children feel valued and worthy of celebration.

Courageous Conversations with Children

One of the things I love about children is how uncomplicated and straight to the point they are. But their straight talking can trigger shame and or embarrassment in us, leaving us feeling winded or on the back foot where we don't always know what to do or say in the moment. Make a conscious choice, because children are watching us. What behaviour and message about race do you want to role-model to children? Empathy and compassion, or embarrassment and panic?

We're human, conversations about race or experiences of racism can and will catch us off guard – they still catch me off-guard and I am an educator. If this happens, please don't beat yourself up. Pause, slow your breathing down and get back into a state where you can respond rather than react. Children are watching how we navigate race and, right now, what they're witnessing is a bit of a shitshow.

It's also really important to revisit conversations and experiences that are left unresolved with children, so we don't leave children feeling confused or filling in the gaps. We must provide them with an opportunity to explore what is happening and give them the language and tools to help them make sense of it. If something happens when you are outside of the home, or it's not appropriate, or it catches you off guard in the moment, providing them (and you!) an opportunity to have a further conversation or to ask questions afterwards, if they would like to, can really help support them. It also gives you some thinking time.

Tools to revisit a conversation:

- 'Remember when you asked me about X? I didn't really know what to say, so shall we talk about it a little bit now?'
- 'I understand why you said that and that you were curious about their skin colour. I wonder how pointing at them and

saying that made them feel? Do you think it might have made them feel sad? I wonder when you may have felt a bit like this?'
- 'I wonder if you see someone who looks a bit different to you again what you might say? Shall we try that instead?'

In an interview with clinical psychologist Chantell Douglas, she explained to me that it is important children feel able to talk about what is happening in their world; to have both their internal feelings and external experiences named and validated to help them understand. This is vital for their emotional wellbeing and social development.

Don't punish young children who are already exhibiting overt racism – that ultimately won't change outcomes, and won't make whatever they have learned from adults, or the feelings they experience, go away. Yes, there needs to be accountability, but this behaviour also needs to be interrogated.

If you role-model vulnerability rather than trying to be some kind of messiah who knows everything, it teaches children empathy, compassion, curiosity and again, that it is okay not to know. It also teaches them the full range of being human – that we are not perfect, that we get it wrong and hurt people sometimes. More importantly, we are not our behaviour – we can learn and do something about it. The more you address your own shame around racism, the less triggered you will become about a child's innocent curiosity or confusion about race.

Racism, sadly, remains a part of society. It is also a huge part of history – so we should be able to speak about it with the freedom and honesty that we do about other parts of history. If you want to try to tackle conversations about systemic racism but the subject feels like too big of a bite, reframe systemic racism as 'fairness and unfairness' and find age-appropriate examples to demonstrate, such as allowing one child to have all the toys and another child to only have one. You could even reference the 'Blue eyes/Brown eyes' exercise by anti-racism advocate and teacher Jane Elliott, where children with blue eyes were treated less favourably than children with brown eyes. Children quickly start to develop a moral sense of justice and hate unfairness – start from there.

Challenging Racism with Children in Public

I purposefully haven't given you many examples of how to address overt racism, because it's easier to spot and, therefore, tackle. Nonetheless, I want to share an experience one of my white students encountered.

Whilst seated on a train, she witnessed a young Black boy and his father enter a train carriage. It was fairly busy with a few free seats. The father asked if his boy could sit on a spare seat on the train next to two white women, one of whom had her bag placed on the seat. She protested and said she didn't want them sitting next to her. Shortly after, she allowed another white passenger to sit there without protest. A heated exchange between the father and the women ensued. My client intervened and gave the little boy (who was becoming very upset) her seat. A little boy who had just experienced racism. My student confronted the women about their racist behaviour towards the child and his father. Her courage then inspired other passengers to speak up, who soon took a stand to call out these women for their 'blatant racism' and others who were sitting next to them who, in small protest, got up and sat on the floor instead.

My student asked the father if there was anything he needed or anyone she could call. She then started talking with the little boy, who was visibly scared. The boy told her he was on his way to a birthday party. They started to talk about Avengers, his favourite superheroes, and he eventually calmed down. He may remember that incident of racism – but he may also remember the nice lady on the train who talked to him about Avengers too.

My student was following this simple formula:

1. **Challenge.** She felt safe enough to challenge the behaviour in the moment.
2. **Move.** She moved the survivors of racism away from harm and gave up her seat.
3. **Offer support.** She provided a distraction and asked if there was any more she could do.

The behaviour could also have been reported to the British Transport Police and station staff. Recording racist incidents on a mobile phone can also be extremely helpful because survivors of racism are so often not believed or not taken seriously. For example, in 2019, senior paralegal Jackson Yamba and his 10-year-old son moved into their new home in Salford and after five days, came home to the graffiti 'no Blacks, no Blacks' spray-painted on their door. [29] Jackson immediately reported the hate crime to Greater Manchester Police, took several images and left the graffiti on the door. Over a week later, appalled that he still had not heard from the police, Jackson shared the image of his front door online and instantly got media attention which seemed to prompt police action.

What does this communicate? Not only the act of racism, but the lack of swift action from the police. Your lives don't matter. Jackson's son was left traumatised and afraid to leave the house. Our children are watching and quickly observe who is valued in society, who is protected in society and who isn't and where they fall within that.

It can also be useful to film if you witness a stop and search happening to a young person by the police that you suspect may be an abuse of power:

1. Risk assess
2. Film
3. Remain safe and respectful
4. Keep your distance
5. Communicate

Let the young person and police know you are there witnessing and filming. Some police may get wound up by being filmed, but the public do not need a permit to film or photograph in public and the police have no power to stop you filming or photographing incidents or police personnel, such as badge numbers and registration plates.

Post-search you could:

1. Let the young person know they can request a receipt from the police for the stop and search (evidence for reporting).
2. Check they are OK.
3. Ask if you can offer further support or call someone.

4. Report it to organisations like stop-watch.org that advocate for fair and accountable policing and also provide guides for parents, caregivers and teachers to tackle disproportionate use of stop-and-search powers.

Raising Black Children and Children of Colour

Positive affirmations can support emotional wellbeing and are especially important for children to help build their self-esteem. If you are raising Black children or children of colour, building resilience, self-esteem, empowerment and ownership over identity are vital in counteracting exposure to racist projections. This helps build their sense of self and, in undoing any negative self-perception. Affirmations can also help children become more aware of their feelings.

Nicola Rae-Wickham, parent and founder of A Life More Inspired, swears by positive affirmations and has created cards for adults and children and says:

> Affirmations have helped increase my daughter's self-confidence and self-worth. I use affirmations with my daughters to help set in motion beliefs and thoughts which carry an alternative narrative of truth. A truth that Black children both need and deserve. One of our favourites is: 'I am more than enough; I believe in myself and my dreams.

One parent, Nuna, shared how she and her husband Kenrick take an approach to raising three kind-hearted, confident and socially conscious Black children. They centre positive affirmations within their day-to-day and started teaching the children affirmations from as young as they could talk. Each affirmation is reinforced with a physical action.

The affirmations evolved as they got older, and they noticed the children started getting extra hard on themselves when they made mistakes. Their daughter started feeling guilty when she got something wrong or lost her temper at her two brothers. Feeling like she was bad and not good. And they realised their words of empowerment had left no room for error. Worried it was breeding perfectionism, they adapted their affirmations to encompass how to recover from failure and gave them permission to make mistakes. The affirmations they created are:

- I am strong.
- I am confident.
- I am smart.
- I am funny.
- I am loving.
- I am beautiful inside and out.
- I am going to make mistakes but it's OK, as long as I try my best.

It's also important to find safe spaces for children in their community whether those are Black history classes, community events, positive role models online and offline, or with family where they have the opportunity to centre the parts of their identity and culture that are othered. Reinforce the fact that, even if they are 'the only' one like them in their class, or their hair is different to the majority of their peers, they are worthy. Their hair is beautiful. Share stories of incredible African warriors and goddesses whose hair was often sacred and intricate hairstyles were used to communicate social ranking, or braids were even used as an act of resistance to communicate escape maps.[30] There is so much glory in the history of Afro-textured hair – help them learn it and celebrate it.

If you are white and raising or supporting Black children or children of colour, reassure them and demonstrate that you are a safe space for them. Show that they can share experiences of racism with you and be heard without being gaslit, shamed or silenced. Or if you say something that is racist, they can tell you and are encouraged to address racism without being shut down and having to deal with your shame spiral or fear of upsetting your white feelings.

One of the young Black boys of the parents I interviewed, aged 10, wanted to share some ideas too:

> If someone is mean to me at school because of my race, I will tell them not to be scared. I would talk to them and show them I am just "me" and just play games with them. If they weren't friendly, I would stay away or tell a teacher.

Such wisdom, yet so simple.

★

Shame is deeply linked to feelings of not being loved, not belonging, being abandoned and like you are inherently flawed. Founder of OutTales, shame resilience expert and one of my podcast guests, Adéwale Adeniji, spoke about his experience moving to the UK from Nigeria when his parents voluntarily put him into foster care at 8 weeks old. He grew up in Kent, with white foster parents and their children until he was 6 years old. The need to belong was ever-present and manifested in two significant instances. The first was when his foster mother was painting a wall white. She came back in to find that Adéwale had painted his body white, saying, 'Now I am a white boy.' The second incident was when he watched his foster mother bleaching the toilet and he asked her what she was doing. She replied: 'I am cleaning the toilet so it will be nice and white.' Moments later, he ingested the bleach.

Adéwale felt a fear of abandonment and a strong sense of that need to belong throughout his adulthood, trying to fit in and losing fragments of himself along the way. Environments where we don't foster belonging can be a breeding ground for shame. A child's desire to belong is vital for psychological wellbeing. Shame can show up when we feel abandoned, or like we don't belong, and can sometimes lead to unhealthy and destructive behaviours, including addiction. As adults, we know how shame makes us feel, how painful it can be and how it can make us feel childlike and small. We don't want to intentionally do that, especially not to children who are bound to make mistakes while trying to make sense of big, overwhelming feelings and their external world. It is especially important not to shame Black and Brown children who may be feeling shame or showing signs of self-hate because of who they cannot help but be. Don't be afraid to consider seeking proactive support from a certified child psychologist or therapist who is also anti-racist.

If shame is a by-product of doing or saying something, encourage children to talk about it. If they get it wrong, let them know that you love them anyway. If they make poor choices, teach them about consequences, responsibility, accountability and making better choices while reinforcing that you love them. Let them speak about what is causing them shame and big feelings; allow them to reflect and, if necessary, apologise. If age-appropriate, give them ownership, allow them to elicit some of their own ideas what they can do differently next time.

OK so let's re-cap and wrap it up.

1. Use age-appropriate language
2. Remove emotion and keep it factual
3. Claim your identity – normalise talking about your own skin colour as a part of your identity
4. Own your vulnerability – if you freeze when a child exhibits racial bias in the moment, revisit and own your feelings.
5. Don't bombard – keep it simple and keep it open for them to go away and come back and ask you more at another time, adding depth when they get older and develop more emotional intelligence
6. Get creative – like my interviewee's family who loves art and used paint to explain why they are different colours.
7. Cultivate empathy and kindness – 'What must that feel like if people don't play with them? That must be lonely.' 'What might you do if you see that happening again?'
8. Teach children to value people who are different to them, especially those who are undervalued in society and role-model this by how you treat others, especially Black people, who are, for example, homeless, living with disability and in service roles

9. Use books, TV programmes and diverse toys as tools to discuss topics and opportunities for learning about general difference via current affairs to help your children to start to understand the diversity and difference of people and viewpoints in the world around them as a normal way of life

10. Provide reassurance and sensitivity – if you notice your child starts to obsessively point out visible differences in the moment, reassure them that difference is normal i.e. 'We don't always have to point out differences as it may start to hurt people's feelings. If you had a bump on your head or a pimple and people kept pointing it out, how might that make you feel?'

11. Expose them to books and characters that may help them deepen their understanding of children different to them, whilst encouraging them to understand more about their own identity

12. Create a safe and neutral place at home or school where children can come back to conversations about race and difference in a non-judgemental setting so you can both be vulnerable and curious

13. Provide opportunity for reflection – What do you think of that? What could you do? Who can you tell if you see racism or hear unkind words at school? How do you think that friend would feel if they heard you say that? Was that kind? Give them time space to think, process and come back and ask questions.

14. Practise – How can you use current affairs, music, magazines, TV programmes to start encouraging children to

notice diversity and talk about difference and give them tools to recognise in the moment?

15. Stay curious and keep it moving – children will zone out when they've had enough so treat this as an ongoing and evolving conversation, just like with adults. That's the beauty of being human with a limitless opportunity to learn and grow, we are never done.

16. If your default response to a child's innocent question about skin colour is shame, embarrassment or panic, then that is a clear signal. You need to lean into this work, unpeel more layers and do more self-enquiry, because that's where you will role-model the biggest change for the next generation.

While I have shared some suggestions and notes on the importance of building self-esteem, resilience and a positive sense of racial identity for children of colour, I cannot do this topic full justice in one chapter, so please seek out further resources. Given the nature of this book, I have intentionally focused the majority of this chapter on parents and caregivers of children with some form of white skin privilege. If you are raising or working with Black or Brown children who are experiencing frequent occurrences of racism at school and you are worried about their wellbeing, please involve your school, the governor and/or guidance counsellor. Racism is a public health issue and schools should be treating it as such. Find local or online support groups, speak to your local doctor who may be able to offer wellbeing support services in the area that promote psychological wellbeing, seek out environments that centre their identity, boost confidence and resilience and, if you have the means, engage a conscious therapist privately.

Resources

Young Minds:
   www.youngminds.org

Childline:
   www.childline.org.uk
NSPCC:
   https://www.nspcc.org.uk/keeping-children-safe/support-for-parents/children-race-racism-racial-bullying/

Consider seeking emotional and psychological support from a child psychologist or therapist who is anti-racist (some I have referenced throughout this chapter) – do not underestimate the impact of racism in children.

Counsellors and Psychotherapists in the Black community can be found here – BAATN: Black African and Asian Therapy Network: https://www.baatn.org.uk/ Black Minds Matter www.Blackmindsmatteruk.com

And if it warrants it, contact the police for advice on dealing with hate crime online or in person and follow companies like Glitch for advice on staying safe online: https://fixtheglitch.org

10. Brokering Change: Tackling Racism at Work

'Without inner change there can be no outer change.
Without collective change, no change matters.'

REV. ANGEL KYODO WILLIAMS[1]

Racism at work has a particular kind of flavour. Subtle. Invisible to most, perhaps even charming to some, but almighty in its power. Outwardly, it can look like a smiling portrait from a United Colours of Benetton advert; impressive mission statements and slick inclusion and belonging policies. But underneath the veneer, you start to notice those smiles are, in fact, grimaces. Racism at work winds you, disarms you and slowly strips away self-esteem. It rips the very essence of who you are out, throws it on the ground, stamps on it and then blames you for it. Workplace racism is the kind of racism that knocks your confidence, requires you to anglicise your name, and blocks career progression. The kind of racism that undermines, micromanages and regularly masquerades itself as office banter or seemingly harmless behaviour that others and fetishes you at after work socials.

Whatever the guise, if you try to challenge workplace racism, it has you branded a troublemaker or 'difficult' and when you don't, it has you regularly questioning your sanity, or just swallowing frequent occurrences through fear of being outcast, or worse, losing your job.

My first memory of experiencing racism at work, was aged 16, working in retail. I remember being woken up on my day off and being summoned to come to the store, after money had gone missing from the till. I was essentially being accused of stealing, even though the day money went missing from the till I wasn't even working. The CCTV, which they had failed to watch before hauling me in, identified the culprit. The second instance of racism, in the same job, was indirect. We were advertising for a new role for a store assistant. I was helping my white manager close the shop and count the takings. While I was doing that, she started to look through CVs that had been handed in throughout the day. She paused on one and started to fumble pronouncing the name before saying 'What kind of ridiculous name is that? If I can't pronounce it then they're not getting an interview.' She threw the CV in the bin – that was the extent of her interview criteria. Perhaps unsurprisingly, given my age, her seniority over me and the fact that I was Black, I did and said nothing. I felt pretty ashamed about it, so much so it's a memory that has stuck to this very day.

Fear of retribution is a common barrier to tackling racism at work. I can attest to that and it came up time and time again in my book interviews and reiterated by the results from Pearn Kandola's Racism at Work study that reports Black or Asian people are least likely to report instances of racism through fear of repercussions.[2] It's easy to churn out inclusion and belonging statements, but they are meaningless if so many staff continue to experience workplace racism and feel unable to bring issues forward. As long as there is an undercurrent of fear at work, racism will continue to be reproduced.

There is generally zero tolerance for *overt* racism at work. Most people know that if they are caught engaging in overt racist behaviour in their place of work, they are likely to lose their job and potentially face charges for inciting racial hatred. Nonetheless, people don't just suddenly shed their racism when they go to work. Instead, it becomes coded. It shows up in non-verbal and verbal behaviour and impacts outcomes, culture, relationships and, for the most part, remains unaddressed.

So how has everyday racism in the workplace become so normalised at work?

★

Racism at Work: Where it All Began

It's hard to believe this but it was not a crime to commit race discrimination in public in Britain as recently as 1965. It was perfectly lawful to refuse my mum or dad work because of their skin colour. It was also a free for all for police brutality and violence on the street. No repercussions, no consequences, not unlawful.[3]

This is what activists mean when we talk about racism as the messy combination of discrimination, prejudice and power. All of this and more allowed the colour bars on Oxford Street to be possible and for employers like Transport for London and Bristol

Omnibus Company to refuse to employ Black or South Asian staff in the 60s because of skin pigmentation.[4]

Civil rights activists in Britain, including Dame Joycelyn Barrow, DBE who co-founded Campaign Against Racial Discrimination with four hundred members, successfully lobbied to make race discrimination illegal, and the Race Relations Act was introduced in 1965.[5] The Act made it illegal to discriminate based on race, colour, ethnicity or national origins in public – the key word being 'public'.[6] This meant racism continued at work, and that employers could continue to refuse work to Black and Brown people. Landlords could continue to refuse housing or charge four times the rate for rat-infested accommodation; even pubs could continue to refuse to serve Black and Brown folk and signs on doors and windows reading 'no coloured' or in the infamous 'no Blacks, no Irish, no dogs' were commonplace.[7] We were seen as and treated as second-class citizens and the law didn't just allow it, it enabled it. Unsurprisingly, the Act the government passed wasn't fit for purpose and, in fact, the Act was totally distorted by police. The first five out of the six convicted under the Act were Black people accused of inciting racial hatred, against white people.[8]

A revision of the Act came in 1968, which really seemed to agitate Conservative MP Enoch Powell. In his 'Rivers of Blood' speech he named the revision of this act, 'dangerous and divisive' and a 'campaign against fellow [white] citizens'.[9] It sparked widespread resistance and defensive fears from MPs and the British public, who felt that introducing a bill would essentially give 'immigrants' unfair rights and encourage a compensation culture.

In a Parliamentary debate discussing the bill on 23 April 1968

Barrister and Conservative MP Sir Ronald Bell said:

'Suppose that now a coloured man wants to buy a house and he is not able to buy it. He will be disappointed; he may suspect it is because he is a coloured man, but he will not be sure, and the matter will probably end there. If the Bill becomes law, he may be tempted by the prospect of damages to make a complaint and then, if there is held to be a prima facie case, the seller will be dragged through the conciliation procedure. The seller will cave in at that point and sign a somewhat humiliating document. He will probably agree, indeed he may be forced to agree, to sell the house to the complainant. If he does not, he will go through the court procedure that I have described. In that case that man, his family, his neighbours and his friends will all be deeply resentful for ever. The coloured man will for the first time have taken a formal hostile step against the native community, with psychological consequences which will remain with him for ever. It is the accumulation over the months and years of thousands of such cases that builds up the tensions from which a flash of violence comes. It is necessary to know what is in store for us in the Bill'[10]

Conservative MP Sir Dudley Smith said:

'I have been told, by a personnel manager, who is extremely worried and who is by no means a racialist, that if, in the course of many weeks, he turns down too many coloured people who fall below his usual acceptable standards, he will have the humiliation of being taken before the Race Relations Board and then possibly be prosecuted, and his firm with him.'[11]

The 1968 revision was eventually passed after complaints about how inadequate the 1965 Act was at actually protecting people from racial discrimination, with over 70 per cent of cases falling outside of what the Act outlined as racial discrimination.[12] Employers simply just denied accusations of race discrimination, as many still do today.[13] The new revision finally made it illegal to refuse work, housing or public services to someone because of their race.[14] But the 1968 Act, unsurprisingly, given the resistance to enforce it, remained insufficient, and racism remained rampant.[15] It didn't recognise indirect racial discrimination, nor did it give an individual rights to go to civil courts or sue an employer for racism at work. This came with a later revision in 1976 that was only instated as a by-product of joining the European Union.

To become a member of the EU at the time, gender equality law was an EU Directive, therefore it was mandatory for countries to have a sex discrimination law to protect people from sexual harassment at work.[16] Britain passed the Sex Discrimination Act in 1975 and, strangely enough, it didn't seem to incite the same resistance as the Race Relations Act, or the same fear of giving too many people unfair rights to sue, even though, there were far more women than Black people in Britain.

The government later passed the 1976 Race Relations Act, which for the first time gave employees the right to sue for race discrimination in court or at industrial (employment) tribunal, but only within three months from when the race discrimination happened.[17]

The Race Relations Act was created at the height of civil unrest; these laws still did not protect human rights for Black and Brown folk, and it's difficult to believe they were ever designed to. For example, even in the 1980s, the police remained protected from these laws. Former Metropolitan Police detective Peter Bleksley, in an interview for BBC Radio 4's *The Reunion*, described how, 'being racist was compulsory in the force.'[18] He shared how commonplace it was in the 80s for police officers to take it in turns to beat up Black men, arrest them for petty crime and torture them to admit to crimes they didn't commit. They would also rip off Rastafarians' dreadlocks and stick them on noticeboards.[19] Police would do this without repercussions because they were protected by law. The Race Relations Act did not apply to the police and other public authorities until it was amended again in 2000, thanks to the tireless campaigning of (yes, another Black woman) Baroness Doreen Lawrence.[20] Baroness Lawrence's son was murdered by racists, and the Met tried to make her family suspects of his death.[21] Are you understanding the full extent of what systemic racism looks like here? It is embedded in law.

The UK's Crown Prosecution Service does not come out unscathed either. It paid out a record-breaking race and sex discrimination settlement of £250,000 to Maria Bamieh and a further twenty-two race discrimination allegations that followed. As a result, the late Sylvia Denman, an academic lawyer, undertook a private investigation and after an 18-month inquiry, found the CPS to be institutionally racist across all services at work in a report produced in 2001.[22] She also found white managers failed to promote ethnic minority lawyers. It would seem racism continues to be reproduced, even by barristers who are there to uphold the rule of the law.

Barrister Alexandra Wilson, in her book *In Black and White*, recounts regular experiences of being mistaken as a defendant in court. She recounts racism as a trainee barrister too and, on one occasion, being approached by a senior white male barrister who told her that 'whilst lower crime rates were "bad for business", the Black community has helped [barristers] out by killing each other.'[23] It seemed to go over his head that Alexandra is, in fact, part of the Black community. In September 2020, she made a complaint to Her Majesty's Courts and Tribunals Service after being mistaken as a defendant on three different occasions in just one day and, at one point, being told loudly to get out of court by a clerk.[24]

This is a human rights issue. It shows the power of law and equally, how little changes at work and in society if mindsets do not change. I don't write this to leave you feeling despondent. (I told you this is big work, not for the fainthearted.) I write this to raise awareness of our reality, because I have come to understand the magnitude of what these employment laws mean. Laws designed to protect human rights actually only protect some and discriminate against others. I write this so that you understand the gravitas of what we are dealing with, why it matters and the important, pivotal and powerful role you play in it.

Systemic Racism and Employment Law: What Lies Beneath

In an interview with leading UK employment lawyers Equal Justice Solicitors, founder Lawrence Davies explained that racial harassment at work has doubled to 31 per cent in the last three years.[25] This is up from 16 per cent in 2017 with outcomes at employment tribunals worse than ever – only 1 per cent are successful.[26] The average award at tribunal for race discrimination cases is approximately £12,000 – a pay-out more than 50 per cent less than the cost of legal expenses, which on average are £30,000. So in layman's terms, if you take a race discrimination case to tribunal and you're part of the 1 per cent who win, you still end up in debt.

There is no financial benefit for employees to take a case to tribunal and there is no financial incentive for employers to take racism seriously. If you have a senior member of staff who is racially abusive to staff, but they're seen as an asset to the company because they bring in several million pounds in sales per year, why would they want to let them go? A £12,000 pay-out and a removal of the member of staff raising the grievance would, let's face it, be far more appealing to any employer who cares more about the bottom line than people.

What is most devastating is that, under current law, if you experience general deliberate bullying and harassment (not based on race or other types of discrimination) – for example, by a landlord or a cyberbully – you have up to three years from the date of the incident to claim. Similarly, if you have an accident at work or a personal injury, you have three years to claim. If you experience racial discrimination at work? Three months, minus one day. This is the same three-month caveat that was enforced when the Race Relations Act was finally amended in 1976 to give employees the right to sue for racism, when race relations in Britain were toxic. The Act also places the onus on survivors of racism to prove that it happened; to prove that the perpetrator was consciously or unconsciously motivated. In contrast, for an employer to enforce a misconduct case a manager doesn't have to prove an employee did commit misconduct, but they do have to have a 'genuine belief an employee is guilty of misconduct'.[27] A mere genuine belief.

This is the birthplace of why so many Black and Brown people and Non-Black People of Colour are automatically disbelieved when they bring forth race grievances: this incessant obsession with gathering receipts. This is why so few make it to employment tribunal and when the rare few do, only a fraction are successful. When someone who experiences racial abuse feels fear so powerfully that they do not feel able to exercise their basic human rights because their employer would rather protect their brand credibility, we have reached a low point.

Davies also explained that if someone experiences sexual harassment and has their case upheld in tribunal, under current employment law, they have a right to reinstatement. What that means is that if you win a sex discrimination claim, and you were unfairly dismissed, you can have your pay backdated, or if you choose, be re-employed. If you are one of the rare few to win a race discrimination case and were unfairly dismissed, you are *not* entitled to have your pay backdated or potential reinstatement. This is what systemic racism looks like and is why your allyship and advocacy is urgent.

Coded Racism and Office Politics

I first started to experience coded racism at work with the usual obsession with my hair, regularly being mistaken as a secretary or note-taker in meetings, and strange water cooler conversations, like being asked if my husband is Black because 'I don't sound

Black'. But it became more persistent when I received a promotion. My change in job title and elevation in terms of responsibility and pay grade seemed to agitate others.

I didn't realise that what I was experiencing back then was racism, but I recognised I was being regularly targeted and treated differently to my peers. The fact that I was elevated and given more responsibility without receiving a pay rise was an early part of the oh-so-common lesson of pay inequity and extraction. When I did pluck up the courage to push for one (and it wasn't much because back then, I didn't believe I was worthy of much), it took months. I had to jump through hoops to get it signed off and was accused of being 'like a dog with a bone' for having the audacity to ask for pay that reflected the extra work and training I had to undergo to take it on.

The more I started to garner more public recognition for my contributions by senior leaders, the worse the behaviour became. As well as being micromanaged, I was excluded from social gatherings and had my career progress blocked with projects that were verbally agreed, then halted after a sudden change of heart. My manager refused to sign off training because, in their own words, it would mean I 'would be more qualified' than them. This persisted for years and utterly corroded my confidence and mental health.

The Trades Union Congress (TUC) 'Dying on the Job' report, published in 2020, revealed that most staff who experience racism said the perpetrators were 'direct managers or someone else with direct authority'.[28] The 2017 NatCen 'British Social Attitudes' survey revealed 26 per cent of respondents 'described themselves as "very" or "a little" racially prejudiced' (and many more are undoubtedly still in denial).[29] Of course, we're going to come into contact with racism from managers at work, so it's no surprise so few report it. So many (understandably) fear retribution.

After a number of years, I decided to raise a grievance. I had pages and pages of evidence, notes and witness statements of harassment. When I finally felt able to report it to HR, I was dissuaded from lodging a formal grievance because 'they hadn't used the policy before' and that 'I might make things worse'. What is the point of spending so much money and time drawing up anti-racism, bullying and harassment policies if we are to be punished or dissuaded from using a fair and due process in a policy created to protect staff? Of course, I did what I was told and the behaviour continued.

My experiences were echoed by the many interviews I held for this book. Black and Brown staff regularly told me of being frequently overloaded with work outside of their roles for which they are not financially compensated. This could be because we are more likely to be deemed as 'subservient' (a common adaptive behaviour both taken on and assumed by people in South Asian, East and South-East Asian and Black communities), to not have our wellbeing considered because dominant groups have been socialised to seeing us working our fingers to the bone, being expected to be strong and able to cope. We're also more likely to 'do as we're told' through fear of repercussions if we say no.

Out of 23,000 university professors in the UK, only 1 per cent are Black.[30] Dr Nicola Rollock's 2019 'Staying Power' report, commissioned by University College Union, explores the experiences of twenty of the twenty-five Black women professors in the UK. It highlights a common culture of disproportionate workloads and undermining and bullying towards these academics.[31] One interviewee, who works in academia, also reported regularly being asked to take on extra work, impacting their ability to complete their own PhD and experiencing regular burnout. They also felt the need to provide support for the Black and Brown students who were not being adequately supported by white supervisors.

Another more coded type of racism was shared with me by an interviewee left humiliated after he brought in sweet treats and food relevant to his culture for colleagues to enjoy and celebrate his birthday. The food got left in the staff kitchen stale, untouched, for a week. Every time he went to the kitchen it was a reminder of his difference. He ended up having to throw the treats in the bin.

Coded racism impacts outcomes and exists in creative and intimate working relationships too, the kind of racism that exposes pay inequity, like in June 2020, when the media campaign #publishingpaidme highlighted racial pay disparities in publishing, with white authors being offered significantly larger book deals than 'BIPOC' authors. The kind of racism that assumes Black authors, as decided by predominantly white publishing teams, won't write books that sell or that there isn't a market for their work. This not only leads to continued under-representation in the publishing industry, but it contributes to an industry that is inexperienced and ill-equipped to support, provide safe spaces for, and market Black talent.

We've explored various examples of racism in healthcare throughout this book. A study by NHS England shows racism at work has worsened since 2016. With 29 per cent of Black, Asian and Ethnic Minority staff reporting to have experienced racism bullying and harassment from within the NHS, with some staff who also experienced bullying from their managers.[32]

If a manager has a penchant for bullying Black, Asian and Ethnic Minority staff, how do you think that might impact behaviour, choices and outcomes? Who are you more likely to overload with work and put on COVID wards with more patients and increase their risk to viral load, and who are you more likely to protect? How might that impact the numbers of Black Asian and Ethnic Minority NHS staff disproportionately dying of COVID?[33]

In February 2021, a white nurse won an employment tribunal after witnessing racist bullying and highlighting that Black colleagues on a children's hospital ward were being given more work than white staff. She was told by managers to 'be a good citizen' and stop talking about the issue. She didn't. She was subsequently removed from the ward, victimised and investigated for misconduct. She raised a formal complaint about the race discrimination she witnessed and received a £26,000 pay-out.[34]

Another issue that came up often was racism passed off as 'office banter'. In June 2020, three police officers in the Cambridgeshire constabulary were reprimanded for a WhatsApp group made up of predominately white constables, featuring racist remarks in response to an image being shared of a Black actor Kayode Ewumi. One wrote the word 'monkey' underneath while another laughed. A complaint was raised by one ethnic minority officer in the group. Those responsible explained their racist banter in the chat as just 'harmless fun'.[35]

In December 2020, it was reported (thanks to an electronic bug being planted) that six police officers in an organised crime unit in Hampshire regularly made racist remarks, wishing death on foreigners and referred to part of the office where a Black officer was situated as the 'Africa corner'. When the tribunal confirmed they were guilty of gross misconduct, one of the officers shouted, 'This is an absolute disgrace. It is absolutely ridiculous. Unbelievable.'[36] He clearly saw no issue with his or his colleague's behaviour. But what allowed this behaviour and culture to run rampant for years? Why did an electronic bug need to be placed for allegations of racism to be believed?

This 'harmless banter' doesn't disappear when the police put on their uniform, and no doubt has a direct impact on how they interact with the very communities they are dehumanising in their WhatsApp chats. Taking into consideration the continued disproportionate stop and searches of Black men to the disproportionate deaths of Black people in police custody that we have explored earlier. Do you think police who spend their spare time making monkey jokes and wishing death on 'foreigners' are more or less likely to treat people from within these communities with respect and due process?

It should be no surprise that racism is so present in the workplace – it's where so many of us spend so much of our time, but there is a lot more to it than that. Racism remaining unaddressed or being swallowed in fear of retribution or being disbelieved, alongside our very patchy inception of employment law has meant racism at work has become institutionalised.

As a bare minimum, employers have a legal duty to provide safe working environments and those who don't are, in fact, breaking the law.[37] They have a duty of care to provide a healthy and safe working environment free from bullying and harassment – not just ergonomic furniture and meeting physical accessibility needs, but psychological safety. That doesn't mean it's a workplace free from challenge or difficult conversations, but somewhere we are treated with respect rather than 'being tolerated'; one where we are welcomed, our culture is not relegated to dustbins or the butt of jokes and where we can be ourselves without fear. We should be able to communicate an issue concerning workplace racism, be listened to and believed and not receive further racism or punishment for doing so.

Equity vs Equality

The 2019 Racism Ruins Lives study of 5,000 respondents by TUC reported a whopping 65 per cent of BME respondents admitting to receiving racial harassment at work.[38] However, workplaces really do love to 'BAME' us. It lumps together millions of experiences and hides vital information about who experiences racism and how differently it shows up depending on who you are. We have to interrogate patterns in the data beyond the smoke and mirrors. For example, a Racism at Work study by Pearn Kandola featuring 1,500 respondents shows that 60 per cent of Black people experienced racism in the workplace, compared to 42 per cent of people who identified as Asian.[39]

Let's break it down further. Even in the Black community, our experiences of racism are compounded by our social location and other intersecting identities. The TUC BME Women at Work report reveals that racism towards Black women in the workplace is even more rife than towards men.[40] When you look even closer, Black disabled women reported even higher levels of racism compared to non-disabled Black women, and are four times more likely to receive physical violence or threats of violence too.

Let's take the ethnicity pay gap reporting, for example, which is still not mandatory in the UK – something that Dianne Greyson founder of #EthnicityPayGap campaign is seeking to change. The gap is a very clear indicator of the pervasive ways racism sticks to institutions. While poverty has always persisted across all communities and ethnicities, what the ethnicity pay gap reveals is that it disproportionately impacts Black and Brown people.[41] When you add the intersections of gender and disability, the results are often even more revealing. And when you dissect class disparities, it becomes even more exposing, with the rate of poverty being much higher for Black and Ethnic Minority families. According to a report by Social Metrics Commission that measures poverty in Britain, '46 per cent of all people living in families where the household head is Black/African/Caribbean/Black British are in poverty, compared to 19 per cent of those living in families where the head of household is white'.[42] Poverty, at this level in a rich country like Britain is a serious social issue. These stats, evidently, do not mean that white working-class people don't live with the consequences of poverty, but that the class inequity they face is *not* as a result of them being white. Instead, it is due to wealth division, permanent shifts in economic structure and political policy.[43] And when you look at the data, it is clear those who are Black and Brown are disproportionately affected and systemic racism, in these cases, *is* also a contributing factor.

If we just look at our history and the fact that, when slavery was abolished in 1833, the government paid compensation to former slave-owning families for their 'loss of property' that British taxpayers were tasked with paying off the debt accrued from this compensation, to the white elite. This was a debt so large it took until 2015 to clear it.[44] Of course that is going to leave a socio-economic disadvantage on the lineage of those who were enslaved and had amassed zero land or generational wealth as a result, and of course it gives a socio-economic advantage to the families who accrued generational wealth as a result. If we have falsely been socialised for centuries to believe that Black folk are inherently inferior, how do you think that is going to manifest into employment rates and valuing staff with pay equity? Of course, it also explains why most people in senior positions are white.

In October 2020 the Office of National Statistics (ONS) reported that the ethnicity pay gap was only 2.3 per cent in Britain. Tabloids latched onto this and used it as a signal to stop talking about race. Surely things couldn't be that bad in Britain, if the ethnicity gap had improved? However, the data had not been dissected, something I picked up instantly. Moreover, ethnicity pay reporting is still not mandatory in the UK which means most employers are still not disclosing ethnicity pay gaps. Therefore, these statistics do not give you an accurate picture. If you dissect the available data further, the ONS took this as the average – including parts of the UK where there are barely any Black folk. This disguises regional variations, making a huge difference to the data. The highest ethnicity pay gap of 23.8 per cent is reported in London (with some public service employees in London facing pay gaps of up to 37 per cent)[45] the city with the highest population of Black, Asian and Ethnic Minority people who are overrepresented in lower-paid jobs. Quite a difference from the 2.3 per cent in the headlines, don't you think?

★

During Black History Month, I delivered a talk to 300 staff about racism in Britain, Black Lives Matter and how to bring allyship into the workplace. We'd arranged for questions to be pre-agreed so we didn't take questions from the audience at the end – a self-care measure that's become very necessary. This was a talk, rather than an interactive workshop. We had not long gotten started: I'd introduced myself, shared my journey to anti-racism, born out of my former wedding business, and started to explain what racism was beyond an overt act of hate. I provided some evidence for the impact of racism before I received an interruption mid-talk: 'When you say we live in a racist society, don't you mean it's just a few bad apples?'

Even though this hadn't been agreed, the inherent people-pleaser in me comes out when I am feeling vulnerable. So I over-extended and instinctively responded with a definition of systemic racism. I provided some more stats to reinforce my previous points and that it's possible to do or say racist things without realising and be a 'good' person. My talk continued back on track, this time I made it to the end before the same person interrupted. 'You've been talking about "so-called" equality throughout this talk. I've just looked at your website and the first five weddings I see, there are no white people. How is that equality?'

I felt the weight of both his anti-Blackness and misogyny in this question. I felt it viscerally and remember almost bracing because it felt like metaphorical lashings. It took two days to work the hyperarousal and hypervigilance, common responses to trauma, out of my body.

Let's pause. Consider the following questions:

1. Would you have even noticed the subtlety of this racism in the moment?
2. Can you recognise it now?
3. What could you have done during these moments or after the talk?

This discomfort of having Blackness centred by my talk, for just forty minutes during Black History Month, was so disarming for the participant that he felt the urge to disrupt the talk and defend his position. He clearly felt challenged and under attack by the subject matter, he decided to hunt down my former wedding business (I doubt very much he was wedding planning in that precise moment) by looking for whatever incriminating evidence he could find online, to try to confirm his bias about me. He did all of this whilst I was talking, which meant he had no interest in what I was talking about or in learning, but just wanted to catch me out. He wanted to put me back in my place. So what did I do? I paused.

As I teach my students, it's so important to slow down your nervous system when it goes into fight/flight mode, so you can respond and not react. This is especially important for Black and Brown folk. I am not saying it's easy, or that you won't always respond in the way you want to. I mean, I really wanted to tell him to fuck all the way off and my body wanted to hit the eject button – it wanted to get the hell out of that unsafe environment, pronto. But I stayed. I took a deep breath in for three seconds and exhaled for five. I asked what his name was, buying some time. Slowing it down some more, I poured a glass of water, took a few sips and placed the glass down. Giving my body time to slow down meant I can get my thinking brain back online, get back in control of the pace, the content and my words, so I could respond, rather than react.

Leaning into curiosity I asked: 'What is your intention with that question?' By throwing a question back to someone displaying racism, it not only buys you more time to gather your thoughts, but most importantly, it holds a mirror up to their behaviour and encourages them to reflect. Sometimes, it can instigate a huge penny drop and an apology, or at least offer both of you clarity. In this case, he began back-tracking.

I wanted to highlight what made him think whiteness should be centred during Black History Month and also in my wedding business, which was birthed to tackle the lack of representation, particularly of Black women. So I spoke about how Positive Action is encouraged under the Equality Act to provide specific needs, improve representation and/or participation of under-represented groups.

'Positive discrimination' – such as only hiring someone because they are Black, not because of their skills – is unlawful. Positive Action, which is encouraged by law with conditions under the Equality Act 2010, means that it is perfectly lawful for an employer to hire someone to take intentional action to compensate for disadvantage, representation and engagement from a particular community who share a protected characteristic (age, sex, sex orientation, disability, race, gender reassignment, marriage, civil partnership, pregnancy, religion or belief) where participation in that activity is disproportionately low. They can use Positive Action to encourage people from disadvantaged groups to apply for positions. We often hear people talk about the utopia of equality when they feel challenged by anti-racism work, and interpret the opportunity to centre Blackness as an attack on equality. Equality means the state of being equal, especially in status, rights, or opportunities. But to bridge the broken gap to equality we need equity first: the state of being fair or impartial.

In this particular talk, I spoke about the difference between equity and equality, using healthcare as an example. I shared that statistically, most of us will be impacted by cancer in some way, about the lots of different types of cancer such as breast cancer or liver cancer. All are deserving of equal attention, with not one type of cancer being more important or less devastating. However, in order to understand the nuances of each type and address the specific set of issues to find cures, we have to shine a spotlight on one. That is how we address specific issues and increase equity. When people in dominant groups, who have been so accustomed to always being seen and catered to, continue to feel like equity is some kind of oppression and personal attack on them, we'll never get to equality.

I heard my colleague Tamu Thomas, founder of Live Three Sixty, once describe equity in a simple way that has always stayed with me. Equality is paying everyone £5 in their bank account today. It assumes we are all living in the same socio-economic circumstances and we all have the same needs. But the reality is if we each got a fiver, we all would not have the same amount of money or the same financial responsibilities. Some would have £5, others £12,205, with some in their overdraft with −£995. Some won't even have bank accounts. Giving everyone the same does not mean we are all suddenly equal or that inequality suddenly fails to exist. Equality is not the immediate goal in anti-racism, intentional equity is.

Equity means directly addressing the systemic disadvantages present that cause more groups to experience social disadvantage than others, to provide work and employment free from discrimination, access to fair education, healthcare, food and safe housing to all etc, and then perhaps resetting everyone's bank balance to 0 and giving everyone £1,000,000.

I also asked this man to get curious about what it is inside him that made him get so agitated at Blackness being centred in attempts to increase equity and that, perhaps, it needs some interrogation. In an attempt to discredit me, his behaviour and my response ended up giving his co-workers a lesson on what everyday racism looks like in the workplace and how you might be able to tackle it in the moment.

★

Addressing Racism at Work

With many accounts of racism reported each year and even more that go under the radar, there's no question, you're going to witness everyday racism unfold in a workplace. Since white folk are statistically more likely to call out overt racism in the moment,[46] but less likely to recognise subtle racism, including in themselves, you need to sharpen your skills at recognising racism beyond overt acts of hate and tackling racism as it unfolds at work, and fast.

Racism at work can be born out of well-meaning initiatives and exchanges. Having a corridor chat with a random member of staff who happens to be Black to 'pick their brains' about Diversity and Inclusion and Anti-Racism policy is one of these guises. What is often overlooked is that experiencing racism is a form of trauma. By doing something like reverse mentoring, given the statistics that reveal racism at work is often perpetuated by senior managers, you are asking Black and Brown people to potentially enter environments that could be re-traumatising because due care, strategy and expertise has not been invested in. If staff had reported repeatedly receiving sexual discrimination from senior managers, it's hard to believe there would be the same suggestion to 'mentor' them. Perhaps, even more pertinent, is when we start to bring the conversation of racism into more majority-white spaces, without due care, it can become incredibly psychologically unsafe for survivors of racism. The fact that so many organisations think they can undo centuries of systemic racism by choosing not to consistently engage in expert help is not only woefully misguided and redolent of how little this issue is taken seriously and how little we have progressed, it is racist.

However, if staff are happy to share their personal experiences, that has huge value. Seeking staff feedback, anonymous surveys, forming focus groups and gaining insight on where improvements can be made is vital. Critically, however, somebody's skin colour doesn't make them an expert in tackling systemic racism, organisational cultural change or managing peer wellbeing and Black trauma, nor does it make them critical race theorists. Thinking that their extra melanin automatically qualifies them to advise you, when it has nothing to do with their role or expertise, not only feeds into an unhealthy relationship of extraction but also puts them at risk of harm and burnout. It is, in fact, also racist.

If this is being suggested, challenge it. Ask which experts can be brought in. If it's already taking place, ask what measures are being put in place to support staff wellbeing as a priority. Are staff being given training to take this on? Are they being given time out of their usual roles to do this? Are they being financially compensated?

I was once told about a production company working with a client to create a new television advert. Just before the casting process began, the company explicitly said they did not want any Black or South Asian people in their advert. Advertising executives responded to the request in the boardroom by nervously laughing. No one called it out. Instead, the production company complied in their casting and so did the advertising agency.

Being anti-racist means addressing this behaviour in the boardroom by:

1. Taking that client on a journey to educate them and encourage them as a global brand to understand the economic and moral benefits of having a brand and advert reflective of all customers that consume their product.
2. Simply holding a boundary by revisiting company values, clearly communicating what they are, standing by them,

upholding them and making a decision to no longer work with racist clients.

If you witness racism at work as an ally, if you feel safe to do so (remember don't conflate discomfort with unsafety), it is imperative to start calling it out. Of course, there will be incidents that need to be – and should be – escalated formally, but the ideal is that we develop agility at discussing, recognising and responding to incidents of everyday racism quickly and informally, so that there are learning opportunities and a change in behaviour; so everyone can feel safe and do their jobs in peace.

Multiple variables will come into play, which means addressing racism might not always feel possible or be appropriate in the moment. Business psychologist and author of *Racism at Work*, Binna Kandola, makes a great and very effective suggestion to pair up with someone. If racism is being witnessed by more than one of you and address it together. Do not underestimate the power of two to disrupt white dominance and also to help avoid the person who is experiencing racism being scapegoated as a troublemaker.

Raising what you've witnessed with colleagues retrospectively can offer processing time and clarity: 'I noticed what I thought was racism in that meeting today, when X said this. Did you notice that too? What do you think? Will you join me?' By doing this, you're gathering buy-in.

Where relevant, unlike the advertising example above, if the racism has directly involved a peer, it's important to try to gather their consent too. Fear of repercussions is huge and they also may not want you to advocate on their behalf. If they're in agreement, take it to management to raise your concerns; they are more likely to acknowledge and address it. This isn't about ganging up, this is about communicating the issue and reducing harm.

And I will share a caveat: if you are not the target and you are witness to racial harassment, and it makes you feel unsafe in the workplace, you are still within your legal rights to flag a concern or report it even if it didn't happen to you directly.

If approaching the perpetrator, try this on for size: 'Can I talk to you for a moment? What you just did there [repeat what they did or said – hold up that mirror to their behaviour], what did you mean by that? I wonder what [insert the name of a peer/friend in a marginalised group targeted] would feel if they heard you say that?'

We don't all have to share the same view at work. We're not robots. But basic respect, common decency and civil behaviour should be a benchmark. A willingness to reduce any harm we enact by our actions (or inactions) should be non-negotiable and being able to communicate when someone is being disrespectful, indecent and uncivil requires open communication.

One of the reasons racism at work is so rampant is because when racism happens, there is such racialised fragility – racism is denied, rarely addressed adequately and, for the most part, it's not even acknowledged. An organisation's poor action or inaction can be even more harmful than the initial incident and can lead to institutional trauma, also known as institutional betrayal.[47] This is when a person experiences further harm from the community they have turned to for support and whom they also rely upon for employment. Lack of action, acknowledgement or validation, and insensitivity alongside silence, can all exacerbate the impact of trauma.

Institutional betrayal can look like not taking any action on a racism complaint. It can look like a generic 'paint-by-numbers' apology, with any or all of the following missing:

1. Acknowledgement of the specific issue
2. Acknowledgement of the harm caused
3. Action to address it

It can look like regularly expecting members of staff to work overtime and not paying them for it. It can look like career blocks and social exclusion when someone reports racism. It can also frequently look like cover ups to protect the institution's brand identity and perception and favouring the maintenance of hierarchical institutional relationships over admitting fault and taking accountability. For example, silencing a member of staff who has experienced workplace racism by having them sign an NDA and giving them a payoff to leave, rather than reprimanding the perpetrator, who happens to be in a senior role and brings in a lot of money for the business. Or another example, brilliantly outlined by Smith and Freyd in their 2014 paper on Institutional Betrayal: 'a bishop may elect to relocate rather than report a member of the clergy accused of abuse to the authorities in order to maintain his standing within the Catholic community.'[48]

Institutional betrayal is rife. Not addressing biased egotistical responses to traumatic experiences at work can lead to inadequate outcomes at best and negligent and racist outcomes at worst. There must be an understanding that these incidents are beyond isolated accounts of bickering staff, but interconnected with systemic social suffering. Failing to take them seriously or to be aware of how institutional betrayal can re-traumatise, impact staff wellbeing, impact outcomes, can lead to devastating consequences.

Of course, racism at work doesn't just happen in the traditional 9–5 setting. It can happen in any place of work, including contractors who visit your own home. One interviewee, a mixed-heritage Black woman shared one standout moment of racism at work and allyship by her white Irish husband. During a visit the husband fell into conversation with the contractor on the subject of COVID and what the future might look like for businesses after the global pandemic. They responded with words to the effect of, 'Well, as long as the foreigners stay out of the country, that's OK. They stay over there, and we'll stay here.'

Her husband told me that he was perplexed. 'It could not have escaped them that I have an Irish accent and am a foreigner by any definition of the word. And my wife, who they met, is of mixed heritage. Her father is Black.' In the moment, he didn't know what to say. But later, he decided to follow up formally with the company, with whom he had a solid eight-year working relationship, directly, by phone and email afterwards to relay the incident and suggest some solutions going forward including diversity training for staff.

The couple received a response from the director of the company stating how disappointed they were to receive this type of feedback from them. Apparently the member of staff did not mean for their comments to be misinterpreted by them. And in response to my interviewee's suggestion on how to move forward, they simply asked the staff member to be more careful with how they express themselves in future.

This response to feedback is a classic example of racialised fragility, finding automatic truth and 'rightness' in white solidarity and finding more offence in having racism highlighted, than having any regard for the actual racism.

My interviewees' email reply was an excellent example of what to do next.

You're disappointed to hear uncomfortable feedback but offer no apology for the content of the complaint. 'X said some words, but I didn't understand them?' You have basically dismissed my account as a 'misunderstanding' on my part. 'X needs to be more careful in the future, but not less racist.'

In short, please return the key to our property by post, immediately.

If you read back my email, you'll see that this was not my intent. Your response is wholly responsible for this outcome...

What my interviewee's husband did was recognise that he froze in the moment. He regathered his thoughts so he could:

- Address it retrospectively.
- Collaborate with his partner, rather than act on her behalf, considering she was most impacted by the incident.

- Escalate the issue by speaking to a senior member of staff on the phone (which by their account, actually went well, it all went to pot when the director got involved).
- Give feedback about the behaviour with suggestions on how to move forward.
- Offer a chance for atonement, no cancelling, just account-ability.
- Follow up what was discussed on the telephone by email to keep a record.

The company was unable to receive feedback on racism, nor apologise (which contributed to institutional betrayal), gaslighted my interviewees' experience and actually caused further harm. The client held a firm boundary and said this behaviour and your response to it will not be tolerated, contributing to the loss of an eight-year client and risk to brand credibility. This is a powerful way to use your allyship by intentionally spending your money with companies that are actively engaging in anti-racist practices and not with those that don't. That doesn't mean these companies are perfect but are those that acknowledge racism, take account-ability and take steps to address it.

Creating Safer Spaces

When organisations say they want to be anti-racist, we have to ask: do they really want to be? A huge component of anti-racism is accountability and atonement – if they're too busy covering their asses that's not anti-racist. Offering fair and due process, respect, being honest about where things have gone wrong and role modelling vulnerability, accountability and atonement is where cultural change happens.

So what can we do? We can rebuild trust.

There is a risk to speaking up about racism. If somebody has the courage to speak up, they are taking a conscious risk that speaking up may result in further abuse, being disbelieved or losing their job. This takes courage and it also indicates some level of trust, or a breaking point and utter despair. If an incident of racism is brought to you, this risk should be acknowledged. This should be handled with care, trust and sensitivity from HR (if escalated) and leadership teams.

1. Believe them: Paranoia about Black and Brown people wanting to go on a revenge rampage and unfairly sue all white people and employers has built up a culture of mistrust since civil rights campaigners campaigned for race discrimination laws to be enforced in Britain. If an automatic culture of mistrust has been built up in your organisation, that is an urgent invitation to interrogate. Everybody has a right to exercise their human rights. If people feel trusted, respected and able to do their job free from racial harm, then surely fear of being sued will become redundant.

2. Acknowledge the incident: 'I am sorry to hear this [name it] has happened to you.' If an informal complaint involves you, acknowledge the incident and your part in it. If formal, it may be appropriate to refer on to someone impartial.

3. Offer support: especially important if they are in visible distress and may need access to immediate resources, such

as a quiet space, access to therapy, working from home, time with a peer mentor or race champion so they can help validate their experience.

4. Ask what they need in the moment. This may be covered by offering support, but you may offer alternative ideas relevant to their experience and current needs.

5. Keep lines of communication open: obviously, you will need to go away and investigate and take some actions. Let them know what you are going to do next and when they are likely to hear from you (or someone else impartial).

6. Keep in contact: Follow up verbally and via email. Keeping in contact lets them know you are taking the matter seriously.

7. Do not break trust: If you say you are going to do something do it. If you can't meet a deadline set, let them know in advance. Manage expectations. This builds trust and sense of safety.

8. Review policy and refer them to it: If a policy clearly outlines what steps will be taken if someone experiences harassment at work – follow the procedure. If you choose not to follow formal procedure, communicate why you're approaching something differently.

9. If the procedure is not adequate to tackle race complaints, time to review it and update it and seek expertise.

10. Continue to listen and ask for feedback: This provides an opportunity for them to let you know how they are doing and if the steps taken are helpful or need review to keep them safe. It also provides an opportunity for them to share further concerns or ask questions. This demonstrates your

duty of care to them and offers some ownership over the situation.

Safe spaces are not free from challenge or difficult conversations, but spaces that intentionally encourage psychological safety. This can look like:

1. Fostering trust, respect and curiosity within a team, especially when experiences are different to our own.
2. Being able to share ideas without being belittled.
3. A dedicated space for marginalised people who share similar experiences (this could include specific staff networks).
4. A space where you are welcomed.
5. Encouraging active listening.
6. Being able to make mistakes free from punishment (though do not mistake being proportionately held accountable for punishment).
7. Being able to give feedback on problematic circumstances or behaviour without receiving social persecution, being branded a trouble-maker, or being punished for holding a boundary and asking for help.

What else makes a safe space? Ask your Black staff and staff who experience regular workplace othering what they need. Collaborate with them and gather feedback anonymously.

Other ways to consistently foster anti-racism in your place of work as a practice is to prioritise constant education that fosters curiosity.

1. Invest in continued social learning such as lunch and learn session: A bite-sized 30-minute talk with 15 minutes' Q&A and provide staff with a nice lunch once a month.

2. Get buy-in for those staff who choose to opt in to take part in a listening session, where staff in a dominant group are solely present to listen, not respond. From that event, ask those who were in an active listening role to submit any questions through via email (to a race champion or staff network for example), have them collated and pre-agreed (this keeps Black and marginalised staff safe) and use these questions as a framework to offer a potential follow up where questions are answered. Again make sure if staff are labouring they are fairly compensated.

3. Use key moments in the calendar to inspire topics of conversation, or creative events.

4. Buy Black history calendars that highlight key moments in history throughout the year and not just during one month – use them as talking points.

5. Foster curiosity and community from within your staff force with regular 'a day in the life'-type interviews for a work podcast or newsletter where staff talk about who they are and what they do from their unique perspective of the world. 'A day in the life' could share snippets into day-to-day-life of staff in various marginalised communities – for example, a member of staff who is also an artist and using art as a means of expression or who has some nifty tips on growing their own vegetables.

So much racial trauma and associated institutional betrayal happens in community; there is so much richness and communal healing that can happen in shared experiences. We spend so much time at work; fostering curiosity about all of the things that make us human beyond our roles can deepen understanding, deepen connection, build respect and build trust.

It's time to move from bystander to changemaker and start engaging when racism unfolds at work. It's important, where relevant and appropriate, to communicate with people directly impacted by racist incidents at work and gather consent and a collaborative approach to find solutions. But sometimes, you just need to hold a firm boundary and say enough is enough. That also means employers need to take responsibility for who they are hiring to represent their company, to start redefining and communicating company values, staff conduct, training and to communicate clearly to no longer tolerate when values and conduct are consistently breached. Being anti-racist and learning to recognise and address racism at work is going to be like learning a new language. You need to practise. Use media or current affairs as talking points to discuss everyday instances of racism with peers and colleagues all of the time, not just when the shit hits the fan. Racism has been lawful, enabled and defended in the workplace in the UK for too long – it's time for it to stop and you play a key role in that.

11. Brokering Change: Action and Advocacy

Change will not come if we wait for some other person
or if we wait for some other time, we are the ones we've
been waiting for, we are the change that we seek.

BARACK OBAMA[1]

So here is the penultimate chapter, where we tie it all together and where you level up. (Side note: if you've found your way here without reading the rest of the book, I see you. Please don't undermine anti-racism work or the labour it has taken to create this resource by trying to skip ahead. And please don't underestimate the unintentional harm you will continue to inflict on others by not doing this work properly.)

When Trump finally left his presidency at the end of 2020 after making unsubstantiated claims of voter fraud, global celebration erupted. However, it most definitely still leaves me uneasy and should not cause complacency. Exit polls show 55 per cent of white women voted for Trump in 2020, even more than in 2016.[2] January 2021 saw a heavily armed mob of majority-white Trump supporters try to stop the change in presidency by breaking into

Capitol Hill; five people were killed in the process.[3] Amidst the storming, insurgents were taking selfies with some police officers who appeared to have lost their power of arrest and seemed more interested in posing for the camera than stopping people invading a secure government building and carrying weapons of mass destruction.

Here in the UK, at the time of writing, a Conservative government remains in power for the foreseeable, and COVID continues to run rampant on this little island, tallying up one of the highest death counts in the world.[4] No one has been held accountable for the deaths of seventy-two human beings in the worst UK residential fire since World War II at Grenfell Tower, as a result of the unlawful use of cladding that remains on many other council flats around the country.[5] At the time of writing, well over a thousand Black British citizens unlawfully detained, deported, or threatened with deportation, denied legal rights, lost pensions have still not received *any* compensation from the 2018 Windrush scandal.[6] The Royal Family has been accused of racism by Meghan Markle and a damning Human Rights report ordered by the House of Commons and the House of Lords, published in November 2020, revealed the seismic failure of the Equality and Human Rights Commission and the British government to address systemic racism.[7] It also reports that 85 per cent of Black people are not confident that they would be treated the same as a white person by the police, while over 75 per cent of Black people in the UK do not believe their human rights are equally protected compared to white people and it barely received a murmur in the press.[8]

Whether Trump's 'Make America Great Again' fan club

persists, or Conservative MPs like Boris Johnson are in power, they are just pawns. While their leadership has, no doubt, dangerously emboldened and role-modelled hate, we cannot blame any one individual for the state we are in. They are the symptom of the ugliness of white supremacy that has plagued our countries and many others for centuries. We have to examine all of the ingredients that made it possible for the son of a Klansman to become one of the most powerful men in the world and a prime minister who has no issues calling Muslim women 'letterboxes' and Black people 'picannines' to run a country.

I want to give you an opportunity to start to recognise how to put some of what you have been learning throughout this book into practice. Activism can take many forms: your role now is to raise awareness and draw others in to this work; to educate whilst simultaneously recognising this is a journey and the work is never 'done'. You must identify and explore where your skills are most needed. Whilst the most powerful, important and sustainable activism you do will be offline, there is a huge role social media plays in sharing information, supporting differing accessibility needs and enabling more people to learn from each other, but the work does not stop there.

The work is about adopting new practices in your life to reduce the racism around you. This is a commitment to continue to interrogate your own racism whilst starting to expose the racism that is at work, in the law, in education, in media, in politics, in cultures, in healthcare, in families and to understand how this continues to infringe on human rights and impact outcomes. This is for you to also raise awareness, use your influence, skills and circle of influence to start brokering change. Let's look at the areas where you can create change on an individual level.

Media

An industry that is 94 per cent white and 0.2 per cent Black in Britain,[9] media plays a firm role in influencing perception and the opinions we start to form. It can spread negative or one-dimensional narratives about groups of people and propaganda and, at times, even incite hatred for clickbait. Understanding every facet is important: the language used, how it is presented, the questions being asked, when they bring in experts to present complex ideas, which experts they choose to bring in, if they bring in experts at all, the content that is being shared and the content that isn't. Pay attention.

I was once contacted to take part in a video series discussing Meghan Markle's treatment and the role bias may play in media reporting. In the interview I presented facts, examples and gave a brief history lesson. The news outlet contacted me to say how proud they were of the piece; they had learned so much. Their content always gets picked up by a well-known newspaper with whom they have a close relationship. All that pride and excitement soon dissipated when said newspaper chose not to publish my piece. After all, it did happen to be exposing media bias. Apparently, this was the first time that had ever happened in the history of their relationship.

Pay attention to how racism seeps through media by osmosis. Remember the huge role the media played in spreading fear and hate at the height of lynchings in the American South.[10] How it fostered division during civil rights in the UK and spread fear about Commonwealth citizens travelling from the Caribbean and other Commonwealth countries coming to 'take' from white people.[11]

Pay attention to who is given disproportionate airtime on mainstream TV to spread propaganda. Let's take Nigel Farage for example. Former leader of the right-wing United Kingdom Independence Party (UKIP) from 2006–2009 and 2010–2016 and leader of the Brexit Party 2019–2021, Farage weaponised an image of Syrian people seeking asylum, who had nothing to do with Brexit, to promote fear about immigration and was accused of using Nazi-style propaganda tactics as part of his Brexit campaign.[12] In her book *We Need New Stories*, journalist and author Nesrine Malik highlights how, even though Farage has a 100 per cent failure rate of running for a British Parliamentary seat, his media profile on mainstream TV and news outlets would have you believe otherwise. Malik writes: 'By February 2018, the BBC's most prestigious political debate programme *Question Time* had invited Nigel Farage on the show thirty-two times, making him the joint most invited guest in the history of the show. The other was Kenneth Clarke, a sitting member of parliament and former Chancellor of the Exchequer.'[13] Why is he consistently and disproportionately given a platform by mainstream British broadcasters?

Understand the way op-eds (opinion led articles that are written by journalists not affiliated or necessarily in keeping with the editorial agenda of a media outlet) are often a useful tool to spread further divide. Most people cannot tell the difference between opinion and fact or the validity of, for example, one article by a reputable broadsheet presenting facts and another written by someone who has pitched an idea and is being paid to intentionally agitate and have an opinion.

Let's examine this headline of an op-ed published in the *Telegraph* in May 2020 entitled: 'Campaigners are twisting BAME COVID data to further their "victimhood" agenda.'[14]

1. What does this headline communicate about people in Black, Asian and other Ethnic Minority communities in Britain?
2. What assumptions does it make about the perception and bias the author automatically has about these richly diverse communities?
3. Does the general public, who are absorbing biased media reporting, genuinely know the difference between an op-ed and an editorial, or will they just read what they consume from who they deem to be a 'credible newspaper' as legitimate?

In the absence of tighter regulation on incitement, opinion pieces will continue to make it easy for some publications to churn out provocative content that incites racial hatred and spreads misinformation, whilst simultaneously absolving themselves of any responsibility by claiming that it's not reflective of their editorial views.

When the above article was challenged by one of my anti-racism students, a member of staff at the Independent Press Standards Organisation (IPSO) explained they don't have a section on racial hatred because they don't deal with 'taste or offence issues'. It begs the question, why does the Independent Press Standards Organisation, a body that regulates journalists, currently have no reference to hate speech or incitement in their Editors' Code of Practice guidelines?

Compare and contrast these headlines featuring white folk and Black folk engaging in similar activities. For example:

1. 'Manchester City starlet buys new £2 million home for his mum'
2. 'Young Manchester City Footballer, 20, on £25,000 a week, splashes out on mansion on market for £2.25 million despite having never started a premier league match'

Same newspaper, same activities, very different suggestion. Ask yourself:

1. What's the difference?
2. Which one of these do you think is in relation to a Black player and which in relation to a white player?
3. Who is being humanised?
4. What message does this communicate to you?

Pay particular attention to the way the media industry talks about white people who commit crimes and Black or Brown people. Start to notice dog-whistle headlines – headlines using suggestive language to covertly attract the attention of a particular group:

1. 'Young man wading through chest-deep waters after looting a grocery store'

2. 'Two residents wading through chest-deep water after finding goods including bread and soda in a local grocery store'

1. What's the difference?
2. Did you notice the use of language to describe unlawful
   activities?
3. What does the use of 'finding goods' suggest?

Pay particular attention to how the headlines of violent hate
crimes and acts of terror are reported when the perpetrator is
white, and when they aren't:

1. 'Tunisian Terrorist Migrant Grins After Arriving in Italy
   Weeks Before He Was Freed from Detention to Kill 3 in
   Nice'
2. 'Loner suspected of Murdering Jo Cox was in crisis and
   sought help from health counsellor just 24 hours before
   attack'
3. 'Kenosha shooting vigilante identified as high-school
   drop-out'

Ask yourself:

1. Who is being named a terrorist and who isn't?
2. What do the people described as vigilantes, lone wolves,
   'mentally ill' share in common?
3. Who is being infantilised?
4. Does infantilisation add to the perception of innocence or
   withdraw from it?

5.   Who is being humanised and how?

While the media is busy infantilising male terrorists who are white and conveniently framing them as a few individuals who are mentally unwell or having bad days, it successfully masks the terrorism and grooming of young people that is taking place right here in Britain and the fact that right-wing extremism is the UK's fastest growing threat.[15] Websites like Act Early can help if you are concerned someone close to you might be at risk of being groomed.

A comparison of the treatment of Kate Middleton, Duchess of Cambridge and Meghan Markle, the Duchess of Sussex, while pregnant in the headlines. See who you think they're speaking about:

1.   'Not long to go! Pregnant X tenderly cradles her baby bump while wrapping up her Royal duties ahead of maternity leave and X confirms she's due any minute now'
2.   'Why can't X keep her hands off her bump? Experts tackle the question that has got the nation talking: Is it pride, vanity, acting – or a new age bonding technique?'
3.   'X's morning sickness cure? X gifted with an avocado for pregnant Duchess'
4.   'X's beloved avocado linked to human rights abuse and drought, millennial shame'

1.   What do you notice?
2.   Who is white and who isn't?
3.   What do these headlines communicate?

4. How is media bias impacting public perception and how could this impact behaviour and outcome?
5. How could subtle racism be playing out here?

Ask, and explore what responsibility are education establishments and journalism departments in universities taking to educate about this and create the next generation of anti-racist journalists? Write to news outlets to ask them what they are doing to take responsibility and make sure their publication isn't promoting hate speech and propagating harm. Use their complaints procedure.

Write to the IPSO or your local alternative journalism reporting body and ask them if they have a section on hate speech or incitement and if not, advocate for it and make a case as to why it's necessary. The Editors' Code of Practice is updated every two years so, in the UK for example, get writing to the Editors' Code Committee and IPSO. Make your MPs or local government representative work for their money: you can contact your All-Party Parliamentary Media Group office or local equivalent that tackles public policy and ensure proper media regulation is in place, on our behalf.

★

In Society: Human Rights

Pay attention to what is going on in the news and what reports are being published (often without much noise) by the government.

Institutionalised racism isn't currently recognised by law so if an institution such as the police, or even the Crown Prosecution Service are found to be institutionally racist, only 'recommendations' can be made. Unless the law changes, it's up to the institution to implement those recommendations, or not. Public pressure can help.

That's why it is important to use your agency. Regardless of who is in office in your parliament, all parliamentary members act as civil servants and work for us and not the other way around. It's hard to believe it sometimes but that's what we pay our taxes for. Recognise your individual power. If we spent more effort being strategic in our activism and less time mindlessly scrolling on social media, just think how impactful we could be. Believe your words and letters can help drive through change. Write to your local government representative about current issues and ask them what they are going to do to ensure recommendations in public inquiries are implemented.

For example, many victims of the Windrush scandal in 2018 have still not received the promised compensation after losing jobs, homes, livelihoods and rights to marry, and experiencing the trauma of being repatriated to a country many no longer even know – or never did. Many remain in financial difficulty as a result of this human rights infringement by the UK government, so much so that the most senior Black Home Office employee, Alexandra Ankrah, who was responsible for the scheme, ended up resigning, citing that it is systemically racist and not fit for purpose.[16]

It doesn't stop with Windrush victims either. The British government was at it with Chagos Islanders. After the UK separated the Chagos Archipelago from Mauritius in 1965, it made a deal with the US, allowing them to use its largest island as a military base. Chagossians were forcibly removed from their homes by Britain in 1971 and relocated to Mauritius and the Seychelles. It was only in 2002 that some were given the right to British passports. British Chagossians reported that West Sussex Council offered to pay for flights to an Indian Ocean island rather than provide them with housing assistance in the UK, which is potentially unlawful. According to a report about the scandal by journalist Katie McQue, published in the *Guardian* in 2019, one housing officer said he 'didn't like the Chagossians coming to the UK and asking for houses.'[17]

And as we've mentioned, we have a report revealing how damaging systemic racism is in Britain with 75 per cent of Black people not believing their human rights are equally protected as those of white people.[18] Use your agency. How can you use your skills to help? Who in your circle of influence might help with this? Are people you know directly impacted? What can you do to support them personally? What can you do to raise awareness?

- Write to your local government representative (yes, in the old-fashioned way – in the UK, MPs have to respond when it's in writing) and, if they're active on social media, let them know you've written and get their attention there too. And remember:
- Be prepared to be persistent. Don't just write once and give up, change won't happen with half-arsed attempts so, if you don't get a reply, be proactive and write and email again and tag them on social media.
- Don't write a generic letter – you're more likely to get an automated reply. Be specific:

- Stick to the facts and, if you have personal experience of the issue, add it.
- Ask a question that has to be replied to.
- State what you want them to do.
- Leave your full name and address so they can contact you.

A top tip I received from one of my anti-racism students who works for MPs in the UK is to remember that, more than anything, they need your courage and backing, rather than berating, to be strong on this. Many will already be on your side and may have been too afraid to speak up – especially if your government representative is progressive.

Here's an example:

Dear X,

I am writing to you about the recent Human Rights Black People and Racism Report commissioned by the House of Commons and the House of Lords.

I am extremely concerned that over 75 per cent of Black people in the UK do not believe their human rights are equally protected. The report also found the Equality and Human Rights Commission to have failed to adequately provide leadership and gain trust in tackling racial inequality, protect human rights and promote the racial equality of Black people in Britain. Additionally, the report noted the failings of successive governments to act in response to the several reports and reviews and that continued failure, 'shows that something is wrong with the architecture' which is supposed to protect human rights and promote racial equality.

I also noticed X in the news/this report by X that shows this remains a serious issue.

I hope you will agree that this is utterly damming and demonstrates a country-wide failure to protect the human rights of all British Citizens.

What are the next steps you will be taking to ensure the government will;

Take swift action and address the recommendations in this report?

Prioritise this human rights issue?

Promote racial equality of Black people in Britain?

I look forward to both your response and details of how you will be combatting this within government.

Yours sincerely,
XXXX

(Don't forget your address and other contact details.)

★

Law

In the previous chapter, we touched upon race discrimination in employment law and the 'three month minus one day' rule birthed in the middle of huge racial tension and civil rights movements in the UK. Identify if this is something you can help with directly – where are your skills needed most? If you're drawing blanks, you can still play an important role by simply sharing and raising awareness of this law.

I hope this book inspires you and others to take the reins to campaign against this discriminatory three-month law. Petition and, if you can, use your allyship alongside a politically-astute person who works in discrimination rights law to overhaul the Equality Act, with the intention to root out the racism that remains embedded in law and start from a fair foundation, so it actually serves the communities it is supposed to protect.

You can also help by making sure Black and Brown folk and Non-Black People of Colour know about the importance of getting legal protection with any home insurance policy. This should cover most legal fees if they find themselves needing to go to tribunal and being unable to afford to pay to exercise their basic human rights – not a long-term solution that's available for all, but something that could help now. Also consider joining trade unions, finding organisations that offer legal aid, or contacting organisations like the Citizens Advice Bureau who offer impartial, free legal advice if someone needs help but is not sure what to do.

I also asked discrimination lawyers Equality Justice Solicitors what law firms can do to take responsibility because ultimately, they are all well aware of the 'three months minus one day' rule. They all know that the payout for race discrimination cases is horrendously and disproportionately low in comparison to other discrimination cases, but will still charge high fees. Firms could agree to enforce industry-wide fixed fees for race discrimination cases. Check out the Solicitors Regulation Authority (or equivalent) as a governing body – what's their stance on this? Can you help with enforcing that?

Society: Community Action

Here's where you can get creative – how can your skills help others directly and indirectly, online or in person? What's going on in and around your local community?

Grassroots movements and social justice activists are hugely overworked and often grossly underfunded, ending up burned out, in debt, or both. That, of course, has a direct effect on our ability to impact social change and pay for the staff and resources so desperately needed to make the work more impactful.

This is where paying it forward becomes a superpower. Can you volunteer a number of hours per month to help race justice workers? Having skilful and trustworthy volunteers who care about impacting change can be an absolute godsend, I can attest to that. It puts your allyship in action, and takes the pressure off those who need it most, so that they can concentrate on what they do best – activism, not admin.

- Do you have wealth privilege?
- Can you invest or partner with an individual or small business owner or charity with a social justice mission?
- Can you donate towards a bursary so others who do not have wealth privilege can engage with formal anti-racism education?

Between 2009 and 2019, only 0.24 per cent of private investment in the UK went to Black entrepreneurs, totalling just thirty-eight businesses over an entire decade. Out of those, only one Black female founder received funding.[19] The culture of extraction and exploitation from enslavement has generated disproportionate wealth distribution. It is these oppressive structures, or their by-products, that many racial justice workers are trying to dismantle, while still having to operate within them. This has led us to where we are today, needing to approach the same establishments that uphold these structures for funding. Lack of financial investment or support often creates huge barriers to access and economic growth.

- Can you invest, sponsor or donate money?
- Can you donate your expertise?
- Can you provide business mentorship or do you know someone who can?
- Can you provide investment advice to help racial justice workers to counteract loopholes, or do you know someone who can?
- Can you help with grant applications?

Your help doesn't always have to be monetary either:

- Can you help with professional social media, web or graphic design?
- Can you offer time, administration, marketing or planning skills?
- Can you offer a wellness service to support healing and wellbeing?

- Can you offer food, or even accommodation?
- Do you have access to a venue where you can donate space to hosting events?
- Do you have a second home or holiday property where you can offer subsidised rent or a complimentary stay?

Don't underestimate what a powerful tool rest is for activists and communities impacted by racism. White supremacy wants us to be worn down; rest re-resources and nourishes us and is another useful way to pay it forward. Cornwall initiative Cornwall Grenfell Hugs gathered pledges and acts of kindness from local residents and businesses to give Grenfell Tower survivors, their bereaved loved ones and firefighters a chance to have some respite, welcoming 480 Grenfell Tower survivors and guests to rest and enjoy a complimentary holiday in the beautiful countryside.

What about art and creativity in your community?

- What Black talent can you uplift, mentor, nurture or support?
- What diverse artists' work can you raise awareness of, buy from, showcase in a gallery, place of work, or local café?
- Are you connected to a museum? Hold them accountable to be more transparent about the artefacts they are exhibiting that were stolen during colonial invasion. Can there be events, or an education series on the history and origins surrounding them?

What can you do to make national days like Remembrance Day more inclusive of Black and Brown soldiers? Soldiers who fought with pride for Britain and received persecution while doing so, who all too often remain invisible.

- Can you share and seek out more stories about Black soldiers like Arthur Roberts and Walter Tull, or the first Black woman to join the British armed forces, Lilian Bader?
- How can you involve your local community to better connect with surviving former soldiers from both the British Indian Army and the British West Indies Regiment?
- How can you honour and respect all who served?

Climate

Lots of us are engaged in climate change discussions and action. As we know, it is communities in previously colonised countries who are most impacted by the climate crisis and, simultaneously, they are also the ones who contribute to it the least. Many have been campaigning for years after experiencing catastrophe after catastrophe as a direct result of colonial invasion from the West. A 2019 study by University College London (UCL), exploring earth system impacts of the European arrival, reported that the European colonial invasion of the Americas and the mass genocide of so many native people that went hand in hand, wiped out Indigenous populations by 90 per cent.[20] This meant that agricultural land was left unattended for so long that it contributed to changing the environment causing the earth's temperature to cool down in the late fifteenth and sixteenth centuries. This indirectly caused the deaths of 56 million people, globally.

Start to understand the connection between climate change and racism and learn, as I did from geographer and environmental activist Teju Adisa-Farrar, about how the environmental movement was appropriated in the late 60s by white folk who derailed the conversation from Indigenous, including Black African communities. These marginalised communities were trying to find ways to gain access and deal with the long-term impact of, not only the exploitation of people, but prolonged resource extraction and land exploitation, by creating better environments for themselves. The white West, on the other hand, made the movement solely about clean air and animals.

You can support with the education of community environmental groups who have become disconnected from their original function of environmental justice and, in doing so, run the risk of continuing to exclude the very people most impacted by overexposure to pollution, poor-standard accommodation and barriers to healthcare, including Black and Brown folk right here in the West, referred to as the Fourth World. Discover more about the link between colonialism and the climate with grassroots activists like Teju Adisa-Farrar or organisations like UK-based Climate in Colour.

> '*All racism is environmental, because we cannot separate ourselves from the environments that we live in.*'
> TEJU ADISA-FARRAR[21]

★

Influence in Healthcare

I heard and shared so many heartbreaking accounts of what racism looks like in healthcare. From racism in the therapy room, to Black women being four to five times more likely to die in childbirth and the very real past and present impact of medical apartheid.

Trust in healthcare has been broken again and again and it will not improve until there is first acknowledgement of structural racism. This needs to be coupled with intentional steps to rebuild trust, continuous education to embed anti-racist practices, seek out representation and improve visibility of inclusive and Black medical professionals such as A&E doctor and presenter Dr Ronke Ikharia to help re-engage Black communities where uptake and participation are low.

If you work in maternity, learn about cultural competency and the impact of medical racism in birthwork and more from organisations such as Abuela Doulas founded by Mars Lord. Do outreach work, partner up with organisations that already successfully engage with these communities, host events and feedback sessions. Can you volunteer your time to help charities advocating for human rights in childbirth like Birthrights?

Do you work within a medical or healthcare setting? Do you take into consideration social suffering? These are the socio-political and economic circumstances and social forces that lead to suffering, such as the accumulative and consistent exposure to living with racism. Or is the impact of social suffering being completely ignored, not only in therapy, but on mental health assessment forms that ask service users what has contributed to their ill health? If racism isn't even on there, we have a problem.

What can you do to address community concerns about access to healthcare to make it more inclusive, less clinical and more human?

For example, are you studying to be a therapist? Put pressure on training providers to offer anti-racism and more than a one-hour Diversity and Inclusion workshop as continuous study and reflective practice. This is so that therapists can competently work with and name 'race' in the therapy room without getting fragile or feeling challenged when clients talk about the impact of experiencing white supremacy, or simply know when to refer on.

What can you do to help raise awareness and build relations with impacted communities after centuries, decades and continued medical experiments on Black bodies? To improve services, you have to first understand how that impacts current behaviour such as lack of participation in clinical trials and why even I, thanks to James Marion Sims's obsession with butchering Black women, dread being anywhere near a vaginal speculum. Can you offer your expertise or volunteer with your local Patient Liaison Group or similar at your GP?

More generally, use social media to spread awareness and spark conversations about racial disparities in healthcare; they are so often hidden in plain sight. Write to your MP to ask them what they are doing to investigate the higher death rates of Black women in childbirth and the even higher number of Black women who have potentially fatal near misses.

Offer support if someone you know feels they are not receiving the care they should. Can you be a witness, or suggest they take a witness with them to their next appointment? Remember the power of two. Suggest that they write down questions or concerns, so they remember to ask everything they need to in appointments. And if your memory recall is impaired when you're anxious, ask your doctor's permission to record your consultation on a phone so you can refer back to the information when you get home.

Do they know about their right to complain via patient experience services like the Patient Advice and Liaison Service (PALS)? and if they haven't been able to resolve internally via PALS, to escalate complaints to the General Medical Council, Health and Social Care Ombudsman or similar regulatory body. The NHS has a core value to treat everyone with respect and dignity. If that isn't happening every patient has a right to have that corrected again and again.

★

The Church

To be anti-racist means you cannot ignore the complex link between white supremacy and Christianity. Well, to be fair, you can, but to continue to be ignorant to this relationship, is a choice to hide one's racism in religion.

The Church of England and ninety-six Anglican Priests benefitted from the equivalent of £46 million in compensation from slavery, paid to them as slavers.[22] The Church of England owned plantations in the British West Indies and the income generated from slavery went back to build Churches in Britain. Let's not forget John Newton's role as a human trafficker and Reverend (see page 206).

And there have been Catholic churches engaged in cover-ups of priests, found to engage in paedophilia, who have been sent on to do 'missionary' work with unsuspecting Black vulnerable children in central Africa, rather than to jail.[23]

This type of persistent institutional betrayal has led to the development of Black churches in the UK, born out of racist treatment from majority white churches. There are numerous accounts, both historical and present-day, of Black people being refused entry to worship, white pastors refusing to shake hands of Black churchgoers, having racism dismissed, when expressed, with 'it was a long time ago' comments, and being ignored or looked at in disgust by white Christian churchgoers.

I draw your attention to this to demonstrate that not one institution, no matter how noble the cause, is immune from the grasp of white supremacy. A place of worship is an institution made up of human beings, some of whom may have the capacity to twist the core function or purpose of religion for their own gain. We see that across the board with extremism being used in the name of religions that are usually peaceful.

Being anti-racist means getting curious about, and then addressing, how white supremacy and anti-Blackness show up in your place of worship. It means being honest about the Church's firm role in slavery and how, during colonial invasion, European colonists would often force natives to practise a Eurocentric Christianity in preference to their previous belief systems, and used religion to justify the enslavement of Africans.[24] It means having curious, honest conversations about where Jesus came from, his ethnicity and what he was more likely to look like than the blond-haired blue-eyed mainstream depictions, and using sources that reflect this. It means holding leadership to account when it comes to encouraging education, addressing racism and building trust in Black communities and other communities that do not feel safe in your place of worship. It means actively working to invite these communities to come to your place of worship and to take part in events, children's ministries or in services. It looks like intentionally cultivating representation that is reflective of the local community from leadership, to front of house and intentionally including Black people to make this sacred place a safe one of belonging for all.

Claiming you are a safe space and actively taking steps to demonstrate you are one, are two different things. Ask people in your place of worship who are underrepresented what a safe space means to them. Make eye contact, seek feedback and respond to it.

Spirituality and Wellness

Spiritual and wellness spaces are synonymous with bypassing global racial injustices that impact many humans' ability to live in peace, in favour of oneness and 'love and light' and other reductive rhetoric. But the people who would most benefit from wellness, spirituality and healing are often the most excluded.

In my work, I hear multiple accounts of students not feeling welcomed in yoga and wellness classes: from feeling uncomfortable being the only Black person in class, to size and ability exclusion or being priced out of classes. Lack of eye contact from other students and teachers were common, with accounts of teachers only making efforts to correct white bodies and not Black bodies. Many people of Indian heritage, to whom yoga practice most belongs, do not feel welcome in yoga classes because so many teachers have moved away from the practice's origins; dismissing communal and devotional practice in favour of bendy bodies and tricks (as well as the constant butchering and mispronunciation of the Sanskrit word 'namaste').

So ask yourself:

1. Are you taking steps to make sure your wellness reaches all, especially those who would most benefit from healing?
2. As a fellow student, can you make efforts to make eye contact and personally welcome people?
3. If a teacher, are you educating your students and honouring the essence of the practices of what you are teaching?
4. Can you offer modifications for different bodies and abilities?
5. Can you offer online classes?
6. How else can you make classes more accessible?

In spirituality you can also take steps to create safe environments and welcome people into spaces, to make spaces more intentionally inclusive of Black and Brown folk.

For example, Buddhist angel Kyodo williams runs regular meditation practice and welcomes all. However, she intentionally centres Black, Indigenous and People of Colour and LGBTQ+ people in the space – people who are often excluded or experience persecution in spiritual spaces and in wider society. She does this not only by intentionally welcoming them to the space by name, general address and eye contact, but in her advertising. She also invites them to share their feedback and experiences of practice first. She, and other wellness practitioners like my herbalist also offer a sliding scale payment for their classes and invites those who have wealth privilege and can afford to pay more, to do so and those who cannot to pay less. This is equity in wellness.

★

Influence in Education

Schools and universities play a huge role in the next generation. We're either preparing children and young people to be well-rounded individuals who contribute to society, to learn how to function with lots of different types of people, to respect and understand difference as not something to be feared but as something perfectly normal to be valued and celebrated, or we're not. We're either being honest about the British Empire's monumental role in how this little island has generated so much wealth, and the ripple effects of that, or we're continuing to teach sanitised, warped truths about our history. We're either invested in educating young people as best we can, so as not to continue to contribute to breeding ignorance and racism, and another historically illiterate generation or we're not.

The next generation play such an important role in how this journey pans out. They learn from us and repeat unhealthy patterns of behaviour or they evolve and grow and do better. Whether you're a parent, a caregiver or a teacher, you can play an important role. Ask the following questions:

1.   What's in the curriculum?
2.   Who's teaching it?
3.   What books are in the library?

4.   Who's on the reading list?

If you're a teacher, how can you be intentional with inclusion? How can you share Black inventors like Lewis Howard Latimer who invented the incandescent light bulb (the part that makes our light bulbs shine), or Black musical pioneers like Rosetta Tharpe, a queer Black woman who founded Rock 'n' Roll and inspired people like Elvis, who even covered some of her music. Share information about Black leaders and activists like Beverley Bryan, who ran Saturday schools and decolonised her classroom in Britain. What stories can you find of Black talent in your local area or subject?

Can you help with fundraising initiatives to fund a wider selection of books for the school library, telling inclusive stories and by authors that are representative of the world children need to live and function in? Seek advice from experts like Lavinya Stennett, historian and founder of The Black Curriculum, Liz Pemberton, founder of The Black Nursery Manager who specialises in training in early years sectors or academic Dr Nicola Rollock, who specialises in racial justice in education.

Include contributions, inventions, work, philosophy, science, literature, designers, histories from Black people all of the time, not just during Black History Month. So many teachers tell me that they feel uncomfortable or ill-equipped to talk about race or address Black history in the classroom. Bring in historians like Stella Dadzie or organisations like Black History Walks to inspire teaching staff and expand their knowledge and make history fun for all learners, especially those so often left out or dehumanised by some of the teaching narratives. There are so many stories and histories to share before and beyond enslavement that do not involve Black trauma. Seek them out.

Here's a hypothetical scenario for you:

You're at a community meeting about decolonising the curriculum and making it more inclusive. The head teacher says, 'I have mostly white children at my school. What evidence is there to suggest white children will benefit from changing the curriculum and adding more Black history? What's the benefit for white children?'

Firstly, notice how this statement makes you feel. Notice what happens in your body. Now consider the following:

1. What does this statement assume?
2. How is racism showing up in this statement?
3. How do you respond?
4. What thoughts can you challenge with fact?
5. What else can you do?
6. Who else could you involve?

Schools have a duty of care to all students and to ensure safeguarding measures are being adhered to. Can you engage in a parent-teacher association, or write to the Governors' Board to bring awareness concerns, areas for improvement, training and the importance of embedding anti-racism to the forefront?

We've addressed the impact of racism on children and young people and discussed how important a sense of belonging is in this book. Research has also shown there is a direct link between sense of belonging and student success. How are all students made to feel welcome and included?

One of my interviewees and Professor Binna Kandola shared a great example of how to nip common othering that happens in the classroom in the bud. During a lecture, an academic shared something pertaining to Black history. All the white students turned to the few Black students in class, who felt very uncomfortable, but the lecturer didn't notice at the time and continued. The Black students approached the lecturer afterwards and explained what happened. At the start of their next class together, the lecturer explained what had happened in the previous class and asked them not to expect some people to be more passionate than others just because they're Black. That history is all of ours and gave a call to action to treat one another with respect.

That was the end of it. No big drama. The Black students were listened to, believed, and most importantly, action was taken to address the situation swiftly. The students felt heard and safe, which also created a sense of trust and belonging.

Students in higher education have powerful influence. They are essentially paying customers, with the backing of powerful student unions. So if anti-racism is not being taken seriously at a university, if it is not featuring in a course or training, if supervisors are not sympathetic to students' experiences of studying while Black, students should be encouraged to use their agency, give feedback and ask for improvements.

The examples I have given here are, of course, just a starting point. The reality is that some teachers, parents and caregivers will want to push forward with a more inclusive curriculum and to centre anti-racism. Others absolutely won't and will see it as 'Anti-British'. These are the conversations that will matter in your allyship. This is where you need to dig in, roll your sleeves up and lean in.

★

Relational: Social Media

Online advocacy might seem like you're going down an internet rabbit hole, but it can be a really useful starting point in allyship and is a relatively easy and accessible way to engage. However, as I've mentioned, Black women receive a grossly disproportionate amount of online hate. Social media can be cesspit of hate and false information and provides a convenient way to connect those who have hating someone, or a group of people, in common.

Connecting with like-minded people to say and do shitty things to others, is not healthy, but it is addictive – even if you feel you're on the side of 'right'. If you find yourself doing so, get curious about why you are engaging in this behaviour. Self-interrogate when you're shaming, naming and dehumanising others, particularly when they encounter misfortune, sometimes even when they've died – the latter is something I've seen and challenged on my own timeline.

Gathering to collectively hate online reeks of superiority. Feeling morally superior to a person or group of people is exactly what we are trying to eradicate. As a recipient of online abuse myself, I can say that no one deserves to receive online abuse and when you find yourself gathering to hate, you more than likely have an unmet need that needs attention. If it's connection you crave, there are healthier ways of connecting with other humans than finding someone in common to hate.

When someone is being racially abused online (and notice I use the word 'abused' and not 'trolled' intentionally because the majority are human beings hiding behind anonymous accounts to enact abuse and, at times, hate crimes) there are a number of things you can do to support the person experiencing abuse, whilst also holding the online perpetrators accountable and without getting drawn into name calling. They crave attention, don't give it to them. Instead, you can:

Actively show support

Amplify the voices of the people/person that is being abused. If relevant, spread awareness of their work. Send them words of support; I cannot tell you how helpful it is to have support from others when you are being harmed online.

Offer support

If you have skills or access in your circle of influence to offer tangible support, offer it. Share information about organisations, such as Glitch, founded by Seyi Akiwowo, that offer online safety tips and classes, and are a brilliant resource that I have personally used to keep myself as safe as possible.

Challenge thought with fact

Many conversations about racism go nowhere because far too many people confuse their misinformed opinions as fact.

For example: If an online user says, 'But what about knife crime and Black-on-Black violence?' you can counter with:

1. 'This feeds into the fear-driven, racist belief that Black people, especially Black men, are inherently violent.'
2. 'There is no biological evidence to suggest this.'
3. 'People of all communities commit violence against one another, including white people.'
4. 'This suggests Black folk don't deserve to live free from racism until Black people stop killing other Black people.'

Share TV interviews, books, or research you've encountered to back up your points, for example: 'I watched X and found it useful. Researchers have found common key indicators[25] to young people engaging in knife crime are not determined by race, but poverty, lack of education, exclusion from school, overexposure to domestic violence and family breakdown. You can read more about it here: X.'

Reporting and accountability

Report accounts to admins because, believe it or not, they have a responsibility to keep users safe online. Take screenshots as evidence, as people have a habit of deleting their posts when they get called out. If they are inciting racial hatred online, report it to the police and share any evidence with them. You can also do this via websites like report-it.org.uk.

It can be easy to just demand a racist tweet is deleted and an apology issued. Individual racist views don't just miraculously disappear when a tweet does. Accountability is where change happens and that doesn't come from half-arsed apologies. Online hate is on the rise, in addition to contacting and reporting issues to social media platforms directly, you can also contact All-Party Parliamentary groups (or equivalent) in local government who have a responsibility to tackle online hate. They also hold responsibility for setting and ensuring digital safety standards are adhered to by companies.

Of course there is a caveat with social media reporting as we've all seen demonstrated it took alt-right figures like Tommy Robinson who was able to engage in online extremism on platforms like Facebook and Twitter for years before being banned. Donald Trump was able to incite racial hatred for four years, which emboldened white supremacists to organise the Capitol Hill riots that resulted in five deaths using social media platforms. In contrast, more often than I would like, I have reported being called a 'nigger' on Instagram, only to get a 'this does not breach our community guidelines' automated response.

This is, in part, because tech algorithms are biased, because the majority of people who code them are also biased and predominantly white and male. This is part of a bigger issue and why initiatives like CodeHergirls, Black Codher, Colourintech and Coding Black Females are necessary. Contact social media platforms to ask how they are going to improve online safety and make their platforms safe for all users or, if the mood strikes, take a stance like former footballer Thierry Henry who quit social media until companies take a stance on online racism and bullying.[26]

Engage or disengage?

Generally, you can tell the difference between those who are just lurking to spread hate on the internet and those who are grossly misinformed. If it's the former, follow the advice in 'Reporting and accountability'. If it's the latter, engage with curiosity and educate instead of spreading more hate. There's more than enough hate out there and your energy can be better served supporting the people being abused or engaging those willing to listen – offer to open up your DMs to talk about it more.

A great example of how engaging in online conversations can sometimes make profound changes to people with extreme thinking is that of Megan Phelps-Roper, who was indoctrinated into the Westboro religious cult by her family and was on picket lines from the age of five. They were extreme in their ideology and would attend war veterans' funerals with placards reading 'Thank God for 9/11' and 'Thank God for Aids'. Westboro is anti-war, anti-gay, anti-Jewish, anti-Black, anti-Muslim and quite frankly anti-human. Everything changed when Megan joined Twitter and started having dialogue with strangers on the internet. Notably, David Abitbol, founder of blog Jewlicious, helped her see the contradictions, examine her internal conflict and ultimately make the huge decision to walk away from her entire family and choose a new way. David used curiosity, respect, fact, and humour in his communication with Megan, providing logical challenges to her ideology to educate, not hate.

In an interview for *Gloss* magazine, Phelps stated that it was the online community that helped her change her ways. 'I felt safe – which allowed me to be more open and vulnerable than when I was in a physical space with other people, It permitted conversations to take place over time... When people stopped trying to shame me, started trying to really understand me, and took the time to respectfully challenge my ideas, that was when the magic happened. They helped me see things from their perspective by taking mine into account. We should never underestimate the power of compassionate engagement to change hearts and minds.'[27]

Don't get distracted

No matter how tempting, don't get drawn into debating the existence of racism online and offline. It is nothing but a smoke-screen distracting you from addressing the real issues at hand. Stay focused.

Curiosity and compassion

These two generally go hand in hand. When you feel like raging at someone's sheer ignorance, that's usually a sign to turn up the curiosity dial. Here are some questions you can ask:

1. What makes you think that way?

2. Tell me more about this, so I can better understand where you're coming from.
3. My understanding of X is this – what do you make of that?

Curiosity meets them where they are at and turns it into a conversation.

This is what I do most days I choose to engage online. Compassion doesn't mean not holding someone to account or holding a boundary when they do something harmful to me – quite the opposite. At the end of the day, I want to see mutual transformation, I want people to stop being racist and I have learned that that doesn't happen when one of those ingredients are missing or when I just want to retaliate – if it's the latter, I now just tap out and spend my energy with people that want to engage, looking after my mental health and tending to my needs instead.

*

I have a masterful example of online compassion to share.

Rain Dove is a model who uses their platform to combat pretty vile hate and ignorance towards people in LGBTQ+ communities. I've always been inspired by their capacity to hold compassion when receiving abuse – but the one that floored me, and made the press was this.[28]

Parent: My child is sick due to you.

Rain: Oh no! Did I give them the flu?

Parent: No, mental problems, she wants to be a boy

Rain: Did he tell you that?

Parent: She asked for a strap thing for her chest for Christmas.

Rain: They may not be wanting to identify as male then. Many people wear binders and still identify as female or non-gender. How are you feeling about it? Does it feel heavy?

Parent: My child hates her body because of perverts like you is how I feel in my opinion

Rain: I can imagine it must feel a bit like they are rejecting you when they reject parts of their body. For you to be spending your time reaching out to me, it shows you must care a lot about their happiness and wellbeing.

The exchange goes on for quite some time and ends with the parent thanking Rain, and Rain giving her recommendations on where to buy a safe chest binder for her child.

Most of the time when people lash out online and project shitty behaviour to strangers on the internet, it is almost always about them and their own stuff. For those of us in marginalised identities, just our very existence and identity winds people up. Also remember sometimes (though not all), you are not always engaging with adults, or people with emotional maturity. There are also various ranges of mental health and those things need to be taken into consideration when deciding how and if you wish to engage or not. Regardless of Rain's capacity for compassion, I've witnessed first-hand how being exposed to regular hate still has an impact.

So what were Rain's ingredients?

1.   Curiosity
2.   Compassion
3.   Education
4.   Accountability

5. Boundaries

I am not saying it is easy, but in the years I've been doing this work, I have seen over and over again that if your intention is to sow seeds and offer curiosity, it is more likely to lead to a conversation rather than conflict. You might not be the one who 'changes' them (if that's your intention, check your ego) but believe that you *could be*. Nobody is too old or too far gone. They will not get it all in one go (I mean, did you?) so you don't need to teach them everything, but you will most definitely be sowing important seeds. Of course, for Black and Brown folk, you have full permission to tap out and protect your peace and mental health. You do not have to debate your humanity with anyone.

Addressing Public Fallouts Online

In November 2020, Sainsbury's launched a series of three adverts featuring different families of various ethnicities for their Christmas advert. One of these sequences featured a a dark-skinned Black family. The anti-Blackness this advert received was ugly. Apparently Black people celebrating Christmas was 'absolutely sickening', 'totally inappropriate… a PR failure', with some taking to social media to ask, 'Where are the British people?' and, 'Is this Nigeria?

The fear of Blackness, of that imagined white genocide, that was being centred was rife. In response, I asked my online anti-racism community to be *intentional* and do the following:

1. Show support (to the recipients of racism and the brand).

2. Educate not hate (challenge thought with fact).
3. Continue to focus on their own unlearning so they become better equipped at recognising racism, calling in relatives that say similar things in response to this advert and not responding to racism with shock and dismay.

When public fallouts happen like this, it is really important to show your support to the brands who are taking steps to improve representation. Generally speaking, brands are risk averse. Many are still operating from ingrained racist beliefs and see Black as risky. Let them know you love the new advert – write to CEOs, let them know you want to see it again. Drown out the bullshit or it will confirm their bias and they'll quickly default and go back to homogenous casting with white or 'safer' light-skinned families. Spend your energy to send love to the talent in adverts too. Because beneath all of this online hate, there are human beings and, in this case, a real family being abused by grown adults, for being Black and singing about gravy. Remember, our children are watching.

★

Relational: In Person

This is where you have an opportunity to make a real, huge impact: in relationships with friends, family, children, co-workers, neighbours and general public. The same rules apply as with your online engagements. Foster curiosity, compassion, accountability and boundaries, especially with people in your circle.

It's easy to let coded racism pass by at the dinner table or in a family WhatsApp group. It's easy to laugh along, or leave the room to avoid being 'an outcast'. It's easier to just let your Dad keep saying the word 'half-caste' to describe mixed Black and white children, to prioritise the comfort of white family members, rather than address racism and reduce harm, while making excuses because they are old or, 'That's just the way they are.' If you don't attempt to tackle their racism, you can bet we experience it when they leave their homes. It's not something that just magically happens in your house.

Here's where you have to turn your courage up a notch. The risk of being ostracised and being branded boring, miserable, or obsessed with race is high.

Scenario: Gran keeps using the word 'coloured' to describe Black people.

You: What do you mean when you say 'Coloured' Gran?

Gran: You know, people with darker skin.

You: Do you mean Black people?

Gran: Yes, them.

You: It's OK to say 'Black' Gran. In fact, 'Black' is preferred than saying 'Coloured'. That language is harmful/racist now, Gran.

Gran: In my day, we couldn't say Black.

You: I know, Gran. It's hard to keep up. Language is always changing. If you're not sure, you can ask me anytime, I know you care about people and would want to know if you're using racist/offensive/harmful language. I get it wrong too sometimes.

This is why it's important to bring people in on your

anti-racism journey rather than turn into a teacher dictating to them. It doesn't work if it comes from a place of superiority. So:

1. Be aware of when you're getting frustrated with their lack of 'desire' to wake up.
2. Hold a mirror up to your own behaviour.
3. When was a time where you didn't get it?
4. When was the time you were saying the exact same thing?
5. What were the ingredients that hooked you in and woke you up? Start there.

If you go into the 'I'm better than you, idiot' self-righteous phase, please know, that's not allyship. That's you proving you're better than them, and you're not. You just know more than them in this area; it doesn't make you inherently better. This is the same energy that drives cancel culture, misdirected rage or guilt and this bizarre expectation for people to know everything and always say the right thing. I'm not here for that. It's arrogant, it doesn't help us and it definitely isn't anti-racist. Accountability? Yes. Cancel culture? No. We need to wipe out any sense of superiority. We've had enough of that.

One student contacted me to say she was finding the work hard and avoiding having confrontations about racism with friends and family. 'They just won't listen. I don't want to end up in confrontation, so I don't try.'

My response? 'What would happen if you treated it as a conversation rather than a confrontation?'

We're not at war, troops. This is about human connection and genuinely wanting to see mutual transformation.

1. Show, don't tell. Talk about your journey and the times when you got (and get) it wrong or felt censored.

2. Share how conversations about race made you feel uncomfortable and still do.

3. Explain how you manage when you're finding it hard.

Feeling hopeless, overwhelmed and helpless are common responses to anti-racism. Here's a scenario to help you engage with peers who are overwhelmed and apathetic:

Scenario: 'I care about this stuff, I really do. But I just don't have time. I don't have time for this, I am stressed, I have kids with additional needs. I am doing my best, I am sorry if that is not good enough. What more can I do?'

Consider this response: 'I hear you. It can feel really hard. Even though all of these things are true and knowing there are people who also experience difficult days like this as well as racism, what *can* you do?'

This question acknowledges their situation and helps them come up with their own ideas and feel more in control. What do you do when you're feeling overwhelmed? Offer support while holding them to account. If they get stuck, help them with ideas they can factor into their usual everyday routine so anti-racism doesn't feel like an add on.

For example, instead of finding time to read, perhaps they could listen to anti-racism podcasts or audiobooks while cleaning at home or shopping. Centring wellness and also learning from Black and Brown practitioners might help them manage stress and wellbeing. Could they read stories to their children at bedtime with Black protagonists? Intentionally shop with, or tangibly support Black businesses and their owners? We can always do something to be actively anti-racist based on our current capacity and it doesn't have to be big or confrontational.

Concerns often come up from white students when a Black public figure is seen to be upholding racist views in media or online, such as: believing Black people have a victim mentality, denying systemic racism, believing white supremacy is rare and down to a few individuals, and generally blaming Black people for their own victimisation. Their white friends share this content as a means to prove racism doesn't exist and they get completely stuck on how to address it.

Creating pawns out of Black people who uphold contradictory views that go against the general interest of the majority of Black people, is a powerful and historical racist tactic used by white folk to delegitimise racism and weaponise the 'good Black person model minority' narrative. It's also regularly used by white folk to avoid engaging in anti-racism to both hide behind and validate their own racist beliefs in the process.

It's important you:

1. Use this as an opportunity to call your friend in, and address *their* racism.
2. Get curious about why they seem to find it difficult to believe evidence from experts and accounts of racism from majority groups.
3. Centre the problematic content being shared by the Black public figure and avoid psychoanalysing the Black person or attacking their individual character.

Remember that not everyone will get it in the moment. You can come back and revisit conversations, recommend films, articles, podcasts, current affairs and other resources to help you foster their curiosity and keep dialogue open. Revisiting also gives them processing time and you time to gather your thoughts and work on your responses.

★

It goes without saying, not everyone will like you drawing attention to their ignorance; you're going to be front and centre of other people's racialised fragility and rage. You're going to be branded 'mad' or a 'troublemaker'. Some people will react badly. Sometimes *you'll* react badly. Some people will completely disengage. Sometimes you will freeze and sometimes you'll feel in despair and want to give up; sometimes the penny will drop so viscerally you'll feel incredible.

One of my students shared this with me: 'As a white person in an all-white space, I'm noticing how "weird" it is to be anti-racist. People think you have lost it, gone mad, or dismiss it as being radical, idealist, inappropriate and, my best one yet, "unprofessional". It's quite scary, but it doesn't stop me. Instead of the outright revolution I was first expecting in anti-racism, I realised there are many non-confrontational things I can do that are really helping open up conversations that are already making changes. My anger has turned into project planning!'

Whatever response you get, keep going. Build your anti-racism muscle. Keep coming back to the work. Keep sowing seeds and bringing people into being better – you never know the impact you are having towards something greater than you.

Over to You

How effective your allyship is will be determined by how much you engage in this work and continue to interrogate when your racism sneaks in. When you go back to the rhythm of the status quo, you have to be vigilant.

Master your apology

Master your capacity to receive feedback and give apologies with grace and ease, especially in close friendships. If you learn one thing from me about apologies, let it be this:

Please don't ever give an 'I'm sorry you feel that way' apology. They are not meaningful. They come from a place of feeling like you have to apologise, rather than because you want to. If you can't listen and take responsibility for any harm your actions or inactions have caused, whether intentionally or not, don't bother apologising. Because if you're honest, you're not really doing it to atone and reduce harm, but to make yourself feel comfortable again. That's not an apology.

An apology is for the other person, not for you. According to Harriet Lerner, author of *Why Won't You Apologise, Big Betrayals and Everyday Hurts*, having a big platform of self-worth will be a huge contributing factor in your capacity to be able to apologise for serious harm.[29]

One anti-racism student shared, 'I can safely say, this is one of the hardest things in my journey. To be wrong, as a man means you aren't as good, you're second best and you don't think your ego can take it, so you fight to defend yourself, even if you are in the wrong. When I started saying "I'm sorry" all relationships improved, including the relationship with myself.'

In your anti-racism journey, be transparent and manage expectations upfront. You are going to do or say things that are harmful or racist in this work over and over again; consider setting a boundary: 'If I unintentionally do or say something racist, no matter how awkward, please let me know. I am actively working on being anti-racist and reducing harm and am open to receiving feedback.'

Here are some sentence stems you can use to meaningfully acknowledge and reduce harm:

- I'm sorry I offended you (not '*if* I offended you' – you did, whether you intended to or not. Own your words, own your behaviour.)
- I didn't know that was your experience. Do you mind telling me more so I can better understand? (Remember they have a right to say no to this.)
- I'm listening and I will continue to hold this in mind.
- I'm sorry for hurting you.
- I'm sorry for doing X or saying X (be specific about what you are apologising for, vague apologies are non-apologies.)
- I apologise. I care about you and this relationship. Please let me know if there is anything I have missed so I can make things better going forward.

When you are feeling defensive, acknowledge it:

- I care about you and I want to hear you. I am currently feeling defensive and finding it really hard to listen. I am sorry my actions have hurt you; can we speak about this again, or in a little while when I am better able to listen?

And perhaps most importantly, before or after an apology show gratitude for being given feedback:

- Thank you for letting me know.

It's far easier not to bother giving feedback on racism. So if someone has taken the time to give you feedback, it means they care about the relationship, their wellbeing and reducing the risk of harm to others – or they're just brave enough to run the risk, because there is a real risk of receiving further racism when we give you feedback. A thank you is acknowledgement of that. And also, you'd rather know, wouldn't you?

Remember, when you do or say something racist, if you aren't sure what you did, reflect on it in your own time. If you're having a shame spiral, don't inflict further harm by placing the burden of forgiveness on the person that's just experienced your racism. If them holding a boundary and giving you feedback on your racism sends you into a shame spiral, express it with your own support network or other white folk doing this work who can help you unpack it. It's not Black folks' role to do that for you. Our aim in apologising is listening in order to respond and take accountability, not listening in order to react and defend our position.

Also remember that just because you apologise does not mean they need to accept your apology. They're under no obligation to forgive you. This is about the other person, not you feeling comfortable again. By apologising and meaning it, it doesn't mean you are bad or wrong, it means you're choosing to serve something greater and taking responsibility for your racism – or, in fact, any 'ism'. A meaningful apology is the very first step to atonement and should be backed up by action and a change in behaviour. It is *not* the end goal.

Decentre yourself

Remember, this isn't about you.

Notice the following:

- How much time you're taking up in meetings/environments where Black people and People of Colour are being centred.
- How often you speak over Black people.
- How hard you find it to actively listen without centring your own experience.
- How effective you are at holding space for others.

If someone is giving feedback on their experience of racism and you feel yourself finding ways to delegitimise their experience, you might start to focus and comment on the tone of delivery. If you notice muscles in your body start to reflex, if you go into an agitated, defensive state, that is a sign you feel under attack and are now functioning to protect your identity. You have stopped listening and you've definitely stopped being anti-racist.

How someone expresses their experiences of being persecuted or racially abused is none of your business. Their expression of anger and their feelings have nothing to do with you.

You might get called racist. It might feel horrible, I don't doubt that, but it is not the worst thing in the world to be called a racist. Not even close. You won't implode and if you own your inherent racism, if you own that part of you that you are working on, it won't have any power over you anymore.

Being anti-racist will not always make you popular. People will want, with all their might, for you to stop talking about racism and to go back to the way things were. You'll become fatigued; at times it will feel all consuming. You will be met with frustration, fear and resistance, and apathy, from yourself and others, time and time again. That is why it is so important to consistently build your resilience and prioritise self-care – we just cannot be effective when we are burned out.

Remain self-aware:

- What is your body communicating with you? What sensations are you experiencing?
- Ask yourself: Why is this challenging me?
- How is my mental health today?
- Am I choosing white comfort over doing the right thing?
- What is the fear?
- What do I need in this moment to feel less fear and more courage?

Continue with regular self-enquiry:

- How has being in the majority made you feel superior in life?
- How has your race protected you?
- How was I just complicit in racism?
- How would it feel if the playing fields were levelled out? If you are not the default, not always catered to? Would you truly welcome that or feel threatened by that?

And an important call to action:

- Who are the people in my life I need to have *real* conversations with?

Which approaches worked for you when you were sleepwalking through racism? This is going to be one of the most powerful questions to ask yourself when engaging with peers who aren't quite there yet. What pulled you in and what didn't?

This isn't about being perfect, this is about being present. Perfectionism is a function of white supremacy, so get comfortable with being imperfect and messy.

Before we end this chapter, I want to share a story about being of service. I remember finding out the unexpected news that one of my mum's dearest friends, had been diagnosed with motor neurone disease. Her name was Fatima. She had been in my life since I was a toddler and we first met when we were all neighbours – my brother and I grew up with her son and daughter, no doubt connected by our shared experiences of receiving racism from another neighbour. That wasn't all that we shared, of course. We went on trips together, her daughter and I went to dance school together, various girls' trips including Blackpool, countless Chinese buffets – lots of belly laughing and really great memories. We even went, on one particular memorable holiday, to meet her family and visit their home country, Morocco. Fatima was vivacious and generous to others, and mostly, she was utterly hilarious. Driving was not her forte, shall we say, and she would often leave me and my mum in hysterics over some of her driving adventures, including when the satnav told her to 'go right at the roundabout' and she, quite literally, did.

As always, life takes over, you start going on your own path, you move and those frequent trips start to dwindle, you're in different rhythms and the previously frequent visits become once every few years. I hadn't seen Fatima for a long time when I found out she had been diagnosed with this cruel disease that seemed to attack her body at lightning speed. I felt cheated and guilty all at once. After treatment in hospital had little impact, it didn't take long before she was moved into a hospice. I've been in that place too many times before so I knew what that meant. I remember feeling fearful and not knowing what to say. I really didn't want to go and, in fact, my mum had told me not to, because I wouldn't want to see her that way. I shared my fear with my husband, and he said seven words that had me cooking Caribbean soup for her husband, Mohammed, and heading down the motorway to see her: 'It's not for you, it's for her.'

I hadn't announced my arrival, I just turned up. I hadn't seen Mohammed or Fatima in years. And was greeted by Mohammed's big warm smile and bright eyes when he exclaimed, 'Look who's here!'

By this point Fatima could only move her head and blink her eyes. She turned towards me and her eyes lit up and then filled with tears, which rolled down her cheeks. I kissed her on her forehead. 'Hello stranger,' I said, as I wiped her tears away.

I understood powerfully in that moment not to underestimate the gift of just showing up. Of doing something for others, no matter how scared or uncomfortable you are. Though desperately sad, there was nothing to be afraid of. In fact, I found stealing a few more moments of time; an unexpected peaceful chance to be truly present. Being there and seeing her face was a gift for me and a memory I will never forget. A few days later, she passed away.

This work isn't solely for you. It's for humanity. Your fear, though loud as hell at times, is valid *and* it is not more important than serving something greater than you. Show up and be of service because you are rare; there are not currently enough of you courageous enough to be truly anti-racist. So your role is to do the work with care, honesty and integrity and to bring as many people along on this journey with you. Don't underestimate the ripple effect this has. When you just allow yourself to see people in all their humanity and be of service, it is quite the gift.

12. Courage is Contagious

'Fear is contagious – so is courage'

CAN DÜNDAR[1]

In preparation for writing this book, I researched and interviewed a number of case studies, analysed thousands of comments and messages and I noticed there was an overarching and universal emotion that came up time and time again – fear.

Fear of the 'oppressor'.

Fear of the 'victim'.

Fear of unknowingly being responsible for another person's pain.

Fear of receiving racial abuse.

Fear of causing offence.

Fear of saying the wrong thing.

Fear of retribution.

Fear of losing control.

Fear of losing power.

Fear of not being believed.

Fear of being hated.

Fear of nothing changing.

History has shown, and continues to show us that we are repeating cycles and patterns of behaviour on a global level, different manifestations of the same thing, hoping that this time around we pay attention, listen, face our collective suffering and heal. It is up to us, and only us, to consciously and intentionally work to break that cycle or in another decade there will need to be another book just like this, having the same conversation.

Where you go next is up to you. The responsibility and choice is yours. Will you choose to adopt the practices in this book and change or recoil into the performative wings, hoping nobody will notice you've chosen, this time consciously, to continue to uphold white supremacy? Because that's the important difference between today and when you first started this book – now you know.

Being anti-racist is ultimately about evolution. It's about putting an end to this cycle that continues to dehumanise people. To have the courage to not only confront the status quo but turn it inside out. It's about being able to tolerate your fears of being hated whilst simultaneously wanting to belong. Being a better human isn't about getting it right, or never experiencing vulnerability or fear, it's about learning to be present with fear, getting it wrong and doing it anyway.

★

It was 24 November 2019 and the nerves were back. Upset stomach, clammy palms, overheating. I was about to stand face-to-face with one of my biggest fears. I remember looking down at my feet in bright orange stilettos, standing on a red circular carpet, feeling powerful anxiety at the pit of my stomach. Flight, fight or freeze was in full swing. Quite frankly I was ready to walk out, in fact, I was ready to run.

I was completely overcome by this overwhelming concoction of fear and anxiety taking over my body. It was unexpected because, as a professional speaker, I'm used to being on stage, and as a former actress and singer, I've been on stage many times with an audience of thousands. But this feeling was profoundly different. Standing there, I had never felt more naked on stage. This was me with no script, no costumes or characters to hide behind. No backing singers to cover me when I flunked notes. Just me.

It was in those thirty seconds before I was due to start, it suddenly hit me. I realised that when I agreed to do a TEDx talk about microaggressions, I never actually considered the magnitude of standing in front of a 600-strong white-majority audience, in Germany no less, to share one of my most painful and life-defining memories of racism. To talk about the audience's inherent racism and how it impacts me. I remember scanning the room looking for corners I could discreetly vomit in in case I didn't manage to make a quick enough exit.

Then I stopped holding my breath, and instead of feeling scared, felt a comforting warmth from the spotlight on my face, shining a welcome light among the darkness that surrounded me. And something shifted.

I surrendered.

That was the moment that fear evolved into courage and in an instant, I'd never felt more like I belonged on a stage in my life. It was like I was being held up and propelled forward by every single person who'd had their voices suppressed, by those who simply couldn't find the words to even begin to express the impact this daily trauma has on us. I knew, in that moment, I was there to serve not only my 7-year-old self, but everyone else's too.

You could hear a pin drop.

And then I started to speak.

'Hello, my name is Nova.'

★

When I met journalist Can Dündar backstage, I didn't know who he was, other than a fellow TEDx speaker, but I did notice he had a warm and inviting smile and I instantly felt very safe around him. So I looked for him during my talk and he was the first person who greeted me afterwards. He came to me with extended arms and gave me one of the most reassuring hugs. He said, 'Thank you for inspiring me with your courage.'

I was touched and thought he was just being kind and I didn't realise the significance of those few words until a couple of hours later when it was his turn to stand on that famous red circle.

Can Dündar is a well-known author and journalist from Turkey. He was the editor-in-chief of a leading centre-left news-paper called *Cumhuriyet*, until he was arrested in 2015.

His newspaper had exposed the Turkish government for sending military weapons to Syria, in what was known as the National Intelligence Organisation scandal. Can was threatened by officials and told in no uncertain terms to publish those findings and if he did, he and all those responsible for the article, would be imprisoned.

This gave Can an impossible decision to make. Serve humanity and let the wider public know the truth about the gross violence and human rights travesty and corruption the government was enabling, and avert further harm being caused. Or serve himself and remain complicit. The latter would be understandable, because with those kinds of threats, you wouldn't choose to send yourself and your colleagues to prison.

He didn't make his decision alone – he consulted the editorial and legal teams. The fear must have been all-consuming but the decision was unanimous. Can and his team decided to serve something greater and published the story as front page news.

This decision led to an assassination attempt on his life, which was captured on video, where his wife can be seen courageously placing her body between the gunman and her husband without a second thought. The shots missed them both. Can was imprisoned without due process or cause and placed in solitary confinement. He had his human rights stripped away from him for disrupting the status quo, uncovering corruption and speaking truth to power.

Throughout all of this, through creativity and community with other journalists who had also been unjustly imprisoned, Can never lost hope, nor regretted his decision. His courage inspired an 80-year-old journalist to turn up outside of prison with a chair to peacefully protest about Can's arrest. This inspired hundreds to do the same and within a few weeks, this increased to thousands. Can is now living in exile with his wife in Germany, and is still serving humanitarian causes.

The courage it must've taken to go against the grain, to do what was right even though the risk was insurmountable and incomprehensible to most of us. Fear has always been a weapon used to make us feel scared of the other. Can said we have to be brave enough to challenge the oppression. By author Brené Brown's very definition of integrity, Can chose courage over comfort. He chose what was right over what was easy, he practiced his values, boldly and without just professing them.[2] He role-modelled them. And yet, there he was, not only recognising my courage, but thanking me for it and for inspiring him. Well, as you can imagine, there were tears and I was deeply humbled.

Whatever we do – from speaking up in a meeting room or outside the school gates, to risking our freedom for something we believe in – our courage can have a profound and powerful impact on each other and the world around us.

While I acknowledge at times the state of play can feel hopeless, in the twenty-four months since typing my first word of this book, I have also seen a seismic shift in the number of people, especially women, who are waking up from the deepest of slumbers. There are parents who want to raise socially conscious and anti-racist children. Teenagers who are not willing to go along with the grain and are unashamedly holding adults to account. Even civil rights activist and author Angela Davis expressed during a talk for the Southbank Centre in September 2020 that she never expected to see such a shift like this in her lifetime. After everything she has been through, that revelation is profound.

So it's time to assemble. There are legions of like-minded people who want to live in a world where there is peace, justice, equity first and then equality for all. People who are responding to a silent call to courage and are realising, perhaps for the first time, that rather than waiting for another great like Dr Martin

Luther King Jr. to lead us, each of us are part of the solution to bring forth that change.

This is *big* work. It will go down in the history books.

★

One white student who chose to engage in anti-racism work is also an educational psychologist and is bringing what she is learning into the workplace. She shared how colleagues were so motivated, they've set up anti-racism groups. When she delivers presentations, she courageously starts with, 'My name is X and I am racist.' She delivers these to service leaders and professional teams covering the entire county to discuss what she has learned from her anti-racism journey and how racism impacts young people, especially those at higher risk of social exclusion due to intersecting identities and what they can start to do to address it in their industry. These teams then visit schools asking teachers what they are doing to work in an anti-racist way and supporting teachers and colleagues to go on their own anti-racist journey.

She shared with me these educational psychologists' and professional teams' work across:

- 45 secondary schools
- 350 primary schools
- 10 SEN schools
- 3 pupil referral units

In total, they have reached around 170,000 children and young people. This is just one person's circle of influence and this is just the ripple effect this one student is having in the workplace alone. Don't underestimate the power of one.

Black and Brown folk often reach out to me and share how my courage is inspiring them to speak their truth, or how they feel when white people in their life do this work properly:

'It feels like freedom.'

'It feels like I can breathe. I hadn't even realised I was holding my breath around them until recently. I can finally stop holding my breath.'

'Gosh. It makes all the difference in the world. The emotional and psychological trauma of having to code-switch, of worrying about white fragility...the constant feeling of not being able to be myself and trying to appease to belong, fall away.'

I receive hundreds and hundreds of comments and messages like this. What makes them most profound is what they share in common – that they don't have swathes of friends in their life doing anti-racism work, usually just one. You have a chance and a responsibility to change that.

Let the seeds you have sown take root. Don't ever underestimate your influence and the people you are inspiring along the way, by sharing about your vulnerability and your journey with others like you, online, in the workplace, your place of worship, calling others in along the way. They might not be making the loudest noise, but they are watching, they are processing, they are learning and they are taking inspiration from your courage.

There is no one-size-fits-all journey. That's why, when people ask me, 'What can I do to help? What can I do to be a better ally?' my response will always be: 'Unlearn your racism.' Because it is in that discovery – in having the courage to face your own racism head on, and then hold up a mirror to it — that you will uncover the unique role you play in helping to dismantle racism. Acknowledging your complicity, feeling the shame and pain associated with it, facing it, giving yourself the gift of healing, then liberating yourself from it, peeling back those layers and allowing yourself to live in your full humanity, that's what makes your journey yours. I cannot impress this on you enough: this work is about all of our humanity and collective healing. How you show up and what you will be able to contribute, not only depends on your social location and skills but mostly, your commitment to travelling on your own unique journey to becoming anti-racist.

'When you're close to your suffering you're close to your humanity, and when you're close to your humanity you become a mirror that reflects other people's humanity back to them.'
BUDDHIST LAMA ROD[3]

Leaning into allyship is about waking up and gaining a new level of consciousness over and over again. Making the decision to intentionally move out of the cosy corner of your complicit comfort zone, indeed takes courage. You may well lose friends and might even have to take a step back and hold firm boundaries with family. There will be times when you will feel seduced into giving up, where you feel far from courageous and when fear begins to feel too powerful and perhaps even more significant than disrupting racism.

Consider forming an accountability group with like-minded people doing this work. This will help you disrupt apathy, which will be your biggest nemesis. Connect with people who will hold a high standard for you, support and hold compassion for you, but will not collude with you or enable your racism. The magnetic undercurrent of white supremacy is a force to be reckoned with and will tempt you to go back to your comfort zone when it gets too hard. Your accountability group will propel you forwards, they will inspire you and they will help you keep momentum.

Don't get complacent. Set your intentions at the beginning of every week. What can I do to be actively anti-racist today? Who and how do you want to serve?

If it feels tough when other white folk get on your last nerve (because they will), don't give up. Up your self-care and keep going, because every meaningful interaction is a chance to disrupt racism and an opportunity to reduce harm. What is on the other side? The joy, the connection, being able to live in integrity and with honesty, where your words match your behaviour. No longer having to carry the burden of the lie of white supremacy and fear of being found out. The range of joy you will experience, but mostly, the gifts that come from serving something greater than you: deeper connections, reducing harm and actively aiding yours and others' healing. These gifts all help you live in your full humanity, while they too, can finally, live in theirs.

*

'When you know better you do better.'
DR MAYA ANEGLOU[4]

So, this is where I leave you. This is where my labour stops and your allyship starts. This is where you make a conscious choice to stop colluding with racism, take the baton, pick up the pace and advocate alongside us. This is where you have a chance to rewrite history, to break the cycle and start a chain of communal healing instead of continued trauma.

Continue to hold yourself and others – brands, institutions, government and most importantly, people you love – accountable for their racism. As Angela Davis once said, 'You have to act as if it were possible to radically transform the world and you have to do it all the time.'[5]

If you are truly anti-racist, you become the work. You will get it wrong, you will have inevitable hidden spots when you thought you knew better and it might smart a little and knock your confidence but bounce back, decentre, shake it off and get back to work. Interrupting racism, or anything that is perceived to threaten a dominant group takes an extraordinary amount of courage.

So it's time to be brave. To be better. To show up, agitate, listen and learn to hold space for others. To be vulnerable so you can take consistent action and use your humanity as a superpower. To create a tidal wave of change.

Epilogue

Before I leave you, I just want to share one final note. I thought courage was standing on that red TEDx circle, until February 2020.

Therapy, wellness and healing, as you will have come to realise, have always played a central role in my life. It has had to, not only to help me do my job and support others, but to also support my own wellness and build resilience from living in a racist society. But after navigating microaggressions in one-too-many therapy sessions, I was yearning for something deeper. Both the training and therapy I had, while helpful in many ways, did not scratch the surface for dealing with the trauma of racism. I was tired of being half catered to and I no longer wanted to carry the burden of racism.

It was in conversation with one of my course graduates, and now dear friend, Selina Barker, the first person to enrol on my anti-racism course, who now being awoken to the impact of racism, suggested doing a spiritual healing retreat at the time called The Bridge. I was sceptical. I sensed that I would, as I often am, be the only Black person and, because I wanted to address the impact of racism, I was mindful of not abandoning myself for the comfort of white people around me who would, without a doubt, be triggered by all I had to say. I was frank and asked the co-founder, a mixed-race Black woman and now friend, Donna

Lancaster, if I would be 'the only'. She knew what I meant. She was honest and said, 'Yes, Nova, most likely.'

I expressed my fears, because I was not willing to swallow racism and centre white comfort any longer, as I was holding onto trauma, that was having a detrimental impact on not only my emotional wellbeing, but also my physical health. In fact, ten days after my TEDx talk, I'd had open surgery. I wasn't just going through physical healing – I was craving something deeper, to heal from the inside out, I was craving something ancestral because I knew the enormity of the pain I was carrying could not just be mine.

Donna listened and said: 'Nova, maybe part of your healing is to be able to speak your whole truth in front of white people.' I had been doing anti-racism work for years at that point so, to be fair, I thought I was already doing that. I then went on to deliver my TEDx talk and I definitely thought I was doing it then. But no. Not even close.

I decided to take the plunge. I packed my bags, left my husband for six days, with no phone contact, and off I went. I was, in fact, the only Black person there and the dread in the pit of my stomach felt like the weight of a cannonball. Here we go again, I thought. But something felt different. I just did not have the energy for the usual tap-dancing routine I had learned to perform around whiteness anymore. I was done.

During the retreat, participants had to write a letter to a person or a situation that had caused us harm. We were encouraged to say the 'unsayable'. The majority of my group were ready to rock 'n' roll – they knew who they were writing to, typically an individual. I hung back. Completely perplexed. Who am I going to write my letter to? Dear Racism? It's not any one person, but a community. Donna looked at me, equally perplexed, as if it were entirely obvious who I should write to: 'Nova'. She said. 'Your letter needs to be: "Dear White People…"'

There was just no way. You see, it wasn't just the act of writing the letter, or even the thought of reading it out to complete strangers that triggered huge fear – it was the realisation I had to read it out to the group… of all white people.

Donna invited me to start by just writing the letter and take it from there. Reminding me I had a choice. After writing the letter. I decided to try. I looked at all of the faces of the white people in the room, knowing what they were about to witness. Even in my own healing experience, I was deeply worried about how my words may hurt them, about the enormity of what the colour of their skin represents. That same fear response I had for my TEDx talk was present again, but magnified.

I had a panic attack. Donna knew and she said six powerful words: 'I will hold space for you.'

At that moment, I had another choice. To choose fear and comfort for myself (understandably) as well as white comfort or to choose my healing. I chose my healing.

It took the courage of a motherfucking lion that I did not know was in me. But there it was again, that moment when fear evolved into courage, followed by beautiful surrender. I was free-falling and rooted both at once. I felt extraordinary courage and the warmth of invisible support of all those who had endured far worse and gone before me. I took a deep breath. And I began.

Dear White People…

*

When I came out of surgery, in the recovery room, still under the haze of anaesthetic and starvation, the surgeon was stunned. Pre-surgery, I was told I had around thirteen tumours in my womb. Symptoms commonly linked to epigenetics and the transmission of transgenerational trauma being passed down from womb to womb. The surgeon went on to explain that they didn't find the thirteen tumours they were expecting to remove. Instead, they found thirty-seven. Thirty-seven tumours cruelly mimicking a three-month pregnancy.

It was my husband's gasp and response that stayed with me: 'Wow, that's almost one for every year.' It was in that moment that I made a choice that would impact not only how I show up in the world, how I love, how I take care of my body, how I teach, what I will no longer tolerate, but who I become. Through the interruption of slavery in my lineage and decades of code-switching and assimilation that followed, I got lost along the way. In being courageous enough to make that choice to have surgery, in feeling deserving enough to centre my healing, I was finally able to come back home and have the courage to be who I was always meant to be – myself.

This work is about collective healing. To make a choice about being actively anti-racist, is to choose how you show up in the world and to choose who you want to become. And my choice? To do all that I can to ensure the line of transgenerational trauma stops with me.

Now you have a choice. So make it.

Be courageous. It's contagious.

Endnotes

Introduction

1   James Baldwin, *Notes of a Native Son* (London: Penguin Books, 1955).

2   Angela Saini, *Superior: The Return of Race Science* (Boston: Beacon Press, 2019), 47.

3   June Sarpong, *Diversify* (London: HQ/HarperCollins, 2017).

Chapter 1

1   Button Poetry, 'Guante, "How to Explain White Supremacy to a White Supremacist"', www.youtube.com/watch?v=DbwcXDunxA8

2   Gloria J. Browne-Marshall, *Race, Law, and American Society: 1607–Present* (Oxford: Routledge, 2007), 2.

3   Browne-Marshall (2007), 4–6.

4   David Olusoga, *Black and British: A Forgotten History* (London: Macmillan, 2016), 70.

5   Browne-Marshall (2007), 2.

6   Raj Bhopal, 'The Beautiful Skull and Blumenbach's Errors: The Birth of the Scientific Concept of Race', *BMJ* (Clinical Research ed.), 335:7633 (2007) 1308-1309.

7   Joy DeGruy, *Post Traumatic Slave Syndrome: America's Legacy of Enduring Injury and Healing* (Oregon, Uptone Press 2005) 44–45.

8   Adam Rutherford, *How to Argue with a Racist: History, Science, Race and Reality* (London: Weidenfeld & Nicolson, 2020) 40.

9   Kimberly Macintosh, 'Integration is Not a One Way Process', March 2018, www.runnymedetrust. org/blog/integration-is-not-a-one-way-process/

10   Frank M. Snowden, Jr., *Before Color Prejudice: The Ancient View of Blacks* (Cambridge, MA: Harvard University Press 1983), 88.

11   Snowden, Jr. (1983), 86–87.

12   Kiona N. Smith, 'Ancient DNA Sheds Light on What Happened to the Taino, the Native Caribbeans', February 2018, www.arstechnica.com/science/2018/02/ natives-of-the-caribbean-wiped-out-during-colonization-left-dna-behind

13   David W. Swanson, *'A mark of maturity from white people is moving from shame and defensiveness about what we didn't know, to taking responsibility for hate we should have known'*, September 2020, https:// twitter.com/davidswanson/status/1306396657781769869

14   Shelter Report, 'Shut Out: The Barriers Low-Income Households Face in Private Renting', June 2017, https://assets.ctfassets.net/6sx vmndnpn0s/1V5daqZuWpZ2t5MLOVljTz/b454b87648294c072a 3ce7c81b596eb7/2017_06_-_Shut_out_the_barriers_low_income_ households_face_in_pivate_renting.pdf/

15   Deborah Garvie, 'BAME Homelessness Matters and is Disproportionately Rising – Time for the Government to Act', October 2017, https://blog.shelter.org.uk/2017/10/ bame-homelessness-matters-and-is-disproportionately-rising-time- for-the-government-to-act/

16   Liam Geraghty, 'Black People in UK "Three Times as Likely to Experience Homelessness"', October 2020, https://www.bigissue. com/latest/black-people-are-more-than-three-times-as-likely-to-experience-homelessness/

17   Elisabeth Kübler-Ross, *On Death and Dying* (New York: Macmillan, 1969).

18   Karen D. Pyke, 'What is Internalized Racial Oppression and Why Don't We Study It? Acknowledging Racism's Hidden Injuries', *Sociological Perspectives,* 53:4 (2010), 551–572.

19 Mark Townsend, 'Black People "40 Times More Likely" to Be Stopped and Searched in UK', May 2019, https://www.theguardian.com/law/2019/may/04/stop-and-search-new-row-racial-bias/

20 MBRRACE-UK Report, 'Saving Lives, Improving Mothers' Care: Rapid Report: Learning from SARS-CoV-2-Related and Associated Maternal Deaths in the UK', March–May 2020, https://www.npeu.ox.ac.uk/assets/downloads/mbrrace-uk/reports/MBRRACE-UK_Maternal_Report_2020_v10_FINAL.pdf

21 GOV.UK, 'Detentions Under The Mental Health Act', March 2021, https://www.ethnicity-facts-figures.service.gov.uk/health/mental-health/detentions-under-the-mental-health-act/latest

22 Haroon Siddique, 'Minority Ethnic Britons Face "Shocking" Job Discrimination', January 2019, https://www.theguardian.com/world/2019/jan/17/minority-ethnic-britons-face-shocking-job-discrimination

23 Reni Eddo-Lodge, *Why I'm No Longer Talking to White People About Race* (London: Bloomsbury, 2017).

24 Sir William Macpherson of Cluny, *The Stephen Lawrence Inquiry: Report of an Inquiry*, February 1999, https://assets.publishing.service.gov.uk/government/uploads/system/uploads/attachment_data/file/277111/4262.pdf

25 'Race Relations Bill', *Hansard* HC Deb 23 (1968) 763 cc. 53–198., www.hansard.millbanksystems.com/commons/1968/apr/23/race-relations-bill

26 Peter Walker, Haroon Siddique and Jamie Grierson, 'Dismay as No. 10 Adviser is Chosen to Set Up UK Race Inequality Commission', June 2020, https://www.theguardian.com/world/2020/jun/15/dismay-over-adviser-chosen-set-up-uk-race-inequality-commission-munira-mirza

27 Munira Mirza, 'Lammy Review: The Myth of Institutionalised Racism', September 2017, https://www.spiked-online.com/2017/09/11/lammy-review-the-myth-of-institutional-racism/ and Tony Sewell, Masterclass in Victimhood, September 2010,

https://www.prospectmagazine.co.uk/magazine/black-boys-victimhood-school

28 Commission on Race and Ethnic Disparities, 'Commission on Race and Ethnic Disparities: The Report', March 2021, https://assets.publishing.service.gov.uk/government/uploads/system/uploads/attachment_data/file/974507/20210331_-_CRED_Report_-_FINAL_-_Web_Accessible.pdf

29 Sophia Sleigh, 'Racial Equality Report Chairman Hits Back at Claims Section "Glorifies" Slave Trade', April 2021, https://www.standard.co.uk/news/politics/commission-on-race-and-ethnic-disparities-report-slavery-marsha-de-cordova-b927301.html

30 House of Commons House of Lords Joint Committee on Human Rights, 'Black People, Racism and Human Rights' Eleventh Report of Session 2019–21, November 2020, https://committees.parliament.uk/publications/3376/documents/32359/default/

31 Emma Brazell, 'Laurence Fox Gets "History Lesson" on Sikh Troops Who Died for Britain in WWI', January 2020, https://metro.co.uk/2020/01/21/laurence-fox-gets-history-lesson-sikh-troops-died-britain-wwi-12096944/

32 Jackie Kay, 'Jackie Kay on Arthur Roberts: The Black Scottish First World War Soldier Who Felt Forgotten', November 2018, https://www.theguardian.com/books/2018/nov/11/jackie-kay-makar-poem-black-scottish-first-world-war-soldier-arthur-roberts

33 BBC News, 'UKIP suspends leader's girlfriend after Meghan Markle texts', January 2018, https://www.bbc.co.uk/news/uk-politics-42679187

34 John Blake, 'Don't Use the Royal Birth to Trot Out a Dangerous Myth', May 2019, https://edition.cnn.com/2019/05/06/us/prince-harry-meghan-royal-baby-mixed-race-hope/index.html

35 Salma Abdelaziz, 'Meghan Said Racism Drove Her Out of the UK. Black Britons Ask, "Are We Still Here in 2021?"', March 2021, edition.cnn.com/2021/03/12/uk/ meghan-race-britain-gbr-intl/index.html

36 Lanre Bakare, 'Stormzy: UK is "Definitely Racist" and Johnson Has Made it Worse', December 2019, https://www.theguardian.com/music/2019/dec/21/stormzy-uk-is-racist-and-boris-johnson-has-made-it-worsel

37 BBC News, 'Fulham Schoolboy Dreadlock Ban Overturned', September 2018, https://www.bbc.co.uk/news/uk-england-london-45499584

38 Kameron Virk, 'Ruby Williams: No child with Afro Hair Should Suffer Like Me', February 2020, www.bbc.co.uk/news/newsbeat-45521094

Chapter 2

1 BBC Teach, '"A Diverse Teacher Workforce Benefits All Students, Not Just Those From A BAME Background" – What Does It Mean To Be A Black Teacher In The UK?', n.d., https://www.bbc.co.uk/teach/teacher-support/what-its-like-to-be-a-black-teacher-in-the-uk-today/zhfxdp3

2 Stella Dadzie, *A Kick in the Belly: Women, Slavery and Resistance* (London: Verso, 2020), 126.

3 Akala, *Natives: Race and Class in the Ruins of Empire* (London: Two Roads, 2018) 133.

4 Teju Cole, 'The White-Savior Industrial Complex', March 2012, https://www.theatlantic.com/international/archive/2012/03/the-white-savior-industrial-complex/254843/

5 Michael Brooke 'The Hays Code', 2013, http://www.screenonline.org.uk/film/id/592022/

6 Temi Adebowale 'How the Hays Code—as Seen in Hollywood—Censored Hollywood', May 2020, https://www.menshealth.com/entertainment/a32290089/hollywood-hays-code/

7 'Useful Notes / The Hays Code', n.d., https://tvtropes.org/pmwiki/pmwiki.php/UsefulNotes/TheHaysCode

8   Layla F. Saad, *Me and White Supremacy: A 28-Day Challenge to Combat Racism, Change the World, and Become a Good Ancestor* (2020) 229.

9   Becky Ferreira, 'Hidden Figures' Mathematician Katherine Johnson Defined Her Century and Left a Legacy for Ours', February 2020, https://www.vice.com/en/article/z3bqyy/hidden-figures-mathematician-katherine-johnson-defined-her-century-and-left-a-legacy-for-ours

10   David Lammy, 'The world does not need any more white saviours', February 2019, https://twitter.com/davidlammy/status/1100807912 33226752?lang=en

11   Igor Ryabov, 'How Much Does Physical Attractiveness Matter for Blacks? Linking Skin Color, Physical Attractiveness, and Black Status Attainment', March 2019, https://scholarworks.utrgv.edu/soc_fac/6/

Chapter 3

1   James Baldwin, in *I Am Not Your Negro* (dir. Raoul Peck) Netflix, 2016.

2   Walter A. Stewart, 'The Split in the Ego and the Mechanism of Disavowal', *The Psychoanalytic Quarterly,* 39:1 (2017) 1–16.

3   'Koos Couvée, 'Deaths in British Police Custody: No Convicted Officers Since 1969', August 2013, https://www.opendemocracy.net/en/opensecurity/deaths-in-british-police-custody-no-con-victed-officers-since-1969/

4   INQUEST, 'BAME Deaths in Police Custody', June 2021, https://www.inquest.org.uk/bame-deaths-in-police-custody

5   Paula Akpan, 'Say Their Names: 12 Victims of Police and State Brutality in the UK, *Vice News,* June 2020, https://www.vice.com/en/article/qj4j8x/remembering-police-brutality-victims-uk

6   Simon Hattenstone, 'Ultraviolence: the Shocking, Brutal Film About Deaths in Police Custody', October 2020, https://www.

theguardian.com/film/2020/oct/12/ultraviolence-ken-fero-documentary-injustice-deaths-police

7   Eddo-Lodge (2017), 42–44.

8   Hattenstone (2020).

9   Abi Rimmer, 'Ethnic Minority Staff: Trust Boards Still Do Not Reflect NHS Workforce', *BMJ*, 368:m618 (2020).

10 'Oprah with Harry and Meghan', ITV, March 2021

11 Rory Tingle et al, 'Kate and Camilla Break Cover Day After Devastating Accusations from Sussexes Trashed Their Husbands for Not Being Protective and Understanding Enough to 'suicidal race-victim', *Daily Mail,* March 2021, https://dailymail.co.uk/news/article-9339229/Royals-break-cover-amid-fall-onslaught-damaging-allegations

12 Alex Finnis, 'What Did Piers Morgan Say About Meghan Markle? How the GMB Presenter's Relationship with the Duchess Crumbled', March 2021, https://inews.co.uk/culture/television/piers-morgan-meghan-markle-relationship-what-say-good-morning-britain-quit-explained-906776

13 Piers Morgan, 'PIERS MORGAN: Stop Playing the Victim, Harry – You and Meghan Brought the Negative Press On Yourselves, and Just When You Turn Things Around, You Ruin it All', October 2019, https://www.dailymail.co.uk/news/article-7528951/PIERS-MORGAN-Harry-Meghan-brought-negative-press-yourselves.html

Chapter 4

1   Russell Howard, 'Daryl Davis on converting 200 white supremacists to leave the KKK', *The Russell Howard Hour*, November 2017, https://www.youtube.com/watch?v=HLtp13Rw8Kc

2   Gina Torino, 'How Racism and Microaggressions Lead to Worse Health', November 2017, https://centerforhealthjournalism.org/2017/11/08/how-racism-and-microaggressions-lead-worse-health

3 Nadia-Elysse Harris, 'Changes in DSM-5: Racism Can Cause PTSD Similar to That of Soldiers After War', May 2013, https://www.medicaldaily.com/changes-dsm-5-racism-can-cause-ptsd-similar-soldiers-after-war-246177

4 Guilaine Kinouani, 'Working With Racial Trauma in Psychotherapy', *Therapy Today*, October 2019, https://www.bacp.co.uk/bacp-journals/therapy-today/2019/october-2019/articles/working-with-racial-trauma-in-psychotherapy/

5 Caroline Tien, 'COVID-19 Symptom Lists and Detection Tools May Exhibit Racial Bias', December 2020, https://www.verywell-health.com/covid-symptom-detection-racial-bias-5093649

6 Nicola Davis, 'Higher Covid Deaths Among BAME People "Not Driven by Health Issues"', October 2020, https://www.theguardian.com/world/2020/oct/16/bame-people-more-likely-to-die-from-covid-than-white-people-study

7 Winston Morgan, 'Genetics is Not Why More BAME People Die of Coronavirus: Structural Racism is', June 2020, https://www.theguardian.com/commentisfree/2020/jun/04/genetics-bame-people-die-coronavirus-structural-racism

8 Abdul Razaq, Dominic Harrison, Sakthi Karunanithi, Ben Barr, Miqdad Asaria, Kamlesh Khunti, 'BAME COVID-19 Deaths – What Do We Know? Rapid Data & Evidence Review', *The Centre for Evidence-Based Medicine*, May 2020, https://www.cebm.net/covid-19/bame-covid-19-deaths-what-do-we-know-rapid-data-evidence-review/

9 Nursery & Midwifery Council 'Read the Code Online', 2015, https://www.nmc.org.uk/standards/code/read-the-code-online/

10 Zing Tsjeng, 'It's Time We Stopped Downplaying the UK's Anti-Asian Racism', March 2021, www.harpersbazaar.com/uk/culture/culture-news/a35692226/ its-time-we-stopped-downplaying-the-uks-anti-asian-racism/

11 Zosie Kmietowicz, 'Are medical schools turning a blind eye to racism?' *BMJ*, 368:m420 (2020).

12 David Batty, 'BAME Trainee Doctors in "Climate of Fear" Over Racism', February 2020, https://www.theguardian.com/education/2020/feb/14/bame-trainee-doctors-in-climate-of-fear-over-racism

13 Rob Picheta, 'Black newborns more likely to die when looked after by White doctors', August 2020, https://edition.cnn.com/2020/08/18/health/black-babies-mortality-rate-doctors-study-wellness-scli-intl/index.html

14 James Marion Sims, *The Story of My Life*, in Harriet A. Washington, *Medical Apartheid: The Dark History of Medical Experimentation on Black Americans from Colonial Times to the Present* (New York: Harlem Moon, 2006), 61.

15 Harriet A. Washington, *Medical Apartheid: The Dark History of Medical Experimentation on Black Americans from Colonial Times to the Present* (New York: Harlem Moon, 2006), 2.

16 Joy DeGruy, 'Post Traumatic Slave Syndrome' Lecture, London, 2008.

17 Kelly M. Hoffman, Sophie Trawalter, Jordan R. Axt, and M. Norman Oliver, 'Racial Bias in Pain Assessment and Treatment Recommendations, and False Beliefs About Biological Differences Between Blacks and Whites', *Proceedings of the National Academy of Sciences of the United States of America*, 2016.

18 Derald Wing Sue *Microaggressions in Everyday Life: Race Gender and Sexual Orientation* (London: Wiley 2010).

19 Monnica T. Williams, 'The Link Between Racism and PTSD', September 2015, https://www.psychologytoday.com/gb/blog/culturally-speaking/201509/the-link-between-racism-and-ptsd

20 Mental Health Foundation, 'Black, Asian and Minority Ethnic (BAME) communities', www.mentalhealth.org.uk/a-to-z/b/Black-asian-and-minority-ethnic- bame-communities

21 Pearn Kandola, 'Racism at Work Survey Results', March 2018. https://pearnkandola.com/app/uploads/2018/03/RaceSurveyReportFNLNewBrand.pdf

22 Kashmira Gander, 'The racist human zoos that time forgot', November 2016, https://www.independent.co.uk/life-style/racist-human-zoos-time-forgot-a7425286.html

23 Maya Angelou, *On the Pulse of Morning,* 1993.

Chapter 5

1   Gloria Steinem, *The Truth Will Set You Free, But First It Will Piss You Off!* Thoughts on Life, Love and Rebellion (New York: Random House, 2019).

2   Paul Foot, 'Tearing up the Race Card', *London Review of Books,* 17:23 (1995), https://www.lrb.co.uk/the-paper/v17/n23/paul-foot/tearing-up-the-race-card

3   Alexandra Sternlicht, 'Unilever To Rename 'Fair & Lovely' Skin Lightening Cream; Critics Call For Its Discontinuation', June 2020, https://www.forbes.com/sites/alexandrasternlicht/2020/06/25/unilever-to-rename-fair--lovely-skin-lightening-cream-critics-call-for-its-discontinuation/?sh=c9d894b1e8e9

4   Rutherford (2020), 40.

5   Akala, *Natives* (London: Two Roads, 2018).

6   Kathleen Pogue White, 'Surviving Hating and Being Hated: Some Personal Thoughts about Racism from a Psychoanalytic Perspective, *Contemporary* Psychoanalysis (2013) 401.

7   Andrew Woodcock, 'Racism: Equalities Minister Says Anti-Discrimination Drives Can "Create Prison For Black People"', October 2020, hwww.independent.co.uk/ news/uk/politics/racism-kemi-badenoch-reni-eddo-lodge-critical- race-theory-b1208279.html

8   Hardeep Matharu, 'Priti Patel Cannot Make Herself a Poster Girl For a "Non-racist Britain"', June 2020, https://bylinetimes.com/2020/06/15/priti-patel-cannot-make-herself-a-poster-girl-for-a-non-racist-britain/

9 M.S. James, 'Black Deaf or Deaf Black? An Investigation of Identity in the British Black Deaf Community', Unpublished Doctoral thesis, City University London, 2000.

10 Katherine Eban, *Bottle of Lies: The Inside Story of the Generic Drug Boom* (New York: Ecco Press, 2019) 340.

11 BBC News 'Coronavirus: France Racism Row Over Doctors' Africa Testing Comments', 2020, www.bbc.co.uk/news/world-europe-52151722

12 Washington (2006), 36.

13 Alex Matthews-King, 'Mental Health Act "Needs major reform" as Black Patients Four Times as Likely as Whites to Be Sectioned', December 2018, https://www.independent.co.uk/news/health/mental-health-act-detained-sectioned-ethnic-minority-bme-report-nhs-a8669246.html

14 Sarah Bellamy, 'Performing Whiteness', June 2020, https://www.theparisreview.org/blog/2020/06/08/the-performance-of-white-bodies/

15 Stonewall, 'Racism rife in LGBT community Stonewall research reveals', https://www.stonewall.org.uk/cy/node/79551

16 Aamna Mohdin, 'Calls for Overhaul of Pride in London After Series of Resignations', March 2021, https://www.theguardian.com/world/2021/mar/20/calls-overhaul-pride-in-london-after-resignations

Chapter 6

1 Brené Brown, *I Thought It Was Just Me: Women Reclaiming Power and Courage in a Culture of Shame* (New York: Penguin Random House) 2007.

2 Brené Brown, 'Shame v. Guilt', January 2013, https://brenebrown.com/blog/2013/01/14/shame-v-guilt/#close-popup

3 Ethan Kross, Marc G. Berman, Walter Mischel, Edward E. Smith, and Tor D. Wager, 'Social Rejection Shares Somatosensory

Representations with Physical Pain', *Proceedings of the National Academy of Sciences of the United States of America*, 108:15 (2011) 6270–6275.

4   Alexandra Wilts, 'Donald Trump Says "No Politician in History Has Been Treated Worse" Than Him', May 2017, https://www.independent.co.uk/news/world/americas/us-politics/trump-russia-comey-latest-news-no-president-treated-worse-speech-quote-a7741571.html

5   Gareth Cook, 'Why We Are Wired to Connect', October 2013, https://www.scientificamerican.com/article/why-we-are-wired-to-connect/

6   William Shakespeare, *A Midsummer Night's Dream*, 1605.

7   Olusoga (2016), 239.

8   James Walvin, *How Sugar Corrupted the World: The World Corrupted, From Slavery to Obesity* (London: Constable & Robinson 2019) 72–73.

9   Stella Dadzie, Black History Walks: African Women Resistance Leaders (Lecture), 2020.

10 Dadzie, 109.

11 Ibid., 66-67.

12 Christer Petley, 'How Slaveholders in the Caribbean Maintained Control', n.d., aeon.co/ideas/how-did-slaveholders-in-the-carib-bean-maintain- control

13 Stella Dadzie, Black History Walks: African Women Resistance Leaders (Lecture), 2020.

14 Michael J. Pfeifer, *The Roots of Rough Justice: Origins of American Lynching* (Chicago: University of Illinois Press, 2011) 4.

15 Grace Elizabeth Hale, *The Making of Whiteness: The Culture of Segregation In the South 1890–1940* (London: Vintage, 1998) 201.

16 Ibid., 201.

17 NAACP, 'History of Lynching in America', n.d., www.naacp.org/history-of-lynchings/

18 'History of lynchings', www.naacp.org/history-of-lynchings

19 Hale (1998), 207 and 215.

20 Roberta Senechal De La Roche, 'Why is Collective Violence Collective', *Sociological Theory*, 19:2 (2001) 126–144.

21 Hale (1998).

22 Hale (1998), 201 and 234.

23 Ibid., 213.

24 Howard Smead, *Blood Justice: The Lynching of Mack Charles Parker* (New York: Oxford University Press, USA, 1988).

25 Hale (1998), 237.

26 Hale (1998).

27 Pfeifer (2011), 41.

28 Jacqueline Jenkinson, 'Black Sailors on Red Clydeside: Rioting, Reactionary Trade Unionism and Conflicting Notions of Britishness Following The First World War', *Twentieth Century British History*, 19:1 (2008), 29–60.

29 Olusoga (2016), 459-460.

30 Ibid., 457.

31 Hale (1998), 223–224.

32 Hale (1998), 213.

33 Hale (1998), 219.

34 Hale (1998).

35 Ibid., 219–221

36 Ibid., 221

37 Mo Costandi, 'Pregnant 9/11 Survivors Transmitted Trauma to Their Children', September 2011, https://www.theguardian.com/science/neurophilosophy/2011/sep/09/pregnant-911-survivors-transmitted-trauma

38 Rachel Yehuda et al., 'Holocaust Exposure Induced Intergenerational Effects on FKBP5 Methylation', *Biological* Psychiatry. 80:5 (2016) 372–380.

39 Signe Dean, 'Scientists Have Observed Epigenetic Memories Being Passed Down For 14 Generations', April, 2018, www.sciencealert.com/scientists- observe-epigenetic-memories-passed-down-for-14-generations-most- animal

40 Resmaa Menakem, *My Grandmother's Hands: Racialized Trauma and the Pathway to Mending Our Hearts and Bodies* (Central Recovery Press: Las Vegas, 2017).

41 Bellamy, 'Performing Whiteness' (2020).

42 Guilaine Kinouani, 'Working With Racial Trauma in Psychotherapy', *Therapy Today* (October 2019).

43 Guilaine Kinouani, 'Working With Racial Trauma' (2019).

44 Kehinde Andrews, *Back to Black: Retelling Black Radicalism For the 21ˢᵗ Century* (London: Zed Books, 2018) 73.

45 Angela Saini, 'In the Twisted Story of Eugenics, the Bad Guy is All of Us', October 2019, https://www.theguardian.com/commentis-free/2019/oct/03/eugenics-francis-galton-science-ideas

46 Deutsche Welle (dw) 2019, 'Germany Extends Holocaust Compensation to Include Survivor Spouses', https://www.dw.com/en/germany-extends-holocaust-compensation-to-include-survivor-spouses/a-49438399

47 Randy Cordova, 'Maya Angelou's 2011 "Arizona Republic" Interview', 2014, https://eu.azcentral.com/story/entertainment/books/2014/05/28/maya-angelou-arizona-republic-interview/9682587/

Chapter 7

1 Funmi Olutoye, 'If Black Lives Matter, Why Am I Losing Longtime White Friends Who Refuse to Acknowledge My Suffering?', *Independent*, June 2020, https://independent.co.uk/voices/black-lives-matter-george-floyd-death-protests-racism-white-facebook-memes-a9552926.html

2 MIT News, '3 Questions: Moya Bailey on the intersection of racism and sexism', January 2021, https://news.mit.edu/2021/3-questions-moya-bailey-intersection-racism-sexism-0111

3 Kimberlé Crenshaw, 'Demarginalizing the Intersection of Race and Sex: A Black Feminist Critique of Antidiscrimination Doctrine,

Feminist Theory and Antiracist Politics, *University of Chicago Legal Forum,* 1989.

4   'The Intersectionality Wars', 2019, www.vox.com/the-high-light/2019/5/20/18542843/intersectionality-conservatism-law-race- gender-discrimination

5   Rachel Cargle, 'When Feminism Is White Supremacy in Heels', August 2018, www. https://www.harpersbazaar.com/culture/politics/a22717725/what-is-toxic-white-feminism/

6   Pew Research Center, 'An Examination of the 2016 Electorate, Based on Validated Voters', August 2018, https://www.pewresearch.org/politics/2018/08/09/an-examination-of-the-2016-electorate-based-on-validated-voters/

7   CNN politics, Exit Polls, 2020, edition.cnn.com/election/2020/exit-polls/president/ national-results/21

8   Dadzie, *A Kick in the Belly* (2020), 105, 108–111.

9   Stephanie Jones-Rogers, *They Were Her Property: White Women as Slave Owners in the American South* (New Haven; London: Yale University Press, 2019).

10   Dadzie, *A Kick in the Belly* (2020), 109.

11   T. Morris, *Southern Slavery and the Law* 1619–1860 (1999), 305–306, via Dr Joy DeGruy, *Post Traumatic Slave Syndrome* (2017), 60.

12   Adam Hochschild*, Bury The Chains: The British Struggle to Abolish Slavery* (London: Pan, 2012), 22.

13   Ibid., 130–131.

14   Joy DeGruy, London, 2008 and The Negro Population, Department of Commerce and Labour, Bureau of the Census, 1905, Walter F. Wilcox https://www2.census.gov/prod2/decennial/documents/03322287no8ch1.pdf

15   Dadzie, *A Kick in the Belly* (2020), 141–143.

16   Washington (2006), 65.

17   bell hooks, *Ain't I a Women: Black Women and Feminism* (London: Pluto Press, 1982), 55–54.

18   Ibid., 55.

19   Jones-Rogers (2019), 12.

20 Ibid., 8–9.

21 Ibid., 11.

22 Dadzie *A Kick in the Belly* (London: Verso, 2020).

23 Ibid., 147

24 Nosheen Iqbal, 'June Sarpong: "I Don't Have the Luxury of Being Mediocre"', October 2020, https://www.theguardian.com/culture/2020/oct/11/june-sarpong-i-dont-have-the-luxury-of-being-mediocre-interview-bbc-diversity-books

25 Kayleigh Dray, 'We Need to Talk About the Real Problem with "Unlikeable" Women', 2018, www.stylist.co.uk/life/strictly-come-dancing-alex- andra-burke-unlikable-unlikeable-women-sexism-feminist-double- standards/177967

26 Holly Christodoulou, 'GLOVES OFF "Incredibly Irritating" Meghan Markle is "Weak, Manipulative and Spoilt", Blasts Eamonn Holmes After "Uppity" Row', 2020, www.thesun.co.uk/news/10712664/meghan-markle-eamonn- holmes-radio-spoilt/amp/

27 Amnesty International UK, 'Women Abused on Twitter Every 30 Seconds – New Study', December 2018, https://www.amnesty.org.uk/press-releases/women-abused-twitter- every-30-seconds-new-study

28 Amnesty International UK, 'Diane Abbott Talks About "Sheer Levels of Hatred" She Receives Online', September 2017, https://www.amnesty.org.uk/press-releases/diane-abbott-talks-about-sheer-levels-hatred-she-receives-online

29 ITV News, 'Corbyn Defends Diane Abbott After She Stumbles Over Maths in Interview Gaffe', May 2017, https://www.itv.com/news/2017-05-02/diane-abbott-suggests-10-000-new-police-officers-pledged-by-labour-to-earn-30-per-year-in-interview-gaffe

30 Charlotte England, 'Philip Hammond Gets Cost of HS2 Wrong by £20bn in Radio Interview', May 2017, https://www.independent.co.uk/news/uk/politics/philip-hammond-hs2-cost-wrong-ps20bn-radio-interview-highspeed-railway-4-today-programme-election-2017-a7742006.html

31   Jon Sharman and Benjamin Kentish, 'Boris Johnson: 15 of the Conservative Leader's Most Calamitous Mistakes and Gaffes', July 2019, https://www.independent.co.uk/news/uk/politics/boris-johnson-prime-minister-leader-mistakes-gaffes-iran-libya-muslims-europe-sacked-a9016666.html

32   Jon King, 'Diane Abbott Death Threat: Pensioner who Threatened to Torch MP's House in Vile Racist Letter Gets 12-Month Community Order', May 2018, www.hackneygazette.co.uk/news/crime/pensioner-roy-douglas- brown-trolled-mp-diane-abbott-12-month-3593514

33   Sky News, 'US Open: Serena Williams Calls Umpire "Liar" and "Thief" in Furious Showdown', September 2018, news.sky.com/story/amp/naomi-osaka-wins-us- open-after-serena-williams-suffers-meltdown-11493671

34   Brooke Newman, 'The Long History Behind the Racist Attacks on Serena Williams', September 2018, https://www.washingtonpost.com/outlook/2018/09/11/long-history-behind-racist-attacks-serena-williams/

35   hooks (1982), 57.

36   hooks (1982), 53–54 and 58.

37   Ibid., 57.

38   Ibid., 54.

39   Mike Savage, 'R. Kelly: The History of Allegations Against Him', August 2020, www.bbc. com/news/amp/entertainment-arts-40635526

40   hooks (1982), 62.

41   Stuart Jeffries, 'Dido Belle: the Artworld Enigma Who Inspired a Movie', May 2014, https://www.theguardian.com/artanddesign/2014/may/27/dido-belle-enigmatic-painting-that-inspired-a-movie

42   hooks (1982), 62.

43   Kenya Evelyn, 'Outrage at Whites-Only Image as Ugandan Climate Activist Cropped From Photo', January 2020, https://www.

theguardian.com/world/2020/jan/24/whites-only-photo-uganda-climate-activist-vanessa-nakate

44 Claire Reid, 'A woman has complained to John Lewis because its advert is "Too Black"', December 2016, https://www.ladbible.com/now/film-and-tv-a-woman-has-complained-to-john-lewis-because-its-advert-is-too-black-20161201

45 Warwick University Library, 'Post-Windrush: African Caribbean migration between 1948–1957', n.d., https://warwick.ac.uk/services/library/mrc/studying/docs/racism/windrush/

46 Amelia Gentleman, *The Windrush Betrayal: Exposing The Hostile Environment* (London: Guardian Faber Publishing, 2019) 104.

47 Ishmahil Blagrove Jr., 'Notting Hill Carnival – The Untold Story', August 2014, https://www.standard.co.uk/reveller/attractions/notting-hill-carnival-the-untold-story-9653208.html

48 Ray Funk, 'Notting Hill Carnival: Mas and the Mother Country', December 2009, https://www.caribbean-beat.com/issue-100/notting-hill-carnival-mas-and-mother-country#axzz6z5a7nkR9

49 Dadzie, African Women Resistance Leaders (Lecture), 2020.

50 Beverley Bryan, Stella Dadzie and Suzanne Scafe, *The Heart of the Race: Black Women's Lives in Britain* (London: Virago, 1985), 130-132.

51 Gentleman (2019), 110.

52 Bernard Coard, 'Why I Wrote the "ESN Book"', February 2005, https://www.theguardian.com/education/2005/feb/05/schools.uk

53 Dadzie, African Women Resistance Leaders (Lecture), 2020.

54 1000 Londoners, '#197 Dame Jocelyn Barrow is Knighted For Her Work in Race Relations', 2017, https://www.youtube.com/watch?v=vRo02yOmWk8

55 Patrick Vernon and Angelina Osborne, *100 Great Black Britons* (London: Robinson, 2020), 69.

56 1000 Londoners, '#197 Dame Jocelyn Barrow is Knighted For Her Work in Race Relations', 2017, https://www.youtube.com/watch?v=vRo02yOmWk8

57 Obi Orjiekwe, 'Vanessa Feltz Phone in – Black Men Who Hate Black Women', 2012, https://www.youtube.com/watch?v=1F1-4Y8sIBM

58 Stand Up To Racism, 'Solicitor for Belly Mujinga's Family on the Struggle for Justice', 2020, https://www.youtube.com/watch?v=9dB6CUGH3d0

59 *Belly Mujinga: Searching for the Truth* [TV], BBC Panorama, 2020, https://www.bbc.co.uk/programmes/m000nh49

60 BBC News, 'Sarah Everard: Body Found in Woodland Confirmed as That of Missing Woman', March 2020, https://www.bbc.co.uk/news/uk-england-london-56371163

61 Sophia Ankel, 'After Kate Middleton Paid Her Respects at Vigil to Sarah Everard, Police Moved in and Started Arresting Women', March 2021, https://www.insider.com/kate-middleton-attends-sarah-everard-vigil-police-arrest-demonstrators-2021-3

62 Leah Sinclair, 'What happened to Blessing Olusegun?', March 2021, https://www.standard.co.uk/news/uk/what-happened-blessing-olusegun-death-sussex-b924027.html

63 Sky News 'Police Officers Charged with Misconduct Over Photos Taken at Sisters Murder Scene, April 2021, https://news.sky.com/story/met-police- officers-charged-with-misconduct-over-photos-taken-at-sisters- murder-scene-12289446

64 Ancient Origins, 'A Serendipitous Skull Discovery in Ethiopia: Is This the Oldest Known Modern Man?', April 2017, https://www.ancient-origins.net/human-origins-science/serendipitous-skull-discovery-ethiopia-oldest-known-modern-man-007905

65 *Africa's Greatest Civilization* [TV], PBS, 2017.

Chapter 8

1 AFROPUNK, 'RADICAL SELF CARE: ANGELA DAVIS', 2018, https://www.youtube.com/watch?v=Q1cHoL4vaBs

2 Audre Lorde, *A Burst of Light: and Other Essays* (New York: Ixia Press, 1988).

3   GOV.UK, 'Our Health and Wellbeing Today', 2010 assets.publish-
     ing.ser- vice.gov.uk/government/uploads/system/uploads/attach-
     ment_data/ file/215911/dh_122238.pdf

Chapter 9

1   NAACP Legal Defense and Educational Fund, Inc., 'The Sig-
     nificance Of "The Doll Test"', n.d., https://www.naacpldf.org/
     ldf-celebrates-60th-anniversary-brown-v-board-education/
     significance-doll-test/
2   'Interview with Dr. Kenneth Clark', conducted by Blackside, Inc.
     on November 4, 1985, for *Eyes on the Prize: America's Civil Rights
     Years* (1954–1965). Washington University Libraries, Film and
     Media Archive, Henry Hampton Collection., 1985, http://digital.
     wustl.edu/e/eop/eopweb/cla0015.0289.020drkennethclark.html
3   Erin Blakemore, 'How Dolls Helped Win Brown v. Board of
     Education', March 2018, https://www.history.com/news/brown-v-
     board-of-education-doll-experiment
4   Black History Walks, 'The Amazing James Baldwin' (Lecture),
     Tony Warner, 18 May 2020.
5   BBC News, 'The Child Immigrants "Bussed" Out to School to
     Aid Integration', January 2017, https://www.bbc.co.uk/news/uk-
     england-leeds-38689839
6   Black History Walks, Amazing James Baldwin (Lecture 3), Tony
     Warner 1 June 2020; https://www.huffingtonpost.co.uk/vicki-
     butler/bussing-uk-segregation_b_1938803.html
7   'All Change – a New Government, New Equality Machin-
     ery', 2007, www.runnymedetrust.org/uploads/publications/
     pdfs/351BulletinSept07.pdf
8   Bryan, Dadzie and Scafe (1985), 22.
9   Bernard Coard, 'Why I Wrote the "ESN Book"', February 2005,
10   Bryan, Dadzie and Scafe (1985), 142.
11   Rebecca Speare-Cole, 'Heartbreaking Video of Girl, 4, Call-
     ing Herself 'Ugly' Goes Viral as Hairdresser Assures Her She's

Beautiful', March 2020, https://www.standard.co.uk/news/world/
girl-ugly-hairdresser-instagram-live-viral-video-a4384511.html

12 BBC News, 'Children Whitening Skin to Avoid Racial Hate
    Crime, NSPCC Finds', May 2019, https://www.bbc.co.uk/news/
    uk-48458850

13 Andrew Scott Baron and Mahzarin R. Banaji, 'The Development
    of Implicit Attitudes', *Psychological Science*, 2006.

14 Jeffrey Kluger, 'Your Baby Is a Racist—and Why You Can Live
    With That', April 2014, https://time.com/67092/baby-racists-
    survival-strategy/

15 Maria Trent, Danielle G. Dooley and Jacqueline Dougé, 'The
    Impact of Racism on Child and Adolescent Health', *Paediatrics*,
    2019.

16 DeGruy (2005) 61 and 102.

17 Stephanie Huber, 'What Do The Blind Think Of Racism? These
    Answers Might Surprise You', https://www.buzzworthy.com/
    what-blind-think-of-racism/

18 Evan P. Apfelbaum, Kristin Pauker, Samuel R. Sommers, and
    Nalini Ambady, 'In blind pursuit of racial equality', *Psychological
    Science,* 2010.

19 Ibid.

20 Steven Ross Pomeroy, '"They All Look Alike": The Other-
    Race Effect', January 2014, https://www.forbes.com/sites/
    rosspomeroy/2014/01/28/think-they-all-look-alike-thats-just-the-
    other-race-effect/?sh=2829d7f33819

21 Oscar Williams, 'British Journalism is 94% White and 55% Male,
    Survey Reveals', March 2016, https://www.theguardian.com/
    media-network/2016/mar/24/british-journalism-diversity-white-
    female-male-survey

22 Pomeroy (2014).

23 Po Bronson and Ashley Merryman, *Nurtureshock: Why Everything
    We Think About Raising Our Children Is Wrong* (London: Ebury
    Press, 2011), 51.

24 Louisa Adjoa Parker and Chris Matthews, 'Eight-year-old opens up about sickening racial abuse in Cornwall', October 2019, https://www.cornwalllive.com/news/cornwall-news/eight-year-old-opens-up-3416277.amp

25 Frankie McCamley, 'Exclusions for Racism in Primary Schools in England Up More Than 40%', January 2020 https://www.bbc.co.uk/news/education-50331687

26 YMCA, 'Young and Black: The Young Black Experience of Institutional Racism in the UK' YMCA, October 2020 https://www.ymca.org.uk/wp-content/uploads/2020/10/ymca-young-and-black.pdf

27 Akala, *Natives* (London: Two Roads, 2018) 66–70.

28 Whitney Crenna-Jennings, 'A black Caribbean FSM boy with SEND is 168 times more likely to be permanently excluded than a white British girl without SEND. Why?', December 2017, https://www.tes.com/news/black-caribbean-fsm-boy-send-168-times-more-likely-be-permanently-excluded-white-british-girl

29 Josh Halliday, 'Salford Man Targeted with Racist Graffiti "Overwhelmed" by Support', February 2010, https://www.theguardian.com/uk-news/2019/feb/18/salford-dad-jackson-yamba-targeted-with-racist-graffiti-overwhelmed-by-support

30 Siraad Dirshe, 'Respect Our Roots: A Brief History Of Our Braids', June 2018, https://www.essence.com/hair/respect-our-roots-brief-history-our-braids-cultural-appropriation/

Chapter 10

1 angel Kyodo williams, Meditation Class, 2021.

2 'Racism at Work Survey Results', 2018.

3 Omar Khan, 'How Far Have We Come? Lessons from the 1965 Race Relations Act', December 2015, https://www.equalityhumanrights.com/en/our-work/blogs/how-far-have-we-come-lessons-1965-race-relations-act

4 Eric Silver, 'From the Archive, 16 July 1966: Colour Bar Ends at All London Stations', 2010, https://www.theguardian.com/the-guardian/2010/jul/16/archive-colour-bar-ends-at-all-london-1966 Jon Kelly, 'What Was Behind the Bristol Bus Boycott?', August 2013, https://www.bbc.co.uk/news/magazine-23795655

5 Vernon and Osborne (2020), 69.

6 'Race Relations Act 1965', https://www.parliament.uk/about/living-heritage/transformingsociety/private-lives/relationships/col-lections1/race-relations-act-1965/race-relations-act-1965/

7 Rahul Verma, 'An Important UK Law On Racial Discrimination Is 50 Years Old', November 2018, https://eachother.org.uk/an-important-uk-law-on-racial-discrimination-is-50-years-old/

8 Ian Burrell, 'Black is Fined For Race Slur on Police Insult Police', July 1999, https://www.independent.co.uk/news/black-is-fined-for-race-slur-on-police-insult-police-1108921.html

9 Enoch Powell, Keynote Presented at the General Meeting of the West Midlands Area Conservative Political Centre, Birmingham, 20 April, 1968, Now Commonly Referred to as His 'Rivers of Blood' Speech, https://anth1001.files.wordpress.com/2014/04/enoch-powell_speech.pdf

10 Race Relations Bill, HC Deb 23 April 1968 763: cc.53–198'.

11 Ibid.

12 Jennifer Brown, 'An Early History of Britain's Race Relations Legislation', *House of Commons Library,* 2018.

13 '50 years on From the (Second) Race Relations Act, and the Run-nymede Trust', 2018, www.Blackhistorymonth.org.uk/article/ sec-tion/real-stories/50-years-second-race-relations-act-runnymede-trust/

14 'Race Relations Act 1968', www.legislation.gov.uk/ ukpga/1968/71/ enacted

15 Political Economic Planning, 'A survey of racial discrimination in employment and other fields in the United Kingdom', *International Labour Review,* 1967.

16 European Commission, European network of legal experts in gender equality and non-discrimination, A comparative analysis of gender equality law in Europe, Alexandra Timmer and Linda Senden https://www.equalitylaw.eu/downloads/4553-a-comparative-analysis- of-gender-equality-law-in-europe-2017-pdf-1-mb Briefing EU Policy Delivering for Citizens Promoting equality between women and men M. Prpic and R. Shreeves with A. Dobreva https:// what-europe-does-for-me.eu/data/pdf/focus/focus10_en.pdf

17 'Race Relations Act 1976', www.legislation.gov.uk/ukpga/1976/74/ enacted

18 'Brixton riots 30 years on: What has changed?', 2011, www.bbc.co.uk/news/uk-england-london-13004915

19 Ibid.

20 'Doreen Lawrence finally won her 19-year battle for justice for murdered son Stephen this year', 2012, www.prideofbritain.com/history/2012/doreen-lawrence

21 *Stephen: The Murder That Changed A Nation* [TV], BBC One, 2018.

22 'CPS pays £250,000 to settle race bias case', 2003, www.theguardian.com/uk/2003/sep/05/race.equality

23 Alexandra Wilson, *In Black and White: A Young Barrister's Story of Race and Class in a Broken Justice System* (London: Endeavour, 2020) 37.

24 BBC News, 'Black Barrister Mistaken for Defendant Three Times Gets Apology', September 2020, www.bbc.co.uk/news/uk-england-essex-54281111

25 TUC Report, 'Dying on the Job – Racism and Risk at Work', 2020, www.tuc. org.uk/research-analysis/reports/dying-job-racism-and-risk-work

26 'Is racism real? A report about the experiences of Black and minority ethnic workers – polling findings', 2017, https://www.tuc.org.uk/research-analysis/reports/dying-job-racism-and-risk-work

27 'Employment Tribunals – Legal Tests for Unfair Dismissal Claims – Misconduct', https://www.citizensadvice.org.uk/work/

problems-at-work/employment-tribunals-from-29-july-2013/
making-an-employment-tribunal-claim-is-it-worth-it/employ-
ment-tribunals-unfair-dismissal-claims/legal-tests/employment-
tribunals-legal-tests-for-unfair-dismissal-claims-misconduct/

28 TUC Report, 'Dying on the job – Racism and Risk at Work',
2020.

29 Nancy Kelley, Dr Omar Khan and Sarah Sharrock, 'Racial
preju- dice in Britain today', *NatCen,* 2017, https://natcen.ac.uk/
media/1488132/racial-prejudice-report_v4.pdf

30 Sean Coughlan, 'Only 1% of UK University Professors are Black',
January 2020, https://www.bbc.co.uk/news/education-55723120

31 Nicola Rollock, 'Staying Power: The Career Experiences and Strategies of UK Black Female Professors', *University and College Union,*
2019, https://www.ucu.org.uk/media/10075/Staying-Power/pdf/
UCU_Rollock_February_2019.pdf

32 'NHS Workforce Race Equality Standard: 2019 Data Analysis
Report for NHS Trusts', 2019, https://www.england.nhs.uk/wp-
content/uploads/2020/01/wres-2019-data-report.pdf

33 Sarah Marsh and Niamh McIntyre, 'Six in 10 UK Health Workers
Killed by Covid-19 are BAME', May 2020, https://www.theguard-
ian.com/world/2020/may/25/six-in-10-uk-health-workers-killed-
by-covid-19-are-bame

34 Katie Weston, 'White Nurse "Frozen Out" After Blowing Whistle
that Black Colleagues on East London Hospital Children's Ward
Were Being Given More Work to Do WINS £26,000 Employment
Case', February 2021, https://www.dailymail.co.uk/news/arti-
cle-9286227/White-nurse-frozen-saying-black-colleagues-given-
work-WINS-26-000.html

35 Diane Taylor, 'Three Police Officers in UK Accused of Racist
Remarks on WhatsApp', July 2020, https://www.theguardian.com/
uk-news/2020/jul/09/three-uk-police-officers-accused-of-racist-
remarks-on-whatsapp

36 Vikram Dodd, 'Six Hampshire Police Officers Guilty of Misconduct Over Offensive Comments', December 2020, https://www.

theguardian.com/uk-news/2020/dec/18/six-hampshire-police-officers-guilty-of-misconduct-over-offensive-comments

37 UNISON, 'Tackling Bullying at Work: A UNISON Guide for Safety Reps', https://www.unison.org.uk/content/uploads/2013/07/On-line-Catalogue216953.pdf

38 'Racism Ruins Lives: An analysis of the 2016-2017 Trade Union Congress Racism at Work Survey', 2019, hummedia.manchester.ac.uk/institutes/code/research/projects/racism-at-work/tuc-full-report.pdf

39 'Racism at Work Survey Results', 2018.

40 'BME women and work: TUC Equality Briefing', www.tuc.org.uk/sites/default/files/2020-10/BMEwomenandwork.pdf

41 'Ethnicity pay gaps: 2019', www.ons.gov.uk/employmentandlabourmarket/peopleinwork/earningsandworkinghours/articles/ethnicitypaygapsingreatbritain/2019

42 'Measuring Poverty 2020', 2020, socialmetricscommission.org.uk/wp-content/uploads/2020/06/Measuring-Poverty-2020-Web.pdf,

43 Wendy Bottero and Kjartan Pall Sveinsson (ed.), 'Class in the Twenty-first century', *Who cares about the white working class?*, 2009.

44 Tristan Cork, 'Taxpayers in Bristol Were Still Paying Debt to City's slave Owners in 2015, Treasury admits', 2018, https://www.bristolpost.co.uk/news/bristol-news/taxpayers-bristol-were-still-paying-1205049

45 Pippa Crerar, 'Black and Asian Workers Paid Up to 37% Less Than White Staff at City Hall', March 2018, https://www.standard.co.uk/news/mayor/black-and-asian-workers-paid-up-to-37-less-than-white-staff-at-city-hall-a3779811.html 'Racism at Work Survey Results', 2018.

46 'Racism at Work Survey Results', 2018.

47 Jennifer J. Freyd, PhD, 'Institutional Betrayal and Institutional Courage', n.d., https://dynamic.uoregon.edu/jjf/institutionalbetrayal/

48 Carly Parnitzke Smith, Jennifer J Freyd, 'Institutional Betrayal', *American Psychologist* (September 2014) 578.

Chapter 11

1   Barack Obama, 'Barack Obama's Feb. 5 Speech', 2008, www.
     nytimes. com/2008/02/05/us/politics/05text-obama.html

2   CNN politics, Exit Polls, 2020, edition.cnn.com/election/2020/
     exit-polls/president/ national-results/21

3   Kenya Evelyn, 'Capitol Attack: The Five People Who Died', April
     2021, https://www.the.com/us-news/2021/jan/08/capitol-attack-
     police-officer-five-deaths

4   Statista, 'COVID-19 Deaths Worldwide as of April 26, 2021, By
     Country', April 2021, www.statista.com/statistics/1093256/novel-
     coronavirus- 2019ncov-deaths-worldwide-by-country/

5   British Safety Council 'Improving Fire Safety: British Safety
     Council response to consultation', November 2020, https://www.
     britsafe.org/publications/safety-management-magazine/safety-
     management-magazine/2020/improving-fire-safety-british-safety-
     council-response-to-consultation/

6   Amelia Gentleman, 'Windrush Scandal: Only 60 Victims Given
     Compensation So Far', May 2020, https://www.the.com/uk-
     news/2020/may/28/windrush-scandal-only-60-victims-given-
     compensation-so-far

7   Jack Royston, 'Every Royal Family Racism Scandal Before
     Meghan Markle's Oprah Bombshell', November 2021, https://
     www.newsweek.com/every-royal-family-racism-scandal-meghan-
     markles-oprah-bombshell-1575314

8   'Black People, Racism and Human Rights', 2020.

9   Oscar Williams, 'British Journalism is 94% White and 55% Male,
     Survey Reveals', March 2016, https://www.theguardian.com/
     media-network/2016/mar/24/british-journalism-diversity-white-
     female-male-survey

10   Hale (1998) 204.

11   Gentleman (2019) 111.

12   Oliver Wright, 'Nigel Farage Accused of Deploying Nazi-Style
     Propaganda as Remain Crash Poster Unveiling with Rival
     Vans', 2016, https://www.independent.co.uk/news/uk/politics/

nigel-farage-brexit-poster-vans-eu-referendum-london-remain-breaking-point-a7085396.html

13 Nesrine Malik, *We Need New Stories: Challenging the Toxic Myths Behind Our Age of Discontent* (London: Weidenfeld & Nicolson, 2019) 114.

14 David Green, 'Campaigners Are Twisting BAME COVID Data to Further Their "Victimhood" Agenda', *The Telegraph*, May 2020, https://telegraph.co.uk/news/2020/05/04/campaigners-twisting-bame-covid-data-victimhood-agenda/

15 Mark White, 'Right-Wing Extremism is UK's Fastest Growing Threat, Says Top Counter-terror Cop', November 2020, https://news.sky.com/story/right-wing-extremism-fastest-growing-threat-says-uks-top-cop-in-counter-terrorism-12135071

16 Amelia Gentleman, 'Black Official Quit "Racist" Windrush Compensation Scheme', November 2020, https://www.theguardian.com/uk-news/2020/nov/18/black-official-quit-allegedly-racist-windrush-compensation-scheme

17 Katie McQue, Mark Townsend and Katie Armour, 'Windrush Scandal Continues as Chagos Islanders Are Pressed to "Go Back"', July 2019, https://www.theguardian.com/world/2019/jul/28/windrush-scandal-continues-in-crawley-as-chagos-islanders-told-go-back

18 'Black People, Racism and Human Rights', 2020.

19 'Diversity Beyond Gender', 2020, https://www.extend.vc/reports

20 A Cock, C Brierley, M Andrews, M Maslin, S Lewis, 'Earth System Impacts of the European Arrival and Great Dying in the Americas After 1492', *Quarterly Science Reviews*, March 2019 207:13–36.

21 'Why Black Lives Matter in the Climate Movement: An Introduction to Environmental Racism' – Shado Magazine Event An Introduction to Environmental Racism, 6 January 2021 https://shado-mag.com/events/why-black-lives-matter- in-the-climate-movement-an-introduction-to-environmental-racism/

22 Tim Wyatt, 'Clergy gained compensation equivalent to £46 million today, at abolition of slavery', June 2020, www.churchtimes.

co.uk/articles/2020/26- june/news/uk/clergy-gained-compensa-tion-equivalent-to-46-million- today-at-abolition-of-slavery

23 Nima Elbagir, Barbara Arvanitidis, Katie Polglase, Bryony Jones and Alex Platt, 'How a Catholic Order Dedicated to Protect-ing Children Failed Them', 2019, edition.cnn.com/interac-tive/2019/11/africa/luk-delft-intl/

24 Richard Reddie, 'Atlantic Slave Trade and Abolition', January 2007, https://www.bbc.co.uk/religion/religions/christianity/his-tory/slavery_1.shtml

25 Emily Lindsay Brown Gemma Ware and Khalil A. Cassimally, 'Knife Crime: Causes and Solutions – Editors' Guide to What Our Academic Experts Say', n.d., https://theconversation.com/knife-crime-causes-and-solutions-editors-guide-to-what-our-academic-experts-say-113318

26 Marcus Christenson, 'Thierry Henry Quits Social Media Until Companies Act on Racism and Bullying', March 2021, https://www.theguardian.com/football/2021/mar/26/thierry-henry-quits-social-media-until-companies-act-on-racism-and-bullying

27 Sophie Grenham, 'Losing Her Religion: Megan Phelps-Roper on Leaving the Westboro Baptist Church', n.d., https://thegloss.ie/losing-her-religion/?v=79cba1185463

28 Lili North and Mantas Kačerauskas, 'Non-binary person teaches this hateful parent tolerance and their text exchange goes viral', 2019, https://www.boredpanda.com/non-binary-model-changes-parent-view-rain-dove/?utm_source=google&utm_medium=organic&utm_campaign=organic

29 Kathy Caprino, 'Why Won't You Apologize? Relationship Expert Harriet Lerner Teaches Us How', January 2017, https://www.forbes.com/sites/kathycaprino/2017/01/12/why-wont-you-apolo-gize-relationship-expert-harriet-lerner-teaches-us-how/

Chapter 12

1 Can Dündar, 'Defending People's Right to Know', *TEDxFranfurt*, November 2020, https://www.ted.com/talks/can_dundar_defending_people_s_right_to_know

2 Brené Brown, 'Braving the Seven Elements of Trust', October 2018, https://daretolead.brenebrown.com/wp-content/uploads/2018/10/BRAVING.pdf

3 David Montgomery, 'A Buddhist Teacher's Meditations on Confronting White Supremacy', July 2020, https://www.washingtonpost.com/lifestyle/magazine/a-buddhist-teachers-meditations-on-confronting-white-supremacy/2020/07/20/3f9cf510-b71b-11ea-aca5-ebb63d27e1ff_story.html

4 Oprah's Lifeclass, 'The Powerful Lesson Maya Angelou Taught Oprah', October 2011, https://www.oprah.com/oprahs-lifeclass/the-powerful-lesson-maya-angelou-taught-oprah-video

5 Dorothy E. Roberts, 'Foreword: Abolition Constitutionalism', *Harvard Law Review,* 133 *(*2019*)*.

Acknowledgements

In Gratitude to:

My husband for being my number one fan and giving me space and love to grow.

To every anti-racism writer, activist and academic, especially Black women who have laid the groundwork. Acknowledging all they will have endured to pave the way for authors like me to follow.

In deep gratitude to my invisible support crew who got me through. Your unconditional support carried me every step of the way. Thank you for holding me up, especially when the road got rough: Jonelle Lewis, Donna Lancaster, Layla F. Saad, Sharmaine Lovegrove, Yazzie Min, Susan Ateh, Antoinette Harrison, Nicola Rae-Wickham, Tamu Thomas, Selina Barker. How lucky I am to have found you all.

Thank you to my incredible agent Anwen Hooson for never giving up on me, or the work, even when it got tough. Thank you to Sharlayne at Project Noir and June Sarpong for planting the very first seed to start writing a book. Thank you to every publisher who said *no*. To my publishers and to Kate at HQ for saying yes, and to Lisa for giving me that feedback that opened up my writing. To Paula Akpan and Vimbai Shire, thank YOU for your magic and for seeing me.

To Olivia Knight and Ismay Ozga at Patchwork, there are many reasons why our paths have crossed; this is just one of them. Beyond blessed to have your support and for helping to birth this beautiful cover. Thank you.

In gratitude to each expert for giving up your time and sharing your knowledge with me.

To each interviewee for sharing your experiences, thank you for trusting me.

In deep appreciation to my changemakers and my Zoom crew for holding space – you know who you are, no cookies! To my students for your support and letting me share some of your journeys in this book. To Team Nova, and especially Elizabeth Giblin-Cook for your unconditional support and helping birth this corker of a shout-line.

Thank you to all who sent self-care and joy packages and offered wellbeing support, and to those who let me stay in their homes to write. The Writers Rest will always have a special place in my heart. To Frances M. Thompson, Susie Gething, Aimee Capstick: I appreciate you.

Deep respect to my teachers and those who inspire me and my work:

Black History Walks, Tony Warner and Michelle Yaa Asantewa for providing nourishment and empowerment during a difficult time. Stella Dadzie, what a gift to be taught by you. Dr Joy DeGruy, angel Kyodo williams, Brené Brown, Akala, David Olusoga. Resmaa Menakem – thank you for your support. To my cousin Dr Angelina Osborne and Patrick Vernon thank you for your research, and to Reni Eddo-Lodge, thank you for your work and your spirit, your book *Why I'm No Longer Talking to*

White People About Race ignited a fire in me. The Black Cultural Archives, *The Art of Falling,*

And a big thank you to you, for every follow, every word of support, encouragement and email along the way, and mostly for accepting the invitation to bring this urgent and life-changing work into your lives.

Further Resouces

For more resources please visit:

https://novareid.com/the-good-ally/
www.novareid.com

Reviews hold power in the publishing world. If you have learned from this book and it has resonated with you, I would be grateful if you could pop on over to your online retailer and leave a review. In deep gratitude.

ONE PLACE. MANY STORIES

Bold, innovative and
empowering publishing.

FOLLOW US ON:

@HQStories